More praise for Edmund S. Morgan and

THE GENUINE ARTICLE

"Morgan always has an eye out for the surprises. He delights in the telling exceptions that puncture clichés and teach us things genuinely new and interesting about our shared past."

—Edward J. Reneham Jr., *San Francisco Chronicle*

"Americans have been learning from Edmund Morgan for many decades—not only the distinguished historians he has trained at Yale, or other historians, but the reading public at large. He is the clearest of writers. He can put complex matters in ways that make misunderstanding him almost impossible."

—Garry Wills, *New York Review of Books*

"Morgan [is] one of the most influential and admired historians writing on colonial and early America. . . . He has made a decisive difference in the way we interpret the earliest decades of our history."

—Gordon Wood, *New York Review of Books*

"Far from presuming much specialized knowledge, Morgan asks of his readers only the willingness to wonder about the strangeness of the past and what it can teach us about our condition in the present. His are not the tools of criticism, but rather the classical historical talent of knowing his period. . . . Edmund Morgan is one of the most accomplished American historians alive—himself a genuine article—and the book is a delight." —Daniel Vickers, *San Diego Union-Tribune*

"Morgan is a member of that rare species: the academic who can write with authority and grace, offering insights valuable for their common sense, perspicacity, wit, and persuasiveness. This book belongs in every library; they don't come any better than this."

—Thomas J. Schaeper, *Library Journal*

THE GENUINE ARTICLE

The
GENUINE
ARTICLE

><

A HISTORIAN LOOKS AT
EARLY AMERICA

Edmund S. Morgan

W. W. NORTON & COMPANY

NEW YORK LONDON

Image credits: Page 1: *Paul Revere*, 1768. John Singleton Copley, American, 1738–1815. Oil on canvas. 89.22 x 72.39 cm (35⅛ x 28½ in.) Museum of Fine Arts, Boston. Gift of Joseph W. Revere, William B. Revere, and Edward H. R. Revere. 30.781. Photograph © Museum of Fine Arts, Boston. Page 72: *The Plantation*, 19th century, ca. 1825. Unidentified American artist. Oil on wood. 48.6 x 74.9 cm (19⅛ x 29½ in.) The Metropolitan Museum of Art, Gift of Edgar William and Bernice Chrysler Garbisch, 1963. (62.201.3) Photograph © 1984 The Metropolitan Museum of Art. Page 133: *Samuel Adams*, ca. 1772. John Singleton Copley, American, 1738–1815. Oil on canvas. 125.73 x 100.33 cm (49½ x 39½ in.) Museum of Fine Arts, Boston. Deposited by the City of Boston. Photograph © 2003 Museum of Fine Arts, Boston. Page 261: *Margaret Fuller*, courtesy the Library of Congress. *Blind Boy Fuller*, courtesy the Southern Folk Life Collection, Wilson Library, The University of North Carolina, Chapel Hill.

Manufacturing by The Haddon Craftsmen, Inc.
Book design by Dana Sloan
Production manager: Amanda Morrison

Library of Congress Cataloging–in–Publication Data

Morgan, Edmund Sears.
The genuine article : a historian looks at early America /
by Edmund S. Morgan.
p. cm.
Includes bibliographical references (p.) and index.
ISBN 0-393-05920-0
1. United States—History—Colonial period, ca. 1600–1775.
2. United States—History—Revolution, 1775–1783.
3. United States—Social conditions—To 1865. I. Title.
E188.5.M67 2004
973.2—dc22   2004043354

ISBN 0-393-32714-0 pbk.

W. W. Norton & Company, Inc.
500 Fifth Avenue, New York, N.Y. 10110
www.wwnorton.com

W. W. Norton & Company Ltd.
Castle House, 75/76 Wells Street, London W1T 3QT

1 2 3 4 5 6 7 8 9 0

FOR

KATHARINE MacKINNON MORGAN

AND

DANIEL DAVIES MORGAN

CONTENTS

PREFACE

THE REVIEWS collected here—essays, reflections, studies—were first published in the *New York Review of Books*. I probably could not have written them for publication anywhere else. They amount to a kind of intellectual autobiography, prompted by the *Review*'s policy of encouraging reviewers to explore their own ideas beyond the books, to carry their thoughts in any direction they choose at any length they choose. These pieces are thus a statement of what I have thought about early Americans during nearly seventy years in their company.

My first real interest in early America was sparked by an inspired teacher. At Harvard while a sophomore I was assigned, in the tutorial system then prevailing, to a young man named Perry Miller, who was just beginning to persuade people that the ideas of seventeeth-century Puritans should be taken seriously. Not that there was anything Puritanical or even religious about Miller. Actually, he was an atheist. But that did not prevent him from appreciating the intellectual rigor and elegance of a system of ideas that made sense of human life in a way no longer palatable to most of us. Certainly not palatable to me. But before I met Miller, I had never taken any system of ideas seriously. Now he was able to make the beliefs of the New England Puritans, simply as intellectual constructs, challenge my understanding as nothing else ever had. And the challenge was sharpened by the recognition that these people took their own ideas seriously enough to live by them. Perry Miller became my lifelong friend. I never lost the fascination with early New England that he started and continued to stimulate in conversation and correspondence as well as books, until his untimely death in 1963. I still regard him as far and away the greatest historian of ideas that America has ever seen.

He left me with a habit of taking what people have said at face value unless I find compelling reasons to discount it. My first academic job at Brown University offered the opportunity to test this procedure in a course on the American Revolution. The accepted interpretation at the time discounted the constitutional arguments of the Americans (no taxation without representation) as window dressing for economic motives. The grounds for this claim were the supposed shifts in what Americans said against taxation to match shifts in the form of taxation from "internal" to "external." In searching for documentary examples to illustrate this intellectual vacillation to students, I could find no real shift in the colonists' position. I wound up, instead, with documents demonstrating a remarkable consistency from the first protests of the Stamp Act crisis to the final Declaration of Independence. What Americans said from the beginning about taxation and just government deserved to be taken as seriously as the Puritans' ideas about God and man. In subsequent books I argued that the American Revolution was really what the revolutionaries said it was. And the ideas about government that grew from it after 1776 are still worth study and still deserve to be taken more seriously than they have been for some time by the people entrusted to apply them.

My next specific interest grew from reading what the revolutionaries said in support of their boycott of British goods in the 1770s. What they said seemed to be more about the virtues of work at home than they were about putting economic pressure on the British. I grandiosely proposed to myself a large-scale history of ideas about work in America. Virginia as the first permanent English colony was the place to begin. In reading Captain John Smith's account of his rescue of the settlement, which was falling to pieces when he took charge, I did a kind of double take at his boast that he saved it by putting everybody to work. How much work? Under Smith's regime, by his own account: "4 hours each day was spent in worke, the rest in pastimes and merry exercises."[1] Other accounts assigned a little more time to work: four hours in the morning and two in the afternoon.

What kind of people were these first Virginians and where did they get their strange attitudes about work in the face of imminent disaster? My proposed large-scale study became a history of early Virginia. And since Virginia was where some Americans began importing and exploiting the unwilling labor of others, my investigation of slavery began there too. These roughly have been my interests, represented in the first three topics into which I have arranged the reviews. The fourth topic is a little different, as I will explain in the paragraphs introducing it.

I did not produce any of these reviews alone. Barbara Epstein at the *New York Review of Books* suggested them by sending me the books and then gave me the light-handed editorial supervision for which I will always remain her grateful admirer and true friend. Since I can think only with pen in hand, my writing goes through many revisions, draft after draft, before I can be sure of exactly what I think. My first wife, Helen Mayer Morgan, was a brilliant editor and supported me in all my endeavors. More recently, I have had the assistance of my most discerning critic and beloved companion and wife, Marie Morgan, who could often suggest in every draft words that said what I meant more precisely than any I had chosen. Her own knowledge of American history has contributed many ideas that have shaped the way I approach my research.

That the reviews are now gathered into this book is owing to Robert Weil of W. W. Norton. He persuaded me that others would find in them the coherence that I have tried to explain here. I hope he is right.

Edmund S. Morgan
New Haven, Connecticut
July 2003

Part One

NEW ENGLANDERS

THE FIRST permanent English settlement in America was in Virginia, and four of the first five presidents of the United States were Virginians. But the history of the United States has often been written as an extension of the history of New England. In nineteenth-century histories the Puritanism of the first settlers was an embarrassment to be overlooked. In the twentieth century, however, scholars discovered in Puritanism a set of ideas worth exploring and explaining. This new interpretation began at Harvard in the writings of Kenneth Murdock, Samuel Eliot Morison, and most important (for others as well as myself), Perry Miller. Miller's *The New England Mind*, the second volume of which appeared in 1953, was so magisterial a treatment of Puritan ideas that for a time few other scholars had the nerve to look critically at his conclusions. A new kind of social history, relying heavily on statistics of family and community life, produced a series of studies of social relations in New England towns. Other studies of this period dealt with popular superstitions, witchcraft, sex, lawsuits, dissent. And some of Miller's bolder insights began to challenge intellectual historians, who offered revisions and extensions of his analysis of particular developments. The Puritans have now become the most closely examined group of people in American history. American Puritan studies stands out for the quality and quantity of its practitioners, none of whom has quite matched the brilliance of its originator. A few of the revisionist studies, together with a popular play and film, are considered here.

CHAPTER ONE

America's First Great Man

<hr>

The Journal of John Winthrop, 1630–1649
Richard S. Dunn, James Savage, and Laetitia Yeandle, editors

The Journal of John Winthrop, 1630–1649, abridged edition
Richard S. Dunn and Laetitia Yeandle, editors

WHAT MAKES a great man great? Historians occasionally ponder the question in assessing public figures, men or sometimes women (Queen Elizabeth I), who have given direction to a whole society. It is tempting, and sometimes fashionable, to read them out of history altogether, in favor of the impersonal forces and "-isms" that historians like to discover behind everything. And un-great men and women leading ordinary lives have commanded more attention recently than history's movers and shakers. But if we allow that some individuals were able to change or direct the course of history, it is easier to recognize them than it is to say what enabled them to do it. In America we may acknowledge Washington and Lincoln as great men, and probably Franklin and Jefferson and maybe Franklin Delano Roosevelt and possibly even several more, but we would probably disagree about precisely what it was that made them great, what it was that enabled them to give a lasting direction to the course of events.

These ruminations are prompted by the publication of a definitive edition of the journal kept by John Winthrop, the Puritan governor of Massachusetts who led the English exodus there. From the founding of the first English colonies in North America in 1607 to the beginnings of the Revolution in the 1760s, John Winthrop is the only person who looks like a great man in the sense we are talking about. Captain John Smith might be a candidate. By his own account Smith saved the Virginia colony from extinction at the outset, and he probably did. But his influence on Virginia's subsequent history was nil. Until the Revolution with its stellar collection of "founding fathers," Winthrop was the only public figure who left his mark on the way his society developed in his own time and for long after. He preserved many letters and papers to document his achievement—he was not bashful about it—and the most important by far was his journal. He started it as a diary of his voyage to New England in 1630 but gradually transformed it into a running account of what happened in Massachusetts Bay under his aegis.

The journal has a long history of its own, which contributed in no small measure to the continuing influence of its author on New Englanders' consciousness of themselves and their singular importance in the nation's development. When they began writing their story not long after Winthrop's death in 1649, the first historians evidently had access to his manuscript. Despite the wretched handwriting, William Hubbard and Cotton Mather in the later seventeenth century, and Thomas Prince in the eighteenth, drew heavily on it. Several historians and antiquarians later transcribed parts of it, and the contents of the first two of the three notebooks in which it was written were published in 1790 in an understandably faulty transcription. After all three manuscripts came to the Massachusetts Historical Society early in the nineteenth century, the treasurer of the society, James Savage, a noted antiquarian, deciphered the handwriting more accurately and published the entire thing in 1825–26 and, after more study of the handwriting, a corrected edition in 1853.

Savage annotated the work with his own well-informed but dogmatic opinions about everyone mentioned. His name appears on the new edition, however, not merely because of his skill as a paleographer and historian but because his transcription of the second notebook, covering the entire period from October 1636 to December 1644, is the best we shall ever have: he lost the original when a fire destroyed the law office where he had left it. The new editors have substituted their own scholarly annotations for Savage's eccentric ones and have corrected some of Savage's few misreadings in the first and third note-books. The new edition will stand as a model of editorial scholarship. No one need struggle with that handwriting again. And to make read-ing easier the editors have used footnotes to explain the meaning of archaic words and to translate the occasional Latin tags. They have even supplied a separate abridged edition for readers who might find the full text more than they want to know about early New England, a possibility that would scarcely have occurred to an earlier generation.

The journal is worth reading simply for the sense it conveys of what it took just to stay alive in seventeenth-century Massachusetts. If Winthrop was a great man, he was not above recording the tribula-tions of everyday life for everyday people in a new world: they got lost in the woods, they drowned in storms as they traveled up and down the coast in small boats, their crude dwellings caught fire and burned down and so did their haystacks, they fell through ice, drought spoiled their crops, wolves ate their cattle. These were not trivialities for Winthrop, and he recounted them seriously, always observing the hand of God at work when disasters struck the impious or good for-tune blessed those who walked in His ways and kept His command-ments. But it is his treatment of larger matters that makes him look so large himself.

As governor of Massachusetts during most of its first twenty years, Winthrop presided over a collection of people, some fifteen or twenty thousand, who had already defied a more powerful government than Winthrop's in order to join him in building a society more to their lik-ing than the one they grew up in. They agreed on a great many things. They even agreed that agreement was itself a good thing—but not good enough to override differences in matters of principle, of which they carried a heavy load. They were determined that God's will be done in Massachusetts as it had not been done in England, and their determination kept them busy searching out every implication of every passage in the Bible for directives to guide their conduct. Having escaped the ecclesiastical authority that had hitherto inhibited their doctrinal and ecclesiological investigations, they turned from denouncing what was wrong in England, on which they could easily agree, to discovering what was right in situations where no one had looked for right or wrong before. Here they could not so readily agree. Bringing their non-negotiable principles to minor matters, they could generate controversies that needlessly threatened their whole enterprise.

Winthrop recorded on March 7, 1634, an episode that suggests what he was up against in trying to keep minor matters minor. This was a controversy over appropriate habiliments for the females of the colony.

> At the Lecture at Boston a Question was propounded about vayles: mr Cotton concluded that where (by the Custom of the place) they were not a signe of the womens subiection, they were not comanded by the Apostle [i.e., Paul, in I Corinthians 11:5–16]. mr Endecott opposed, & did maintaine it by the general Argumentes brought by the Apostle. after some debate, the Governor [Winthrop] perceivinge it to growe to some earnestnesse interposed & so it brake off.

Such debates did not all break off so comfortably. The English flag, flown from forts and carried by military companies, bore a red cross against a white ground. John Endecott, one of the leaders of the colony, who had served as governor before Winthrop's arrival and would serve again, took it upon himself to cut out a portion of the cross from the flag flying at Salem, where he lived. He did it, Winthrop recorded, "vpon this opinion, that the redde Crosse was given to the Kinges of England by the Pope, as an Ensigne of victorye & so a superstitious thinge & a relique of Antichriste." Endecott's act of supererogation troubled the other leaders of the colony, who feared that excising this relic of Antichrist looked like an act of rebellion against the sovereign. They puzzled over what to do about it for a year and then admonished Endecott, in characteristic Puritan fashion, because he "did content himself to have reformed it at Salem, not tak-

ing Care that others might be brought out of it allso. laying a
bleamishe allso vpon the rest of the magistrates as if they would suffer
Idolatrye &c. & givinge occasion to the state of England to thinke ill
of vs." In other words, what he did may have been right, but if so he
should have seen that it was done to all the flags in the colony; but on
the other hand, even if it was right, maybe it was wrong because it
might invite interference from England. The upshot of the affair was
to remove the cross from the ensign of the colony's military companies
but to leave it intact on the flag displayed at Castle Island at the
entrance to Boston Harbor, where ships from England could see it.

The episode, and the casuistry accompanying its resolution, appropriately symbolized the problem faced by Massachusetts as an English
colony bent on achieving complete Protestant purity at a time when
Charles I, aided by his Catholic queen and his "Arminian" archbishop,
seemed to be leading the country back to Rome. The king had granted
the government of Massachusetts to a trading company with the usual
provisions for such companies, in which stockholders (known as
freemen) elected annually a governor, deputy governor, and an executive council of "assistants." While their charter forbade the Massachusetts
Bay Company to make any laws for the colony that were repugnant to
the laws of England, in other respects the company's officers could run
the company and its overseas settlement any way they saw fit. But the
stockholders, taking advantage of the omission in the charter of any
specified meeting place, carried the company lock, stock, and barrel to
Massachusetts Bay, where they turned the charter into the constitution
of the colony and opened freemanship, without any requirement to
purchase stock, to all free adult males belonging to a Congregational
church. They thus carried out a revolution, rendered bloodless only by
the three thousand miles of ocean that separated them from the government they would otherwise have had to overthrow in order to do
what they did. In Massachusetts they created what amounted to a
republic, substituting annually elected rulers for an hereditary monarchy and independent self-starting churches for the whole hierarchical
structure of the Church of England.

To carry out so bold a departure from traditional law and order was to incur high risks of disorder, as the leaders of the venture recognized, none more than Winthrop. Governors deprived of the majesty that surrounded a king, and dependent on annual elections, would have their hands full in maintaining authority over an uprooted people eager for righteousness and all too ready to participate in defining it. Winthrop was particularly fearful that the new freemen would use their freedom to involve the colony in dangerous experiments. It was his view that the role of the freemen should be confined to the choice of officers, on whom their election conferred an authority derived from God Himself. The charter specified that the freemen make laws for the company in meetings of a "General Court" four times a year, but Winthrop reasoned that now that the company had become synonymous with the colony, the less legislation the better because legislation called attention to what they were doing.

Success in establishing a godly society in Massachusetts depended in large measure on keeping quiet about it. The transformation of a joint-stock trading company into an independent republic was certainly not what the king had envisaged in granting the company its charter. As news of what was going on in Massachusetts leaked back to England, the king and his advisers tried to recall the authority they had unwittingly conferred upon the Massachusetts venture. Until the Long Parliament challenged the king's own authority in 1640, the governors of the colony had to prevent imprudent measures that might make the state of England think ill of Massachusetts. Even after a Parliament sympathetic to them took control in England, they had to avoid its embrace in order to preserve an independence that a change in England's government might (and eventually did) destroy.

Winthrop understood more clearly than most of his peers what a thin line they were walking between God's will and England's. Hence he continually sought the discretion to act on his own without laws declaring he had the authority to do what he would do anyhow. He could thus conceal the flouting of English laws that the charter required Massachusetts to conform to. What he hoped for was to establish laws by custom and precedent, the way the English common law had come into being. As he counseled the freemen about making marriage a civil rite,

> *To raise up laws by practice and custom had been no transgression; as in our church discipline, and in matters of marriage, to make a law, that marriages should not be solemnized by ministers, is repugnant to the laws of England; but to bring it to a custom by practice for the magistrates to perform it, is no law made repugnant.*

In this instance Winthrop did not prevail, and ultimately it was flagrant violations of the charter by Massachusetts laws that led to royal assumption of the colony's government in 1685.

But while Winthrop lived, it was his constant endeavor to contain conflicts both within the colony and with England. He inaugurated a policy that the colony pursued successfully for fifty years of dodging orders from England by deliberately misunderstanding them. At home he could be high-handed in his insistence on the authority of government. When the freemen presented a petition for repeal of a law just passed by the General Court, Winthrop was offended:

> *For the people, having deputed others, have no power to make or alter laws, but are to be subject; and if any such order seem unlawful or inconvenient, they were better [to] prefer some reasons, etc., to the court, with manifestation of their desire to move them to a review, than peremptorily to petition to have it repealed, which amounts to a plain reproof of those whom God hath set over them, and putting dishonor upon them, against the tenor of the fifth commandment.*

Winthrop himself was always ready to listen to reasons on both sides in any dispute and to give his own reasons for whatever he did. When he was publicly accused of exceeding his authority in a dispute in 1645, he submitted humbly to trial and when acquitted gave the assembled people a little lecture, reminding them that "it is your selues, who have called vs to this office, & beinge called by you, we have our Authoritye from God." Popular elections did not, in Winthrop's view, make Massachusetts a "meere democracie." Yet the principal criticism of Winthrop's use of authority was not that he used it harshly but that he was too lenient. The freemen wanted not only fixed laws but inflexible and mandatory punishments to ensure that God's will was carried out to the letter.

Winthrop had to give in on the issue of fixed laws, but he was able to preserve judicial discretion in meting out punishments, and it seems likely that his discretion prevented many disputes from escalating into unmanageable divisions. For three years, from the elections of 1634 through those of 1636, he was left out of the governorship in favor of more zealous authoritarians. It was during these years that Roger Williams was banished and Anne Hutchinson took the colony to the brink of civil war over a disputed definition of righteousness. Winthrop's return to the governorship in the election of May 1637 signaled the decline of Hutchinson's influence, and Winthrop presided over her trial and banishment that November.

It would be too much to say that an earlier return of Winthrop to the governor's seat could have averted the troubles, for Williams and Hutchinson were both more than a match for him in argument and appealed strongly to the large number of New Englanders who enjoyed pressing principles to their logical conclusions. But Winthrop's success as a governor, recognized so often in the annual elections, was owing to the way he combined authority with leniency to defuse dissent before it became rebellion. He was probably not a charismatic figure, nor did he have the intellectual powers of Williams or Hutchinson, but he carried authority with the confidence that compels respect. The leniency that lesser men complained of grew from strength, not weakness. He could be stern when sternness was needed, but he could afford to give way without losing face when magnanimity would serve better.

To be sure, we know about his success largely because his account is often the only one we have. As the editors of the journal note, "The reader who accepts his presentation will certainly conclude that the author of the journal was much the best and wisest public man in early Massachusetts." True enough, but the other surviving records from early Massachusetts, while not as full in many details as the journal, are not likely to lead an impartial reader to a contrary conclusion. For example, virtually everything we know about Roger Williams and the views that led to his expulsion from Massachusetts comes from a few passages in Winthrop's journal. Williams did not publish any of his own writings until 1643, seven years after his banishment, but these later writings corroborate the very ideas and arguments that Winthrop ascribes to him. What he advocated publicly in Massachusetts was precisely the kind of thing that Winthrop sought to silence as threats to his colony. Williams demanded public denunciations of the Church of England and ultimately denied the possibility of any true church or ministry before Christ's second coming. Yet we learn from Williams himself (as Winthrop does not record it in his journal) that when the General Court was preparing to ship him back to England in disgrace, it was Winthrop who forewarned him and suggested that he flee to Rhode Island. The two maintained a friendly correspondence until Winthrop's death, without either persuading the other of his views. On the other hand, Winthrop took pains to keep Hutchinson and her adherents out of the colony. He regarded her as an instrument of Satan and displayed an unseemly relish in recording her misfortunes as an exile from the godliness and good order of Massachusetts.

In hindsight Winthrop can be faulted as a despot, however benevolent. The freemen in their demand for explicit laws and mandatory sentencing wanted not only to guarantee the enforcement of God's will but also to protect themselves against a despotism that could turn malevolent. Winthrop thought that annual elections were sufficient protection and that the possibility of English interference brought on by open defiance of English law constituted a greater threat to the Puritan experiment than his own style of quiet action and oral suasion. Winthrop's despotism prevented in Massachusetts the proliferation of religious and political views and the civil wars that England experi-

enced when the Puritans destroyed royal authority there instead of
escaping from it to America. And Winthrop did it without exposing
Massachusetts to the tyranny that a Cromwell imposed on England,
and without provoking the reaction that returned England to a royal
oppression which required yet another revolution to overturn.

John Winthrop surely was the wisest, if not the best, public man in
early Massachusetts. He guided a whole society in a truly revolutionary reform. He appears in the journal as so restrained, so judicious,
that it is easy to forget how radical a thing it was that he did. His reluctance to call attention to what he was doing in Massachusetts masks his
resolve from the reader of his journal, just as he wished to mask it from
England. But we catch an occasional glimpse of the iron in his character when he records laconically that a rumor of England's intention to
send troops to bring Massachusetts into line "occasioned the magistrates and deputyes to hasten our fortifications." This was not a man
who would have given up without a fight.

In his quiet determination and conservative direction of radical
reforms Winthrop resembles some of the other men in whom
Americans have found greatness. Washington and Lincoln both
directed radical reforms in a conservative style. Benjamin Franklin followed the same pattern in a more complex way. He did his best to
transform the British Empire to make it acceptable to his countrymen,
and when that proved impossible, he led the fight for independence
through patient diplomacy, as Washington did through a conservative
style of warfare. Roosevelt transformed American social policy while
conserving its capitalist frame. Only Jefferson does not fit the pattern.
His temperament was radical, and his friend Madison had to furnish
the conservative restraint on his actions in public office, where he did
not in fact achieve as significant reforms as the others did. With the
exception of Jefferson, the men whom Americans recognize as great
seem to have pursued and accomplished radical ends by conservative
means. Winthrop was the first.

June 12, 1997

CHAPTER TWO

Heaven Can't Wait

———— ∞ ————

The Puritan Conversion Narrative: The Beginnings of American Expression
Patricia Caldwell

The Life and Times of Cotton Mather
Kenneth Silverman

THE PREOCCUPATION of American historical and literary scholars with the New England Puritans must seem to outsiders like an obsession. For as long as professional scholarship has existed in the United States its practitioners have devoted themselves to analyzing in ever-increasing detail and sophistication the ideas and activities of a set of people whom many Americans would like to forget. Part of the reason may be that the Puritans left behind so full a record of what they thought and did that scholars cannot resist the temptation to make the most of it. But in all fairness there is more to it than that. Quite apart from the intrinsic interest of the complex system of beliefs the Puritans carried with them, their lives give a clue to what it meant at the beginning to be American. And the level of scholarship dealing with them has reached a point where it can address the human condition itself. In the 1970s and 1980s the focus shifted from theology to experience, from doctrine to devotion, and the results have been rewarding.

The two books here are a case in point. Patricia Caldwell's study examines Puritan religious experience through the narratives given by candidates for membership in New England churches. Every candidate was required to deliver before the assembled congregation a spiritual autobiography, describing his or her progression toward salvation, for membership in the church was confined to persons who could convince others, through such a narrative, that they were predestined to reach the goal. The narratives were somewhat of a novelty when they were introduced in the first years of settlement, and Caldwell advances a new and convincing analysis of their origins in earlier recitations of creeds and confessions of faith. She also has some perceptive things to say about how they helped to bind together the communities where they were performed. But these are the least of her achievements. In examining the content of the narratives (recorded by ministers at the oral presentations), she gives us a searching account of how the American Puritan experience differed from the English experience from which it sprang.

In England, where Puritans had to contend against a hostile government and established church or else (during their years of triumph) against a host of heresies, believers found a haven of certainty in their personal dealings with God. When they wrote about their religious experiences, they wrote of passing through tribulations of spirit to find rest and contentment in some inner assurance of salvation. They began with doubt and ended in certainty. American Puritans had plenty of tribulations to record, but in their narratives the tribulations never end, the doubts never cease. Among many of the first generation the trip to America seems to have been a kind of false dawn, looked forward to as a release from affliction but experienced as a spiritual disappointment, because entry into the company of New England saints did not bring the expected heavenly joy. "After I came hither I saw my condition more miserable than ever" became the common refrain. As Caldwell observes, "A certain emotion begins to be connected with the migration: a kind of grim, gray disappointment that emerges in conversion stories as an almost obligatory structural element."

But this disappointment in America required sublimation into disappointment in oneself. And American Puritans became expert at disappointing themselves. Without the surrounding wickedness of the Old World to combat, they contended with their own continuing sins and corrupt nature. Lifelong anxiety and self-deprecation became the hallmarks of the American Puritan. He made a virtue of uncertainty until he came to identify feelings of assurance about salvation as signs of its absence. The only way to be sure was to be unsure. The only distinction it was safe to claim was that of being the chief of sinners, and one of the primary sins to be bewailed and repented was disappointment in America. Nor was it necessary to have made the trip from England to be guilty of it: those who were born in New England could also be taught to mourn their failure to appreciate it. There thus developed a curious love-hate attitude toward the land, combined with self-abasement for failing to live up to the opportunities it offered.

There is much more to Caldwell's work than I can suggest, and it offers striking insights into the nature of Puritan piety, insights that are borne out in Kenneth Silverman's study of Cotton Mather. Mather, a third-generation Puritan, came of age at a time when Puritans were already on the defensive; and, given his ancestry, he had to be more defensive than most. His grandfathers, John Cotton and Richard Mather, were principal architects of the New England way of worship, and his father, Increase Mather, was its leading champion until Cotton assumed the task. Silverman, though he gives his book the good old-fashioned title of *Life and Times*, has little to say about the times (the last quarter of the seventeenth and first quarter of the eighteenth centuries) that has not already been said in greater detail by other scholars. But his treatment of his subject's life is something else, a shrewd and penetrating examination of a complex man.

Cotton Mather may be miscast in the popular mind as the typical Puritan, but he is nevertheless a man to be reckoned with. As with Puritans generally he earns inevitable attention simply because he left so large a record of himself, 388 titles published in his own lifetime and numerous unpublished manuscripts, including one of the most detailed diaries of a diary-keeping age. But again there is more to it than that. It is possible to write books and letters by the gross without revealing much about oneself. Mather has gained notoriety as the arch Puritan and continues to present a challenge to scholars because he does reveal himself and in doing so exhibits the virtues and vices of Puritanism itself.

It is only fair to say that he had endearing qualities, of which Silverman makes as much as anyone can. He was apparently a brilliant conversationalist; people enjoyed his visits. He often displayed a genuine concern for the misfortunes of others. He seems to have had an appreciation, not to say passion, for beautiful women. And of his fifteen children, his favorite was a winning ne'er-do-well son, whom he loved dearly despite the company he kept (which seems to have included Boston's whores and dancing masters).

But it is not these human qualities that have made Mather so challenging to scholars. Nor is it, I think, his very considerable intellectual achievement, to which Robert Middlekauff has given full credit and appreciation in his brilliant study of the family.[1] Although Mather must be the central figure in any study of the intellectual life of New England in his time (as he was even in the work of Perry Miller, who labeled him an impervious intellect and a nauseous human being), his influence on the subsequent intellectual development of New England is open to question. What makes him fascinating, what makes us keep coming back to him, is his palpable display of the tensions and inner conflicts that are evident but more subdued in other Puritans.

The uncertainty about salvation exhibited in the Puritan conversion narratives of Patricia Caldwell becomes in Cotton Mather a false modesty about everything he does. His estimate of his own worth, by comparison at least with all those other chief sinners, was enormous, but he felt obliged to rejoice in the world's failure to share it. "His impulse," Silverman observes, "when he felt unappreciated, [was] to snarl." But he reduced this to what was often a more offensive unctuousness. When the Harvard Corporation passed him by for the presidency, he felt obliged to write a letter to one of its members, thanking him profusely for what he actually considered a calculated insult; and he confided in his diary, "I rejoice, I rejoice, I feel a secret Joy in it, that I am thus conformed unto Him who was despised and rejected of Men." Mather was, in fact, an obvious candidate for the position. He *was* the most eminent minister in New England. But Jesus Christ he was not, and failure to become president of Harvard was not crucifixion.

Mather provoked his contemporaries as much as he provokes readers of his diary today. There was in everything he did an "ambidexter" quality, a word that Silverman aptly borrows from Mather's enemy Robert Calef, who charged Mather with inciting the Salem witch-hunt of 1692. The charge was unfair, but Calef was correct in using the word to describe Mather's attitude toward the trials. On the one hand he condemned the way they were conducted; on the other hand he praised the judges. And the attitude extended into all his dealings with the world; he exhibited, in Silverman's words, "belligerent courtesy, self-flattering modesty, fretful calm, denigrating compliments, unacceptable offers." What Mather gave with one hand he took back with the other; and "his goodwill and good cheer were often deliberately reversed expressions of hurt pride, anger, and discouragement."

This ambidexter quality is never so obvious or so extreme in other Puritans as it is in Mather, but the sources of it surely lie in the conflicting demands that Puritanism made on all its adherents. Puritanism required a believer to find certainty in uncertainty, required him (or her) to rely for salvation on unmerited, predestined saving grace while spending a lifetime doing unrewarded good works, required him to search his soul for the Holy Spirit but denied him access to direct revelation, required him to be pure but told him he could not be. The strain produced by trying to contain these contradictions was never small, and it was easy to fall into heresy by pursuing one requirement at the expense of its opposite. The strain was doubly hard for anyone with Mather's intellectual energy and enlarged ego; and in his secret flirtations with heresy we can see the temptations that led many other Puritans astray.

It was perhaps the failure of the American world to appreciate him adequately that pushed Mather not simply to a characteristically ambivalent attitude toward America, but to a dangerously (for a Puritan) close communication with his Maker. In his discursive historical masterpiece, *Magnalia Christi Americana* (1702), and in various other writings, Mather celebrated America in general and New England in particular. Even while deprecating the country's and his own provinciality, he hailed the founders of New England as holy heroes, of whom their descendants, himself included, were unworthy. But at the same time he clearly thought his contemporaries as unworthy of him as of his ancestors; he saw himself as one of the blessings of life in New England which an ungrateful, backsliding people neglected.

In compensation he sought and obtained recognition abroad, including membership in the Royal Society (which he solicited by proclaiming his unworthiness of it) and an honorary degree from Glasgow. But he hankered after higher recognition. It was given him by angels, who joined him in his study as he lay prostrate on the floor and who communicated to him various future events in which God would favor him. When some of the events failed to materialize, he became more cautious and the angels ceased their visitations. And a good thing too, for he had come pretty close to claiming the direct revelation that all good Puritans knew had ceased with the writing of the Bible. Mather with his theological skill could doubtless have drawn a fine line between angelic and divine revelation, but he was on dangerous ground and he knew it. He drew back, smothered his anguish, and remained a good Puritan. But the price was more snarling smiles, more proud groveling, more indignant rejoicing over insults.

Mather was capable of genuine courage, as he demonstrated in the smallpox controversy. He had been convinced by reading accounts of inoculation performed in Africa that people who took the disease that way were in far less danger than those who became naturally infected, and he was right. In the face of public hostility and the ridicule of professional physicians, he not only advocated the practice but subjected his family to it—and had a bomb thrown through his window for his pains. But this was no more than he expected. He was always doing good and being requited with evil. In a book recommending good works he warned the reader that "a man of *good merit*, is a kind of *public enemy*." In another book he explained how to bear insults the way he did: "Be always really, heartily, inwardly *loathing your self*." And he proudly collected the abusive letters he received, tying them in a bundle labeled "*Libels: Father, forgive them!*"

Silverman's portrait of Mather is sympathetic but unapologetic. By focusing on the way Mather experienced the world, and on his ambivalent reactions to it, he gives us an inside view, albeit an enlarged one, of what it meant to be an American Puritan. If the view is unsettling, it may be because we have not yet seen the last Puritan.

May 31, 1984

CHAPTER THREE

Those Sexy Puritans

———— ∞∞∞ ————

Sexual Revolution in Early America
Richard Godbeer

I F THERE WAS a sexual revolution in early America, it was not because people had revolutionary ideas about sex. In their new communities the settlers made sex outside marriage illegal, as it had been in the world they left behind. But the New World presented new situations that invited defiance or reconsideration of conventional restraints, and Richard Godbeer looks at the results in a book that shows how sex inside and outside marriage helped to shape American society. In three of the places he examines, the usual limitations on sex outside marriage simply did not work.

On southern tobacco and rice plantations, many masters felt that their ownership of slaves carried an exemption from any rules about having sex with them. Thomas Jefferson, we now know, acted as if he had such an exemption, and so did his father-in-law: Jefferson's wife could count six siblings among her father's slaves. No one in Virginia offered to defend such lapses and respectable people felt uncomfortable even talking about them. In South Carolina, on the other hand, where the majority of the population was enslaved, the presence of dark-skinned children resembling their owner was too common to cause embarrassment. "Charlestonians," Godbeer tells us, "discussed this aspect of their sexual lives with a frankness that would have been inconceivable in the Chesapeake." Both colonies enacted laws forbidding miscegenation as well as extramarital sex, but prosecution of highly placed offenders was unthinkable.

A wholly different disregard for the recognized rules could be found in the Carolina backcountry, where, in the absence of magistrates and ministers, the inhabitants engaged in do-it-yourself marriage and divorce, or lived, as the Virginia diarist William Byrd observed, "in comfortable fornication." Since relationships could be made and broken at will, the distinction between marital and extramarital sex was hard to find. Couples who considered themselves married gave little attention to how they got that way. As Godbeer puts it, "The very reason so many couples saw premarital sex as unproblematic was that they considered private declarations to be more significant than public confirmation of their relationship." They continued to feel that way until eastern institutions of law and order overtook them.

Yet another departure from recognized norms occurred along the frontiers when fur traders made matches with Indian women. Indians recognized marriage, and different tribes had their own rules about what it signified, but an exclusive right to sex was not generally one of them. Traders who took Indian wives in Indian territory were obliged to follow Indian rules. In some locations the society's official restrictions gained reinforcement from a fear on the part of whites that intercourse with blacks or Indians might somehow reduce them to the barbaric status they assigned to people of the wrong color. Occasionally some outsider might propound the desirability of intermarriage as a social policy, but those actually engaged in it did not mount a reasoned defense of it or of any kind of sex outside marriage. Indeed there are only sporadic records of what anyone thought about sex in the plantation colonies and along the frontier. In depicting what went on in them Godbeer has had to rely heavily on scattered court records and on the testimony of a few unusual individuals like William Byrd.

The case is quite different in New England, where people never stopped explaining themselves. Godbeer wisely and perhaps inevitably gives his closest attention to their explanations, and his analysis offers fresh insights into the role of sex in the most self-conscious society we have ever known. Since early New Englanders kept such abundant and detailed records of everything they thought and did, they have already enjoyed more than their share of attention from historians, not least in the past fifty years. Yet in the multiplication of studies, while there has been much ado about "gender," there has not been much about sex. The word itself will not be found in the index of most volumes. The only previous book on the subject is limited to what went on during half a century in a single Massachusetts county.[1] Godbeer's is the first serious assessment of the role of sex in Puritan thought and behavior. The result will surprise anyone still harboring the popular stereotype of killjoys in steeple-crowned hats or the images of "grizzly saints" and tormented outcasts that darken the pages of Nathaniel Hawthorne and Arthur Miller.

Puritan theology placed a high value on the affections, specifically on the love that Christ excited in believers, and the most intense love that most people knew or felt was sexual. Hence in Puritan sermons the most common metaphor for Christ was the bridegroom. What He did for believers was what bridegrooms did for brides, and ministers did not hesitate to use the word "impregnate" to describe it. Every true believer longed "for the kisses of Christ's mouth, not for a single kisse, but for kisse upon kisse." Church services were the "marriage bed," and "a maid affected with the love of her beloved, is not satisfied without the enjoyment of the marriage- bed."[2] The conversion experience, required for full membership in a church, was nothing short of orgasmic, a possession of the soul so physical that it required carnal metaphors to describe it. Church records show that substantially more women than men enjoyed a saving soul possession, but no one seems to have found anything incongruous in having men become brides for a sexually defined religious experience. The young John Winthrop, for example, could transform himself easily from Mary Winthrop's husband to Christ's bride. After Mary's death, recalling

that entire and sweet love that had been sometymes betweene us, God brought me by that occasion in to suche a heavenly meditation of the love betweene Christ and me, as ravished my heart with unspeakable joye;

methought my soule had as familiar and sensible society with him, as my
wife could have with the kindest husbande.3

Anyone who has read Puritan sermons will be familiar with this theological appropriation of sexual love. It can also be found in the very
platitudes of Puritan love letters, whose writers habitually remind each
other that their earthly passion must not exceed their comparable
yearning for Christ. Both kinds of love could be understood only in
sexual terms.

IN GIVING meaning to religious experience, sexual union in return
acquired a religious blessing. It was, of course, conferred only on sex in
marriage. Christ was a bridegroom, not a libertine. But marriage without sex was as hollow as religion without the fulfillment of Christ's
union with the soul. Marriage carried an entitlement to the joy of sex.
Women as well as men, Puritans believed, had a right to "that pang of
pleasure" which came from intercourse. The laws of New Haven, the
strictest of Puritan colonies, allowed a wife to divorce an impotent or
unperforming husband, regardless of whether or not she was "fit to
bear children." And Godbeer cites the case of a Massachusetts woman,
aged fifty-four, who left her husband on the grounds that he was not
giving her the sexual gratification that marriage entitled her to.

Surviving court records attest that not all New Englanders waited
for marriage to sanctify the experience. Many unwed mothers and
fathers endured fines or whipping for their haste. But the purpose of
the punishment, as for all crimes and misdemeanors among the
Puritans, was redemption rather than retribution. It was axiomatic that
sin lay deep in every human heart. People who led outwardly model
lives differed from criminals only in the favor God had granted them
by withholding temptation or opportunity. They were all guilty of lust
if not of fornication, of greed if not of theft, of hate if not of murder.
Judges therefore had to keep in mind that only the grace of God saved
them from standing in the place of those they judged. And as God for-

gave penitent sinners, they too should forgive penitent lawbreakers. Couples who succumbed to their erotic urges too soon had only to demonstrate a proper repentance to escape with light sentences and recover their standing in the community.

The courts had also to deal with people who thought that sex before marriage should be permissible for some couples. Marriages in New England were commonly preceded by formal espousals, often public, and sometimes lasting several months. Many people felt that espousals were a sufficiently binding commitment to justify intercourse and acted accordingly. In doing so they were not rejecting the substance of Puritan doctrine. Rather, as Godbeer sees it, they constituted an independent popular subculture that grew alongside and within the official one. From the beginning this extralegal set of attitudes and beliefs affected what the courts enforced, not only in the timing of marriage but also in the tolerance of deviant behavior. People sensed, Godbeer says, "that official ideology was of limited use in making intelligible their actual experience and observations." Sex of all kinds was observable in the close quarters of seventeenth-century houses. Unusual practices and appetites could become common knowledge without anyone feeling obliged to alert the authorities. The people of a neighborhood might even thwart the prosecution of a person whose sexual offenses did not offend *them*. Testimony in prosecutions for sodomy, a capital crime, revealed that New Englanders were sometimes "well informed about sodomitical behavior in their midst" and found it not as horrifying as the laws expected them to. Godbeer's most telling example is the case of Nicholas Sension of Windsor, Connecticut. When he was charged with sodomy in 1677, his neighbors freely disclosed that they had known of his "sodomitical actings" for thirty years. Though the prosecution of his crime went forward, in the absence of willing witnesses the court could find him guilty only of *attempted* sodomy. In the New England colonies it was equally difficult to obtain testimony concerning the only other capital offenses, adultery and bestiality. Convictions for any of these were rare, because the laws required "that no man shall be put to death without the testimonie of two or three witnesses" who had actually seen the act committed.

In the course of the eighteenth century the courts accommodated more and more to popular standards, and by the 1780s popular standards had stretched to give young New Englanders a sexual freedom that was probably greater than any generation enjoyed thereafter for another century or more. It was symptomatic that by the 1750s the courts had lost interest in punishing premarital sex, despite a growing number of pregnant brides, amounting to 30 or 40 percent in some towns by the Revolutionary era. When young men went acourting now, they did not necessarily wait for permission from the girls' parents. Parents allowed their sons and daughters to frolic unchaperoned in late-night sleigh rides, corn huskings, and dancing parties. And the young made the most of the opportunities offered them.

IN AN EFFORT to regain a degree of control, New England families adopted a custom that has puzzled moralists ever since. They encouraged the young men courting their daughters to spend the whole night at it under their own roofs. After the old folks retired the couple slept together unattended. They were supposed to do no more than slumber, but did anyone really expect that a young man and young woman in bed together would simply whisper sweet nothings to each other before dozing off? However shocking to outsiders, the practice had the advantage of giving parents some influence in their daughter's choice of a husband. Or, as Godbeer concludes, "If couples were forced to find secret venues in which to have sex, families and neighbors would have to rely on rumor and guesswork in figuring out who had impregnated their daughters." The practice was common enough to be given a name, "bundling," and there may have been recognized protocols for carrying it on but no solemn ceremonies to spoil the fun. All in all, despite the Revolutionary War, the 1780s and the 1790s in New England were a lighthearted time for the young.

How long it lasted is not clear. That it happened at all seems to have been owing to a number of perhaps unrelated developments: an increased regard for privacy, a loosening of close community ties with a corresponding decline of neighborly nosiness, and—Godbeer emphasizes this—a spirit of personal independence derived from the collective independence from Great Britain. These doubtless brought a general loosening of sexual relations in all the new United States (though relations could scarcely have become looser than they already were in the Carolina backcountry). Everything tightened up in the early nineteenth century with the exaltation of women as the repository of republican virtue and their simultaneous degradation as prostitutes in urban areas, complex developments that Godbeer traces in his last two chapters.

It is difficult to see any of these developments as a sexual revolution. Most people probably still confined their sex lives to their husbands or wives. What Godbeer leaves unsaid in his consideration of the various departures from the norm is the exclusion of the church and clergy from the powers they had enjoyed as custodians of morality in England and most of Europe. Membership in American churches was mostly voluntary and expulsion from membership (excommunication) in congregationally organized churches was the prerogative of the congregation, not the minister. The Anglican church failed to ordain an American bishop, and without one the church courts that monitored sexual relations in England could not exist. Secular courts often undertook to fill the gap by punishing sexual offenses, but the clergy were barred from participation. In the early seventeenth century they had exerted a powerful influence in New England, which has often been called a theocracy. But the existence of real theocracies in the Near East today should call our attention to the care that New England Puritans took not to create one. In the rest of America the absence of clerical powers may have been at first accidental; for the founders of New England it was a matter of fundamental principle.

It could be said that the Puritans left England to get away from theocracy. In England, clerical and political power were scarcely distinguishable. The king was ex officio head of the church, and the whole population were automatically members of it. The church parish was the unit of local government. Bishops sat in Parliament to make civil laws and presided over courts that dealt not only with moral offenses but also with the probate of wills, collecting lucrative fees at every step. Only clerics could perform marriages, and divorce was impossible except by act of Parliament.

The founders of New England, both laymen and clergy, had suffered from this system, and they were determined to bar churches and churchmen from any kind of political power in the new colonies. A "Body of Liberties" adopted in Massachusetts in 1641 prescribed that no action by a church could affect a man's tenure of political office. In that colony during the seventeenth century, when all political offices were elective, no minister was ever elected to one. Ministers could not even perform marriages, which were sacred but secular. Ministers could preach against sexual license, but that was the most they could do. This reining in of the clergy as a matter of principle among the most devout Americans accorded with the attitude that other Americans acquired from the multiplicity of sects that developed during the colonial period, each of them fearful of a power that might be given to others. The prospect of an Anglican bishop in the 1760s drew a storm of protest not merely from New England but from laymen everywhere who wanted to continue running their churches by themselves.

Because of this disarming of church and clergy, when the young people of New England began to kick up their heels in the last decades of the eighteenth century there was no church power to do more than scold them. The real sexual revolution in early America was the secularization of morality. American sexual mores have sometimes been absurdly strict as regulated by law and custom. But until the current campaign to rearm the church as a dispenser of welfare (which I believe to be unconstitutional), the role of the church has been limited to talk. Secular morality has given us a freedom we have long taken for granted, because it prevailed for a century and a half before it was enshrined in the First Amendment. It saved us from the religious wars of the seventeenth century which devastated Europe. It saved us for long from the modern religious wars of the Middle East. Those wars have now spilled over upon us. We are threatened by theocratic morality, which has never excluded war, terror, and slaughter of the innocent as a means of extending religion and religious morality. The First Amendment has never looked so good.

June 27, 2002

CHAPTER FOUR

The Chosen People

—◆◆◆—

Intellectual Life in the Colonial South, 1585–1763
Richard Beale Davis

The American Jeremiad
Sacvan Bercovitch

SOUTHERNERS HAVE long been irked by the tendency of New Englanders to write American history, especially intellectual history, as the story of New England writ large. Richard Beale Davis set out to redress the balance. In three large volumes he compiled the evidence to show that the people of England's southern colonies (Maryland, Virginia, the Carolinas, and Georgia) thought, wrote, and prayed at least as much as those in New England, if not more.

Davis's method is comprehensive and encyclopedic. Drawing on a host of sources, he has produced, in effect, a series of complete monographs on every category of intellectual endeavor: literature, education, religion, science and technology, the fine arts (including landscape gardening), law, economics, and politics. Along the way he gives us 150 pages on the Indian in southern colonial literature and nearly 240 pages on books, libraries, reading, and printing. In each chapter of the book he begins with an overview of the subject and then breaks it down into subtopics and sub-subtopics for a rundown of everything said or done that can be called intellectual, from the abortive Roanoke Colony of 1585 to the beginning of the American Revolution. For example, in the chapter on the Indian, one of the subtopics is "The Red Man as His White Neighbor Saw Him." Under this heading we begin with "Indian Personal Character in General," followed by discrete discussions of Individual Indians, General Impressions of Indian Life, Dancing and Music, Sports and Games, Medicine, Marriage and Burial, Utopias (two plans for Indian communities supervised by whites), White Ideas of Red Origins, and Native Religion and Christian Conversion and Education.

As a reference work these volumes have become standard. Despite continual warnings that the evidence is not all in, Davis combed the printed sources and some of the manuscript ones for a fuller inventory of intellectual activity and artifacts than had yet been attempted for any set of colonies, northern or southern. It is an impressive achievement, and it goes far toward demonstrating the author's main contention, namely that there *was* intellectual activity. The work is not so successful in demonstrating that all this activity was the product of what he calls an "early southern mind" that left as profound a mark on American national consciousness as the New England mind. Indeed the kind of analysis needed for such a demonstration is scarcely attempted. The author seems more determined to accumulate evidence of thought than to perceive its direction. While he succeeds admirably in showing that southerners engaged in thought about a great many different things, his delineations of *what* they thought do not yield a core of ideas that will sustain the notion of a southern mind. He assures us from time to time, and most insistently in an epilogue, that southerners were realists, who saw things as they were, that they loved the soil, that they had a sense of humor and a number of other traits shared with their descendants, but the characteristics he mentions do not add up to a set of ideas held in common.

Again and again he contrasts his genial folk with the crabbed, hysterical, hypocritical New Englanders, but the contrast never develops into extended analysis. It satisfies him to tell us, for example, that southern funeral elegies were secular, unlike the "lugubrious gnarled Calvinist lines of New England versified mourning for the departed," or that Hugh Jones and Robert Beverley (authors of two early accounts of Virginia) were "far closer to the main stream of American historiography, or the American dream, than Bradford or Winthrop or Mather or Edwards." In opening the discussion of the Indian he raises the extremely interesting question of why the captivity narrative, which became a distinct literary genre in the North, was far less common in the South. This and other questions, he says, will be raised in the chapter "and usually answered by implication," but when we arrive at a section devoted to "Accounts of Captivity and Torture," we get merely the assertion that the captivity narrative did not in fact become a literary genre in the South.

Indeed what we get throughout the three volumes is an assemblage of facts, impressive in amount but relatively inert. The reason may be the author's concern for comprehensiveness. This is in many ways a pioneering work, which can serve as a guide for future investigators. But one suspects that the level of analysis may be limited by the material itself. Individual works, like those of John Smith or William Byrd, could certainly be subjected (and have been) to closer analysis than they receive here. But it is questionable that the thinkers of the colonial South had enough ideas in common to warrant generalizations that go beyond the elementary. This is not to say that their thinking was elementary but that they did not think together. They were not collectively self-conscious in the way that colonial New Englanders were. The men and women who settled New England took themselves very, very seriously, not only as individuals but as a group engaged in a historic mission. That is why they were both so irritating and so influential. Posterity has accepted them, despite numerous protests, at their own evaluation of themselves.

The South, on the other hand, though probably the most self-conscious section of the country today, only began to achieve its collective consciousness in the period after Davis's study stops. The Revolutionary generation of southerners first showed a clear awareness of the sectional characteristics that divided them from the North in the 1780s in the Continental Congress. The awareness surfaced also in the debates of the Constitutional Convention of 1787 and still more strongly in the rise of the Republican Party under Jefferson and

Madison in the 1790s. But even then, and well into the nineteenth
century, most white southerners, including Jefferson and Madison,
were uncomfortable about one of the principal distinguishing marks of
the South: dependence on slave labor.

As southern self-consciousness emerged more and more overtly in
the nineteenth century, it was linked more and more to explicit recognition of that dependence and of all the consequences that went with
it. By the middle of the nineteenth century it would be possible to
speak of a southern mind, but that mind was almost wholly engaged in
the sterile task of defending slavery as a beneficent institution, one
which permitted the development of an upper class devoted to high
intellectual pursuits. It is one of the many ironies of southern and
American history that the South became a major source of high intellectual pursuits (*pace* Davis) only when it lay in ruins. With the end of
the Civil War southerners began to write as never before, and from
that time to this have produced more than their share of the country's
literature. In the colonial period, however, southerners did not feel
obliged to defend their way of life or even to reflect much about their
"peculiar institution," perhaps because it was not so peculiar then as it
later became. Davis has little to say about the development of slavery,
because, as he rightly observes, "the growing institution was not a
major element of southern thinking, economic or otherwise, in the
first century after Jamestown." We might extend the statement for
another fifty years or even another hundred. One of the most remarkable things about southern colonial writing is the absence of discussions of slavery. The silence is at times so profound that one suspects it
may in itself be significant, but without the gift of second sight one
cannot write the history of unexpressed ideas. And without ideas held
in common it is difficult to sustain the notion—which at best requires
some heavy sustaining—of a common "mind," an early southern mind.

The case with New England is surely different. The contrast, as
Davis insists, is lugubrious, but it is also, as he does not seem to notice,
a contrast between people committed to a well-articulated view of
themselves as a group and people without such a view. The New

Englanders not only sustained their view through various transformations but managed to impose it on the whole nation of which they became a part. It is, of course, this bit of cultural imperialism that makes Davis so cross with them. Long before 1860 New Englanders laid claim to the national consciousness and gave their own past as a legacy to the nation, whether the nation wanted it or not. The way the New Englanders did it is the subject to which Sacvan Bercovitch addresses himself in *The American Jeremiad*, a book that will surely raise the hackles of those who think that the New England mind has been elevated at the expense of the South.

It is one measure of the success of New England's cultural hegemony that Bercovitch can unblushingly entitle his book *The American Jeremiad*, for the jeremiad, first identified as such by Perry Miller, was a New England specialty. As defined by Miller, it was a sermon in which New England ministers, after the heroic days of the founding had passed, recited the afflictions with which God was now visiting His backsliding people, identified the sins that had provoked Him, and warned of much direr chastisement if the people failed to repent and return to the ways of their fathers. Miller was concerned to show how the jeremiad came to serve as a ritual renewal of New England's mission. But Bercovitch perceives a great deal more in the ritual than Miller did and extends it to cover a multitude of sermonic, literary, and oratorical performances. For Bercovitch, the jeremiad embraces the sermons of John Cotton and John Winthrop (the famous "Modell of Christian Charity") before the settlers landed, and it goes on through the Mathers and Jonathan Edwards to include the sermons of the Revolutionary period, the poetry of Timothy Dwight, the Fourth of July orations of the early nineteenth century, and finally the essays of Ralph Waldo Emerson, Thoreau's *Walden*, the novels of Melville and Hawthorne, and Walt Whitman's *Democratic Vistas*.

It obviously requires some doing to bring all these together without reducing them to triviality. Bercovitch is up to the task. Seen through the jeremiad in his extended understanding of it, a great deal of American social and intellectual history makes a new kind of sense.

Major episodes, not only the founding and development of New England but the Great Awakening of the 1740s, the Revolution, westward expansion, the American Renaissance, even the Civil War, all appear explicable in terms of the rhetorical formula first developed by the seventeenth-century New England ministers.

Bercovitch is not out to replace Miller. In the preface he pays homage to him and expresses his disdain for the "patricidal totem feast following Miller's death, when a swarm of social and literary historians rushed to pick apart the corpus of his work." That corpus, he insists, "remains pretty much intact, and . . . will remain a towering achievement of the American mind." But Bercovitch builds on Miller and on the work of many other historians, making use of their insights to create a pattern of interpretation that brings together seemingly disparate views in a new synthesis. It is difficult to summarize his argument without destroying its subtlety and sophistication. Yet we must try.

The distinguishing characteristic of the jeremiad, as Bercovitch sees it, was not its condemnation of backsliding (though that condemnation was always present and prominent) but its prophetic assurance of a bright future, not God's anger but His special love for His chosen people, not pessimism but optimism. New Englanders, he argues, identified their hopes of eternal salvation with their hopes for the future of their church and their land. Through the migration to New England, the perseverance of the saints became attributed to the society as a whole. The history of New England became sacred history, which would eventuate in the millennium: "the progress of saint and society became identified: one reflected, and verified, the other." With the Great Awakening of the 1740s this vision was extended to involve the whole continent. Cotton Mather had already made the jump in his *Magnalia Christi Americana* (which Miller himself described as "a colossal Jeremiad"). Jonathan Edwards, with his concerts of prayer, saw the Great Awakening as the beginning of a millennial fulfillment of New England's and America's destiny, enlarging the constituency of the jeremiad "from saintly New England theocrats to newborn American saints."

The expansion continued as North America became the battle-ground for the war against Antichrist in the shape of Catholic France. The French and Indian War which ended in 1763 was to be seen as a holy war, in which God's people, having repented of their sins, must inevitably triumph. When the quarrel with England began soon after and culminated in independence, it was the jeremiad that enabled Americans to see their rebellion not as an act of patricide but as one of filial piety. George III was not a father but an affliction, playing the role that drought, disease, and hostile Indians had played for an earlier generation. In casting him off, Americans must return to the saintly ways of their founding fathers, the fathers, that is, who had founded New England.

By this time, however, the saintly ways of the founding fathers had themselves been transformed into something that the fathers might not have recognized. If we may use another author's terms, the Protestant Ethic had been transformed into the spirit of capitalism, and the jeremiad was now used to batter down any dissent from the values that went with capitalism. Bercovitch detects such dissent during the Revolution in widespread popular movements that threatened the stability of government and the dominance of the rich and well-born, a view that not all historians of the Revolution are likely to accept. He adopts the posture of the Progressive and neo-Progressive and New Left historians to declare that "the first aim of legislators after 1776 was to curb popular demands." The Federalists of the 1780s enlisted the clergy in this cause. Through them the jeremiad, "mediating between religion and ideology . . . gave contract the sanctity of covenant, free enterprise the halo of grace, progress the assurance of the chiliad, and nationalism the grandeur of typology. In short, it wed self-interest to social perfection, and conferred on both the unique blessings of American destiny."

Once we have reached this point, the rest of American history falls easily into place. Westward expansion was "a sort of serial enactment of the ritual of the jeremiad. It was the moving stage for the quintessentially American drama of destined progress." Religious diversity was a cultural counterpart of territorial expansion, with every new religious movement enlisted into a common reverence for the American way and its millennial promise. Indeed every kind of dissent, every potential rebellion was reduced to impotence by the success of the jeremiad in sanctifying the American social order. The effect was "to blight, and ultimately to preclude, the possibility of fundamental social change . . . to transform what might have been a search for moral or social alternatives into a call for cultural revitalization." And Bercovitch closes with the frustration of Melville and Hawthorne and the ambivalence of Thoreau, Emerson, and Whitman in their fundamental acceptance of the society whose shortcomings they denounced, just as the Puritan ministers had denounced the sins of the people while holding out the prospect of a bright future in God's love.

This is a dazzling performance. It supplies conceptual links between phenomena where historians have often sensed a connection without being able to describe it adequately, between the Great Awakening and the Revolution, between Edwards and Emerson, between the Puritan vision of a city on a hill and the "manifest destiny" of American expansion. One can quarrel with the author at almost every stage, from the assumption of the optimistic thrust of the jeremiad at the outset to the identification of it with social and political conservatism at the end. One can even question the unstated assumption that other Americans accepted the embrace of New England and saw themselves in the terms that the jeremiad prescribed.

Bercovitch sweeps us along with him so persuasively that we are scarcely aware that we are not dealing with facts at all. If Davis presents us with a set of inert facts, summaries of what people said and did, Bercovitch touches facts only to see beyond them, to translate them into the scheme of the jeremiad—and we have to remind ourselves that the jeremiad itself is a historian's construct, just as the New England mind is a construct, as would be the early southern mind if we could persuade ourselves of its existence. Intellectual history at this level is metaphor.

As metaphor it is not susceptible to empirical confirmation. The

social historians who have attempted to deal with New England's past
by counting births, marriages, and deaths, by comparing tax lists and
church records and court cases, will find little here with which they
can make contact, just as they have found little in Miller to interest
them and have attempted to supersede his work by ignoring it. But it is
at the level of metaphor and unprovable insight that intellectual history becomes most exciting to those who see in it a way of understanding ourselves. Max Weber's insights into the relationship between
religion and society are not empirically demonstrable, nor, despite the
continual efforts to discredit them, are they susceptible to empirical
refutation. The same is true of Freud, whose insights into human
nature continue to excite us, despite the failure of systematic attempts
to support them in controlled experiments. Miller's construction of
the New England mind is of the same order.

   This kind of history, which creates the past for us in new perspectives, has to depend on the author's ability to persuade his readers to
see what he sees, persuade them to rearrange familiar objects in a new
pattern from a new angle of vision. If those accustomed to other angles
are unable to recognize the familiar objects in the new perspective,
they will reject the new view out of hand. But if the author is successful, he will at least give his readers pause and perhaps make them
adjust their historical glasses. Anyone who reads the mass of writing
produced by seventeenth-century New Englanders and then reads
what Miller makes of those writings must be a very dull person if he
fails to see things that he did not see before, if he does not find his
mind stretched into a new understanding not only of New England
but of himself. What Bercovitch has done is to stretch our minds a bit
further in the direction that Miller bent them. And that means, however one may quarrel with him in details, that he has written intellectual history at the highest level.

July 19, 1979

CHAPTER FIVE

Subject Women

—◦◦◦—

First Generations: Women in Colonial America
Carol Berkin

*Founding Mothers and Fathers: Gendered Power
and the Forming of American Society*
Mary Beth Norton

*Women Before the Bar: Gender, Law, and Society
in Connecticut, 1639–1789*
Cornelia Hughes Dayton

THE FIRST English settlers of North America knew they were making history and started writing their own accounts of themselves as soon as they got here. Their descendants have kept it up, and none more zealously than professional historians in the past fifty or sixty years. These three books on women in the colonies can be understood as revisions, amplifications, and syntheses of a rich succession of studies about every aspect of colonial society and culture. Although the line starts with Captain John Smith of Virginia and Governor William Bradford of Plymouth Plantation, it gained a new beginning and the intellectual energy that still drives it with Perry Miller's volumes on the New England mind written in the 1930s and 1940s.[1] Before him there had been plenty of hero worship as well as debunking and some preliminary efforts to take the Puritans seriously as human beings. But Miller, himself an atheist though immersed in the existentialism of his time, found in Puritan theology a system of thought commanding the respect he gave it and communicated to his readers. Miller's analysis of that sys-

tem was itself so thorough and so complex, continually discovering
implications within implications of theological disputes, that all subsequent studies of Puritan thought in New England have been in one way
or another commentaries on Miller.

By conferring intellectual respectability on the Puritans, Miller
also prompted explorations of colonial society that owed little directly
to his own work. Miller's concern was with ideas. Everything that mattered about a people, he believed, could be found somewhere in what
they thought about the way God deals with man. Not everyone has
agreed. Miller's *New England Mind* had nothing to say about ideas that
may have filled the heads of fishermen and farmers as opposed to ministers of the gospel, nothing to say about what is now called popular
culture. And of course it did not say anything about the details of social
structure and problems of daily life that do not hinge on the problems
of eternity.

Social historians moved to fill the gap. Taking their lead initially
from French and English demographers, they gave their attention to
the statistics of births, marriages, and deaths first of New England
towns and then of the plantation societies of the South. County and
town records, rather than theological treatises, became the guide to
understanding the lives of ordinary people and the way they related to
one another. The result has been a huge compiling of information that
indeed could not have been derived or extrapolated from the ideas that
occupied Miller. For example, Miller could not have known that New
Englanders lived longer than their counterparts in England and that
grandparents were therefore much more visibly a part of society than
in England. It would scarcely have affected his analysis of original sin
or predestination if he had known this or other facts that the New
Englanders themselves could not have been fully aware of. But things
like life expectancy, sex ratios, average age at marriage, and family size,
even without the benefit of precise knowledge of them, can have a
direct, even determining, effect on human relations. They set bounds
for an almost autonomous popular culture, which may bear little relation to the high culture with which it coexists. And where the two do

converge, popular culture can translate the abstract principles of high culture into powerful directives of human conduct.

A major point of convergence in many societies lies in the views that govern relations between the sexes, now encompassed by the word "gender." Gender is the guiding concept of the three books noticed here and of a host of other books and of articles in every professional historical journal in the past ten years. The word as currently used, both as a noun and a verb, applies to the rights and duties and functions that a society assigns to people solely on the basis of their sex. A few of these may be relatively unchanging, rooted in the biological differences between the sexes; but more are literally man-made, dictated by the prevailing culture of a particular time and place.

The line between the two is not always clear, and the question of where and how to draw it in any society is an extension of the old and continuing debate over the relative roles of nature and nurture in shaping human character. But at opposite ends of the spectrum the difference is obvious. Bearing children is imposed on women by God or nature or biology, whether in Boston or Burma, but women's subjection to men, whether in the state or the family, is imposed by ideas and attitudes that have no other basis than a society's acceptance of them. Since the gendering of power in the Western world has generally subjected women to men, women's history, which has become a scholarly discipline in itself, has been devoted heavily to ascertaining the degree and extent of subjection that prevailed at different times, tracing its cultural sources and the forces that have altered its extent (it can scarcely be said to have disappeared). Carol Berkin's book is a survey of the differing positions of women in several societies of seventeenth-century America, north, south, and middle, and of the changes wrought in the course of the eighteenth century by commercial growth and by the American Revolution. Throughout she has striven for "a sensitivity to the social construction of gender" and has included chapters on the contrasting roles of women among Native Americans and African slaves.

Something of the scale of recent work on women's history can be gauged by Berkin's bibliographical essay of twenty pages, in which books and articles published in the last fifteen years predominate. Her text is full of what "some historians" have recently argued and how others have disagreed. What seems clear from her survey is that the position of women vis-à-vis men was worse where the settlers were English than it was with the Indians, or the Africans. Even the Dutch, so closely engaged with the English in the seventeenth-century contest to dominate world trade, gave to married women in their colonies a share in property rights that was totally denied them by the English, whether in their colonies or at home. Economic rights were not as gendered in New Netherlands as they were in New England or in New York after the English took it over.

Berkin brings her subject down to earth by focusing on the way gender determined the experiences of an individual woman in each of the societies she examines. She shows how throughout the colonies the subjection of women could be affected by social class. Women automatically gained the same social status as their husbands, and widows might retain it, thus gaining an anomalous superiority over men of lower class. Finally she notices that the pursuit of equality in the American Revolution fell short of recognizing the equality of the sexes. Power in the new republic was still gendered. Berkin's synthesis of recent research offers what Mary Beth Norton rightly calls "the best available introduction to the lives of women in colonial and revolutionary America."

Norton's own *Founding Mothers and Fathers: Gendered Power and the Forming of American Society* is more ambitious, more original, and more challenging. It is limited in the time covered to the period before the mid-1670s, limited in the area covered to New England and the Chesapeake colonies of Virginia and Maryland, limited in the sources used to published court records. The last limitation is serious, because almost all the extant records are of county courts, and for the Chesapeake colonies only those of Maryland have been extensively published. Only two volumes out of several dozen extant seventeenth-century Virginia county records have been published, and only one volume exists of Virginia's central General Court (the rest were lost in the burning of Richmond in the Civil War). As a result, Norton's statements about Chesapeake society are mainly statements about Maryland society. Nevertheless, the records used, however limited, are still voluminous, and Norton's examination of them has been intensive. She has gleaned from them the statistical backing that has become compulsory for social historians; and within the limits she has set herself in time, place, and sources, she has constructed a daring intellectual frame, a formula for understanding how and why the gendering of power operated in the two quite different cultures that developed in New England and the Chesapeake.

Norton divides her study into three parts to show the location of power within the family, in the unofficial community or neighborhood, and in the state, where the ultimate power resided. She recognizes that power may require force but that it is not the same thing as force, that power can be limited by the need for consent, whether in family, community, or state. Accordingly she classifies social and political activities as public or private, and further distinguishes "informal public" (affecting a whole community that included women and children) and "formal public" (involving almost exclusively adult men, who alone wielded the powers of government). Although "private" meant the opposite of "public," it easily became a matter of dispute at the time whether a particular activity was private or not and thus whether it was subject to formal public scrutiny. In general, Norton finds that this question too was gendered: what men said to one another in private could not be held against them, but meetings of women were fair objects for public inquiry or condemnation. Informal meetings of women nevertheless had to be reckoned with by the men who claimed authority over them. Formal public power could be strongly influenced by informal public opinion, in which women could play a leading role. Gossip, characterized by Norton as a female specialty, could affect the credibility of any man in court proceedings or in the conduct of government.

The interplay of formal public, informal public, and private activities comes out in detailed examinations of a variety of episodes. When Mistress Alice Tilly of Boston was convicted by a Massachusetts court of malpractice as a midwife, the women of Boston, who thought they knew more about midwifery than the men on the court, gathered by themselves to protest that she was the best midwife in town. Though they did not get the court to admit it was wrong, they did get her released from prison to practice her profession. Neighborhood gossip affected formal public authority in Maryland when the government appointed Thomas Baker to the bench of Charles County. Baker was reputed to have stolen hogs and was known for "Baudie talk" about local women. When Baker arrived on the court, the informal hostility of his neighbors obliged him to step down. Norton follows a host of such cases through the courts and concludes with a brilliant analysis of the way confusion over the meaning of "private" figured in the trial of Anne Hutchinson, banished from Massachusetts Bay in 1638 for expressing heretical views in public (or, as Hutchinson insisted, private) meetings.

Despite the informal restraints that women might be able to place on the exercise of power, whether in New England or in the Chesapeake colonies, Norton makes clear that in the end men could always prevail over women. Anne Hutchinson gained a large following in the informal public realm and some in the formal, but she nevertheless lost her case and with it her right to live and teach among the people of Massachusetts. Women were excluded from any share in formal public power; and even in the privacy of the family a woman's very identity was subsumed in her husband's: any property she brought to the marriage was his, any debt she owed was his, almost any tort she committed was his.

The great strength of Norton's book is its thick description of the way that male power and female subordination operated, or occasionally faltered, in specific cases. What makes her descriptions challenging is her delineation of the cultures in which she situates the cases, distinguishing New England's "Filmerian" society from the "nascent Lockean society" of the Chesapeake. Miller had believed that the principles directing New England social organization could be found in what the ministers of New England themselves said. Later social historians found the directing forces in statistics unknown to the people they concerned. Norton finds the principles guiding the peoples of New England and the Chesapeake in the early seventeenth century to be best expressed in writings unknown to them. New England society exhibited the principles of Sir Robert Filmer, whose *Patriarcha*, written in the 1630s or 1640s, was first published in 1680 (though he published other works as early as 1648). Chesapeake society, on the other hand, was moving toward the principles of John Locke's refutation of Filmer in his *Two Treatises on Government*, published in 1690. It would have been impossible for anyone in the Chesapeake region or anywhere else to have read Locke in the period of Norton's study, and there is no evidence that anyone in New England read Filmer before or after 1680.

To prove that New Englanders acted in a particular way because they were "Filmerian" and that people in the Chesapeake were becoming "Lockean" is indeed a challenge. It is one thing to show that people were affected by statistics about themselves that they could not themselves have compiled. It is another thing altogether to show that they were moved by a system of ideas they had never heard of. Norton nevertheless is able to make a case. New Englanders may not have known they were Filmerian, but by Norton's reckoning their society was driven by the assumption to which Filmer's name is classically attached, that all government derives not from consent but from a father's natural and unlimited authority over his family. Because a father's power was unlimited, the power of kings must be unlimited. Filmer, an ardent royalist and no Puritan, directed his writings not toward the explication of family duties or family management but toward refuting the claims of popular rights and popular sovereignty made by parliamentarians against the king in the 1640s. Norton, however, also finds in Filmer an affirmation of the need for government to supervise paternal authority in order to ensure its support of public authority. Such a continuing reliance on family government is what makes New England, for her, Filmerian.

It is well known that the settlers of New England came over mainly as families in the 1630s. And Norton shows that New England governments kept a close watch over them to see that the master of each family was living up to his responsibilities. New England fathers gained a larger role in choosing spouses for their offspring than had been the case in England; but they were themselves held to a rigorous standard of sexual behavior, because in a "Filmerian system" any threat to family integrity by either spouse was a threat to the principle on which all government was based.

The Chesapeake could not have a Filmerian system because the settlers did not come as families but mainly as single men bound in servitude. During the period of Norton's study, before the region turned decisively to slave labor, the planters relied on a continuing supply of servants from England, Scotland, and Ireland; and they wanted men more than women. Throughout Norton's period there were as many as four men for every woman; and both sexes, in further contrast to New England, died early deaths. The family, therefore, could not play the role it did in New England in sustaining public order, and governments accordingly did not supervise family behavior as in New England. The Chesapeake can be called a nascent Lockean society, because Locke did not link the origin of government to paternity. He believed that women and children were subject to adult men in the family but that political government originated independently in a contract among men. Government in the Chesapeake rested not on paternal command within families but on gaining the support of men for other men. Power was gendered, but the subjection of women was not as crucial to its operation as was the securing of consent among men.

Norton is thus able to translate social statistics into political theory, indeed into political imperatives. Despite the anachronistic labeling, she is able to portray the organization of society and the order imposed on it as dictated by political ideas later articulated more clearly by Filmer and Locke than they were in New England or the Chesapeake at the time. The trouble with this analysis is that New

Englanders, at least, did articulate a great many ideas of their own, ideas that were decidedly not Filmerian. David D. Hall showed in 1989 that the contours of popular culture in New England conformed remarkably to those of the high culture that Perry Miller depicted.[2] The conformity extended to political ideas. A central idea in Miller's account of New England thought was that of the "covenant," a term the seventeenth century preferred to the modern "contract." God dealt with man in covenants, and so did men with one another. New Englanders, eschewing the hierarchy that Filmer cherished, created their own churches, not under the paternal authority of a bishop or even of a priest, but by a voluntary covenant among the prospective members, who then elected a minister (they could also dismiss him).

Secular societies, too, they believed to originate in covenants. A covenant among the settlers was the only basis of government in the Plymouth Colony until 1685, when it was merged with Massachusetts, in the New Haven Colony from 1638 to 1662, when it was merged with Connecticut, and in Connecticut until it procured a royal charter in that year. In Massachusetts, John Winthop was able to interpret emigration to the colony as consent to a covenant, even though it was a royal charter that officially endowed the colony with power to govern itself. In all the New England colonies in the period covered by Norton governors and legislative assemblies were elected, usually annually, by the freemen of the colony.

Not elected by women, to be sure. Power was gendered, but how can it be said to rest on paternity? Norton finds the ultimate paternity in England's king, three thousand miles away. She insists that in every contest between power resting on covenant and power resting on paternal, that is royal, authority, paternal authority won, as when New Haven had to "submit to the Filmerian imperative" by accepting absorption into Connecticut under Connecticut's royal charter of 1662. It is a fact that the power of England's king was proof against any open colonial claim of self-government. But his authority was no more visible in Connecticut (or in New Haven as part of Connecticut) after

1662 than before. He appointed no government officers there. "Acknowledgments of the need for consent" were not, as Norton claims, a mere ritual in New England. Consent alone, explicitly given in popular elections, placed men in government office before 1685.

In Virginia, on the other hand, that supposedly nascent Lockean society, a governor appointed in England, usually by the king, dominated the colony's government from the beginning. Maryland's governor was appointed by the Calvert family, who owned the colony and also filled its other official posts. If control by a higher authority than popular consent made a colony Filmerian, Maryland and Virginia fit the description better than New England. If government resting on consent is Lockean, seventeenth-century New England fits the description not only better than the Chesapeake but better than most of the Western world, including England, at the time. A good argument can be made for the increase of active royal authority in all the colonies during the eighteenth century, but by then only die-hard Tories were claiming that the king's authority rested on a Filmerian power of paternity.

Norton's analysis is not only anachronistic, it defies the central known facts of political history. Instead of illuminating the gendering of power in the cases she describes, her explanation of them as part of a Filmerian system obscures them. In subordinating women to men, New Englanders were not making a statement in support of absolute monarchy or absolute government, which Puritans abhorred and which Filmer's published writings were unequivocally and single-mindedly designed to justify. What Filmer expounded in a multitude of arguments was not the need for men to dominate their families, about which he says virtually nothing, but the unlimited power of the king to dominate England. Norton constructs a system of thought to fit vital statistics, calls it Filmerian, and then attributes to that system a commanding influence on a people who were distinguished by their passionate adherence to quite a different and contrary system. Miller was closer to the mark in thinking that New England society scarcely needed explaining if you understood Puritan theology.

How much closer is suggested by Cornelia Hughes Dayton's book on the changing legal position of women in New Haven, from its founding in 1638 until 1789. For Norton, New Haven was the "most Filmerian of all colonies" because it manifested the greatest concern to sustain the family and its fathers as the source of public order. For Dayton, as indeed for most historians, New Haven was the most Puritan of colonies, distinguished by "a more 'rigorous working out' of Protestant dissenting notions of secular government than its neighbors, Massachusetts Bay and Connecticut." Filmer, most historians would agree, did not entertain Protestant dissenting notions of secular government or of anything else. What Norton explains as Filmerian Dayton explains more plausibly as Puritan. For example, Norton can treat as a Filmerian concern for maintaining patriarchal public order the paradoxical fact that New England courts (in contrast to English courts) punished men almost equally with women for sexual disorders. Dayton concurs that "New Haven Colony came close to establishing a single standard for men and women in the areas of sexual and moral conduct," but attributes this degree of equalization (or non-gendering) to the Puritan intent "to create the most God-fearing society possible." That intent, documented by all the surviving sources, works better as an explanation than a putative influence of principles designed primarily to create a dictatorial king.

Dayton takes care to emphasize that society in the New Haven Colony was still patriarchal: it placed women clearly in subjection to men. As in other English colonies, a wife had no property rights apart from her husband; and New Haven actually gave widows fewer legal rights to property than English law provided. But Puritan patriarchy was tempered by a larger recognition of women's rights and functions than had been the case in England or than would be the case in New England as Puritanism declined in the eighteenth century. Dayton goes so far as to suggest that although the nineteenth-century pioneers of women's rights "would not have thought of themselves as operating within a Puritan framework, many of their demands had once been met for women before the bar in courts that cleaved to Puritan jurisprudence."

Women in the Puritan system were not reduced to indirect influence through "informal" public activities. In the New Haven Colony women often appeared as litigants, suing for collection of debts, and their testimony in regard to property transactions became crucial, as the courts ignored many of the rules of formal pleading in favor of the memory of witnesses. Women evidently shared in the running of many businesses, and widows often served as executors of their husbands' wills. New Haven, like other Puritan colonies, treated marriage as a civil contract, yet another covenant, and granted women's petitions for divorce as readily as men's. In such cases, although adultery was still legally defined as infidelity by a married woman and not the other way around, a man's infidelity was nevertheless cause for divorce; and, again contrary to English law, custody of the children was awarded to the aggrieved wife. In cases of rape a woman's testimony was sufficient for conviction, as it was for identifying the father of an illegitimate child, for whose support the government made him responsible.

With the waning of Puritanism all this changed. Although Connecticut, too, was a Puritan colony, the signs of decline had already appeared when New Haven was joined to it in the charter of 1662. Connecticut showed its Puritan heritage in granting nearly a thousand divorces between 1670 and 1799, far more than England or any other English colony did. But English law and legal practices gradually replaced the informalism of Puritan procedures, and commercial growth enlarged the geographical boundaries within which men carried on their dealings, dealings that included fewer and fewer women. Women appeared less often as litigants. They could still get divorces but not the custody of their children. The state no longer sought to identify the fathers of illegitimate children or to compel their support of the children. Women's testimony in cases of rape succeeded only when supported by racial bias—Indians and blacks were now the only men likely to be convicted for the crime. Men were no longer prosecuted at all for fornication, which became a female crime, the more heinous as the image grew of women as the pure guardians of virtue on the one hand and dangerous temptresses on the other. Dayton gives concrete and specific meaning and a new dimension to a phenomenon that has often been noticed by other historians, the transition in New England from Puritan to Yankee, from community values to the cash nexus. She shows the complexity of that transition and of the forces that determined the social construction of gender to deprive women of rights and functions they had for a time enjoyed.

It is tempting to see a parallel between the improvement in the status of women wrought by the New Haven Colony in the early seventeenth century and by the moral reform movements of the early nineteenth, of which the women's rights movement was arguably an offshoot. In both cases the desire "to create the most God-fearing society possible" can be seen as a driving force. But religious zeal can as easily attach itself to a magnification of male dominance. Filmer himself drew his arguments from the Bible, his whole case resting heavily on the book of Genesis. What all three of these books show is the strength of patriarchy, that is, the consistent social construction of gender to empower men over women, whatever limits have been placed on the power at different times. The limits in America today are probably more restrictive than ever before (and without much assistance from religious zeal, which is currently enlisted on the other side). Berkin, Norton, and Dayton all show the variety of the limits prevailing earlier, but that very variety suggests not so much the vulnerability of patriarchy as its resilient persistence. It is easier to locate the limits and to identify the proximate causes of changes in them than it is to determine the ultimate sources of the power itself.

Perhaps, as Miller thought, what people believe about the way God deals with man will govern the way they deal with one another. But is God supposed to endorse some kind of patriarchy, however limited? The Puritan God, omnipotent, arbitrary, and angry, required better treatment of women than the reasonable deity who took His place in the eighteenth century. But they both endorsed patriarchy, as did the sentimental God of the nineteenth century by elevating women in order to subdue them. Shall we place the gendering of power in nature or nurture? It seems obviously to belong to nurture, but is nature dictating to nurture? These books, while arguing the contrary, raise a disturbing question.

October 31, 1996

CHAPTER SIX

Witch-Hunting

—⦿—

Entertaining Satan: Witchcraft and the Culture of Early New England
John Putnam Demos

H ISTORY, AT ITS BEST, always tells us as much indirectly about ourselves as it does directly about our predecessors; and it is often most revealing when it deals with episodes and phenomena that we find repulsive. John Demos's subject is witchcraft, not the infamous Salem trials of 1692, but the general prevalence of witches throughout New England before that date. This is not simply a monograph on witchcraft but a major attempt to understand the kind of society and the kind of culture in which witchcraft had a place. To that end Demos employs nearly every conceptual tool available to the historian, including those borrowed from psychology, anthropology, and sociology. Not everyone will find every part of his analysis persuasive, but the book is so rich in insights, so restrained in differentiating speculation from fact, and so broad in range that it would require a firmly closed mind not be instructed by it.

New England was by no means unique in its attention to witchcraft. The number of alleged witches executed there was probably a good deal smaller in proportion to total population than in Switzerland, France, Germany, and Scotland during any comparable period during the sixteenth and seventeenth centuries (the span of the great European witch-hunts). Demos counts 16 executions in New England and 93 indictments, excluding the 20 executions and 141 indictments in the Salem episode. What is important for him is not the number of cases tried in court but the role played by witchcraft in New England life.

Demos gives us, to begin with, a profile of the persons accused of witchcraft. They were predominantly, though not exclusively, women; but contrary to the modern stereotype they were not old hags, living out lonely and bitter lives on the outskirts of society. They were mainly women in middle age, mainly married (though often childless) and actively engaged in their local communities. Many were knowledgeable about medicines and cures; some were midwives. They had a higher than normal record as litigants in court and as defendants in minor criminal cases. They were for the most part socially mobile, more often down than up, and were generally at a low position socially when accused. And finally most of them had a reputation for abrasiveness and quarrelsomeness. Their victims fell into three main categories: young adult men, adolescent girls, and middle-aged women like themselves.

Victims there always were. One did not acquire a reputation as a witch in seventeenth-century New England simply by affecting intimacy with the devil. There had to be harm done to people in the reputed witch's vicinity, either in their persons or in their possessions, harm that the victims were unwilling to attribute to natural causes: cattle that inexplicably sickened or died, children inexplicably convulsed by fits, cream that inexplicably would not churn. In the seventeenth century, as in every other century before our own, there was an abundance of such events. To blame them on witchcraft was a way of making sense out of them, a way of making the world intelligible. But there was more to it than that. Why were some people rather than others singled out as witches? What was the relationship between witch and victim? Where did witchcraft fit in the way a community functioned?

Demos attempts to answer these questions by close examination of individual cases, reconstructing through testimony in court and through genealogical and local records the structure of families and towns and the life histories of alleged witches and victims. A historian has to approach the people of another time on their own terms, to understand them as they understood themselves, but having done so he may strive to make them intelligible in the terms of his own time. In these case histories Demos has couched his analysis in the terms of today, especially in trying to expose the psychological pressures that afflicted those who thought themselves to be victims of witches. Here his addiction to Freudian psychology results in what seem to the reviewer to be some pretty far-fetched speculations.

Witchcraft victims, Demos suggests, were carrying out a regression into infantile attitudes and projecting onto witches a "pre-Oedipal" rage against their mothers, a rage that had been engendered in them between the ages of one and three. The evidence for such a diagnosis, even if one accepts its terms, is tenuous, though not much more so than the evidence supporting the recent attribution of the Salem outbreak to ergot poisoning from diseased rye. (Demos's diagnosis does have the virtue of explaining why most accused witches were women.) Perhaps more plausible is his additional suggestion that the third category of victims, middle-aged women, may have been suffering (along with some of their alleged tormentors) from the trauma associated with menopause, a trauma that may have been unusually strong among New England women. Because they generally continued to bear children until they were unable to, they may have felt the more sharply the loss of what they had regarded as their principal function. In their distress some of them may have been ready to blame any kind of trouble on witchcraft.

But psychological explanations of witchcraft or of any other historical phenomena are conjectural, at best. We are on firmer ground in Demos's reconstruction of communities and his analysis of the tensions within them. Attributions of witchcraft and an eagerness for witch-hunts were usually generated within a community from the bottom up, not from the top down, not only in New England but elsewhere. Even in sixteenth-century Spain the officials of the Inquisition often dragged their feet in witchcraft prosecutions, while local communities thirsted for blood. And in New England the colony magistrates can be found reprieving witches who had been unanimously condemned by local juries. Witchcraft ceased to be a crime under English law after 1736, but popular lynchings and attacks on supposed witches continued into the nineteenth century in both England and America.

IT WOULD be impossible here to reproduce in detail any of Demos's painstaking reconstruction of the local situations in which popular accusations of witchcraft erupted, but what emerges from them is the complexity of all human relations in a pre-industrial town or village. "Imagine," he asks us:

> The brickmaker who rebuilds your chimney is also the constable who brings you a summons to court, an occupant of the next bench in the meetinghouse, the owner of a share adjacent to one of yours in the "upland" meadow, a rival for water-rights to the stream that flows behind that meadow, a fellow-member of the local "train band" (i.e. militia), an occasional companion at the local "ordinary," a creditor (from services performed for you the previous summer but not as yet paid for), a potential customer for wool from the sheep you have begun to raise, the father of a child who is currently a bond-servant in your house, a colleague on a town committee to repair and improve the public roadways. . . . And so on. Do the two of you enjoy your shared experiences? Not necessarily. Do you know each other well? Most certainly.

In these circumstances any conflict was full of implications that affected the whole community, and interpersonal conflicts were the breeding ground for witchcraft and accusations of witchcraft. Hostility and suspicion might build up over the years against an assertive, aggressive woman, who demanded favors of her neighbors and acted aggrieved when she was refused. Her neighbors might resent her demands and yet feel some guilt in denying them. At the same time they would be continually rubbing elbows with her in the rounds of daily life. "The relationships of witches and accuser/victims," Demos

argues, "were not defined by, or limited to, any single strand of experience. On the contrary, such relationships were typically complex,
many-sided, and altogether *dense*." Returning to psychology, he suggests that a "psychic bond" may have developed between supposed
witch and supposed victim, in which each took out aggressions on the
other, so that there was a kind of "veiled complicity" between them.

For the community itself, united to both witch and victim in a
multitude of relationships, witchcraft served as a way of personifying
evil, and thus a way to sharpen moral boundaries. A witch was sin
incarnate. When hostility to her exploded in accusation, trial, and exe-
cution, the community defined itself and affirmed its righteousness by
thrusting the witch out of it. And in normal times, Demos argues, the
threat of such an ejection may have served as a restraint against deviant
behavior by people who might otherwise have defied community
mores. Witchcraft was not an extraneous element in ordinary community life but a persistent, if not essential, ingredient in the human relationships that tied New England communities together. If the
thrusting out of a witch developed into a witch-hunt, as it did at Salem
and at countless places in Germany and France, the community might
be torn apart instead of defined. But as long as the fury was contained
and directed against a single person, a witch trial offered a kind of
catharsis that left the community stronger.

In arriving at this point, Demos mentions almost for the first time
the high culture that has drawn intellectual historians to seventeenth-
century New England. In his many-faceted analysis of the functions of
witchcraft and witch trials, theology has had no place, for, he writes,
"Popular attitudes toward witchcraft and the views of ministers were
not of a piece." He only grudgingly allows "a wide *influence* to clerical
opinion" in creating the religious atmosphere in which popular attitudes flourished.

In thus dismissing theology Demos could have cited the master of
New England intellectual historians. Perry Miller devoted a chapter to
the Salem episode, but he prefaced it by acknowledging that his whole
analysis of *The New England Mind* would suffer little by total omission

of the subject. Nevertheless, if Demos has achieved anything—as he certainly has—he has demonstrated the significance of witchcraft in the minds of New Englanders. It may well be that there was a considerable gap between the complex and sophisticated system of ideas that Miller called the New England mind and the complex web of relationships and attitudes that Demos has uncovered in the ordinary minds of ordinary New Englanders. But it is doubtful in the light of what Demos has shown us that one can be understood without the other, and it borders on the doctrinaire for him to attempt to do so.

It would almost seem that Freudian psychology for Demos has usurped the place that theology held for the Puritans and that in trying to explain seventeenth-century New Englanders in terms that will make sense to the twenty-first century he has in some measure neglected their own understanding of themselves and of the supposed witches among them. It is unlikely that any of them would have been content with an explanation that gave as little attention as Demos does to the role of religious beliefs and ideas in shaping their attitudes and behavior. Whatever else they may have been, they were an unusually devout people, and they supported a learned ministry whose job it was to help them cope with their belief that Satan would entertain most of them in the world to come. What must I do to be saved, saved from sin, saved from evil? was the question they asked themselves and to which they expected answers from their ministries. Although witchcraft did not play a conspicuous part in those answers, it is hard to believe that a people so concerned, when obliged to grapple with witchcraft, could have conceived of what they were doing outside the terms of the theology that explained for them the behavior of imperfect human beings in a world created by a perfect God.

Freudian psychology and Puritan theology offer strangely parallel and mutually exclusive theories of human behavior. Both deal with human beings as products of forces that are given and unchangeable, locked in human biology by original sin on the one hand and by the Oedipus complex on the other. And both explain the development of the self over time in a series of stages that may eventuate in a kind of salvation. The propositions of Freudian psychology, resting on the inarticulate experiences of infancy and childhood, are no more (and perhaps no less) empirically demonstrable than the theological propositions of John Calvin and are equally filled with seeming contradictions that have to be reconciled by high priests in a rarefied ratiocination requiring a special and arcane vocabulary.

What Calvin's propositions have going for them in the present context is that seventeenth-century New Englanders knew the vocabulary and got lessons in the propositions every Sunday. They may have needed witchcraft to personify evil for them, and it may have served that purpose just as Demos argues, but we can misread their understanding of themselves if we leave it at that. Demos tells us that they "seem to have felt persistently vulnerable in their core sense of self. Tremors of uncertainty plagued their struggles to grow and endure as free-standing individuals. . . ." Indeed. That was the lesson they got every Sunday: that tremors were called for, that evil was not confined to witches, that evil lay within all men and all women, that free-standing individuals were headed for hell. Their kind of salvation was not the kind that their descendants hope for on the analyst's couch.

It is possible that modern psychology, anthropology, and sociology can enable us to understand the early New Englanders better than they understood themselves. Certainly Demos enables us to understand them better than we have before. But it is also possible, just possible, that they understood their own and all men's vulnerability "in the core sense of self" somewhat better than we do. They may yet have something to teach us about that.

November 4, 1982

CHAPTER SEVEN

Bewitched

—◦◦◦—

The Crucible
Film directed by Nicholas Hytner (released 1996)

The Crucible Screenplay
Arthur Miller

T O MAKE a successful film from a successful play is probably much more difficult than making one from scratch, just as any carpenter will tell you that it is more difficult to restore an old house than to build a comparable new one. The constraints imposed on the screenwriter, producer, and director by scenes, language, and actions designed for the stage can never quite be ignored, and they can cripple the action of a film. The difficulty is magnified when the play is as familiar as *The Crucible*, its structure all too firmly imprinted on the minds of those making the film and of the audience they are making it for. Arthur Miller, who wrote the screenplay himself, and Nicholas Hytner, who directed it, knew what they were up against. Miller tried "to put the play out of mind as much as possible and proceed as though it had never existed." And Hytner, who felt "as if I was asking Shakespeare for amendments to *King Lear*," nevertheless found Miller quick to "refashion his screenplay as I strove to visualize it image by image."

The film, then, is not the photographed play. Hytner has done his best to take it outdoors and offstage, and Miller has cut his own lines, in fulfillment of his understanding that "the more wordless the film the better." The screenplay is only about half the length of the play.

But seemingly nothing of consequence is subtracted or added. Admirers of the play will recognize most of the remaining lines, the sequence of the actions, and the development of the characters. This is still *The Crucible*, its message delivered intact and in force. Indeed, the clarity of the direction and the quality of the acting make it the best rendition of the author's work that any of us is likely to see either on screen or on stage.

The film opens with the scene in the forest, only referred to in the play, which drives the rest of the action as it did less convincingly in the play: teenage girls, half in jest, half serious, dance to voodoo rhythms and cast spells to bring them lovers. Then suddenly we see Abigail Williams (Winona Ryder), her face covered with blood from a sacrificed chicken as she utters a shocking curse on Elizabeth Proctor. Abigail has already slept with Elizabeth's husband John and is the ringleader of the girls, not only in the forest scene but in the later antics by which they send their elders into a hysterical fear of witchcraft. Abigail, more explicitly in the film than in the play, is ready to bring to the gallows as witches a host of innocent people in order to be rid of the woman who stands between her and John Proctor.

What makes the film frightening, as it did the play, is the wholesale success of false accusations, unsupported by any visible or tangible evidence. John Proctor, who knows that the accusations are false and Abigail a liar, publicly admits to his adultery with her in an effort to discredit her and her followers, but he is no match for her cunning. Her ability to manipulate the other girls prevails over all, assisted to be sure by the foolish insecurity of a minister (Samuel Parris, played by Bruce Davison), by the greed of a large Salem landholder (Thomas Putnam, played by Jeffrey Jones), and by the seeming impartiality of a grave judge (John Danforth,* played by Paul Scofield).

The film and the play are ostensibly about the way mass madness can overcome justice, as it did at Salem in 1692, as it did in the McCarthy hearings at the time Miller was writing the play, and as it has

---

* Danforth's actual name was Thomas and he was in fact provisional deputy-governor of the colony.

before and since in too many times and places. The theme is universal, and the very fact that witchcraft is so easily discredited today only gives greater force to the shock of recognition when we watch the otherwise sober men and women of Salem take fright at its imagined presence. Paul Scofield's brilliant performance makes Judge Danforth so obviously thoughtful and fair, so unmoved by hysteria, that he obliges us to accept the plausibility and thus the horror of the whole thing.

But if madness is the ostensible theme, it is gradually subordinated to the effect of it on the relationship between John Proctor and his wife. Daniel Day-Lewis as Proctor and Joan Allen as Elizabeth create a tension, arising from her knowledge of his infidelity, that comes to dominate the film. Day-Lewis's Proctor is a man with obvious strength of mind and muscle who does not suffer fools gladly but knows his own weaknesses. The film builds toward the resolution of his guilt in defiance of a society that cannot recognize its greater collective guilt. Along the way we see more casually the courage of the innocent who require no inner struggle in laying down their lives for the truth. The film becomes the story of a man who must reckon with himself before he can join the braver souls who step to their martyrdom without a backward look. Proctor's triumph in the end, absolved by a wife who has come to a new understanding of herself as well as him, is not a triumph of righteousness or even of rightness but of humanity, a man's affirmation simply of himself. He goes to the gallows only after he has shown his weakness, only after he has momentarily agreed to a false confession that would have saved his life but dishonored him in his own mind. But he withdraws it and restores his self-respect and his contempt for a world that could do what the people of Salem were doing.

In short, this is a powerful version of a powerful play. It successfully overcomes the restraints laid on it in transformation from the stage. But no play or film depicting real people and real events can escape another set of restraints imposed by what is already known about those people and events. John Proctor, Elizabeth Proctor, Abigail Williams, Judge Danforth, and most of the other characters shown were real people, and much of what they did and had done to them has been established as historical fact, insofar as fact can ever be established. A playwright dealing with historical figures can scarcely ignore what is known or knowable about them. *The Crucible* would lose much of its power if it were not anchored to the notorious witch-hunt already fixed, however loosely, in the minds of those likely to view it. The only question is how closely a playwright must be tied to what is known, for he cannot be tied so closely that his play or film becomes merely a documentary. He is surely entitled to make up things that did not happen. Indeed he must make them up if he is to give us more understanding of what did happen than historians have been able to do in confining themselves to proven facts.

It must be admitted that in recent years historians have discovered a good deal more about witches and witchcraft in general and about the Salem episode in particular than they had when Miller first wrote *The Crucible*. They have drawn profiles of the accused and the accusers, both in Salem and in other communities where they have found isolated examples of witchcraft and witch trials. They have uncovered much about the earlier lives and relations with one another of the people involved: where they lived, how much property they owned, their sexes and sexual activities, their ages, occupations, and education.

The result has been a greater understanding of community life in seventeenth-century New England and of the existing social tensions that burst into accusations of witchcraft at Salem once the mass hysteria there began. But I think it is fair to say that no one quite understands the hysteria, how it began or how it could have continued so long. *The Crucible* tells us how with a certainty that no historian could afford. And the film does it by creating the inescapable reality in which any good film immerses us more helplessly than is usually possible on the stage. The question is, once the projector has shut down and the Dolby is silent, has our experience been one of Salem in 1692 or of some other time and place where things have happened that we have just seen and felt so clearly, but that could not have happened at Salem and so cannot truly explain what we know did happen there?

The makers of the film have recognized that its success depends, at least in part, on our acceptance of its resemblance to reality. They have been scrupulous in making their Salem and our experience of it *look* like the real thing. They shot the outdoor scenes on pristine Hog Island off the coast of Cape Ann, almost within shouting distance of Salem, and the indoor scenes on a sound stage constructed in nearby Beverly. They chose these locations, the producer says, because they wanted "to make the most authentic film possible." Authenticity extended to buildings "authentically stained and aged," to farm animals of the period, to crops of the period growing in the fields, to costumes made by hand (no sewing machines) from antique linens, even to giving the actors an appropriately unbathed appearance, fingernails daily dirtied.

But they did not and probably could not have extended their efforts at authenticity so precisely to the events that make up the film and play. Part of the problem is that the actual events were so complicated that to have reproduced them exactly would have slowed the movement to a crawl. At the beginning of 1692, when the action starts, Massachusetts had been without what we may as well call an "authentic" government for almost three years. Its original popularly elected government (under a royal charter of 1629) had been replaced in 1686 by a dictatorial royal governor. He had been ejected in 1689 in a local revolution coinciding with England's Glorious Revolution. But by early 1692 England's new king had not got around to providing the colony with a new governor or frame of government. The new governor did not arrive until May 1692, to find the jails of Massachusetts filled with accused witches. A provisional, peacekeeping government had not quite dared to set up courts to try the accused. Instead, various members of the provisional governor's council, including the provisional deputy governor, Thomas Danforth, had undertaken to hear and record accusations and testimony and to hold in jail those accused. No trials were held until the new royal governor arrived and appointed a special court of oyer and terminer. It was this court, of which Danforth was not actually a member, that tried and sentenced the witches.

What Miller has done in *The Crucible* is to conflate the preliminary hearings, of which many records survive, with the actual trials, of which few records survive. Danforth could not actually have signed the seventy-two death warrants that Miller has him say he has done in the play. Nor could the Reverend Hale have signed the seventeen he says he did in the film. And though Parris and other ministers did give and take testimony at the hearings, they could not have participated in giving verdicts or pronouncing sentences. The clergy never enjoyed any political authority in colonial Massachusetts, which was not the theocracy that popular legend has made it.

These are perhaps technicalities. The witches were convicted, and probably on the basis of testimony at the hearings. But the conflation of hearing and trial does make for some confused episodes in the film. Giles Corey in the film and play shows his knowledge of the law when he is cited for contempt of court for refusing to disclose the name of a friend who had made statements favoring the accused witches. When Corey rightly points out that there is no such thing in law as contempt of a hearing, Danforth formally transforms the hearing into a court (which he could not have done). Corey is then pressed to death for contempt of court by granite block weights laid upon him, a scene graphically portrayed in the film. It happened: he was pressed to death for refusing to answer, but under quite different circumstances. Corey was himself accused of witchcraft and at his trial refused to plead, refused to answer either guilty or not guilty. English law provided for pressing under weights (*peine forte et dure*) as a means of inducing a defendant to plead, and it was this process that the court invoked against Corey; by refusing to plead, Corey, who saw that he would be found guilty if he did, prevented the court from passing judgment and thus from seizing his property, which he thereby saved for his heirs. Danforth at the hearing could not have invoked the process of putting weights on him nor could the actual court have legally used it as a punishment for contempt.

Again, this is a technicality. Corey was judicially killed, and it may have served some dramatic purpose—though it is not clear what—to have it done for the wrong reason. But how far can dramatic license extend? Have Miller and Hytner perhaps stretched it beyond the elastic limits in basing their interpretation of the Salem tragedy on, in Hytner's words, "the premise that the source of the girls' destructive energy is their emergent sexuality"? A few of the girls in the bewitched group who demonized their elders were old enough to be driven by emergent or already emerged sexuality. But most of them were probably prepubescent. Abigail, whose age Miller acknowledges he has advanced, was no more than twelve. It seems unlikely that she could actually have had an affair with John Proctor several months or perhaps years earlier. It certainly helps the film to have Winona Ryder as a palpably nubile Abigail. Indeed neither the play nor the film could succeed without the sexual chemistry between her and Proctor. Does it matter that she could not have played in life the role that Miller assigns her? On the whole, I think it does not matter. It is notable that the principal accusers in the play and film, and so far as I know in fact, were female. But if their behavior originated in sexual energy, that energy is not exhibited in overt display but is sublimated in the film to their imagined terror under Abigail's direction. Their sexuality, emergent or emerged, is at least as plausible an explanation for their behavior as any that historians have been able to offer.

It does not, however, tell us why the girls of Salem should have expressed their sexuality in so bizarre a manner when others of their age throughout New England did not. We can easily agree with Hytner's observation that "a community that denies to its young any outlet for the expression of sexuality is asking for trouble." But there is no evidence that the young of Salem endured a stricter supervision of their sex life than was common elsewhere. Moreover, though premarital sex was probably a little less common in New England than in old England at the time, seventeenth-century New Englanders were not nearly as squeamish or repressive about sex as is often supposed.

Whatever the role of sexuality may have been, it can hardly explain the readiness of judges, juries, and the people of Salem generally to believe the wild accusations of young girls. And despite

Hytner's designation of sexuality as his premise, he and Miller have given us an historically valid and wholly convincing depiction, without sexual overtones, of the way the court supported the girls' accusations by its perverse use of confessions. The court took a confession as evidence of contrition, as the cancellation of a supposed contract with the devil, and therefore, in a species of plea bargaining, as sufficient cause for acquittal. But the devil supposedly made his contract at gatherings where a number of his devotees paid him homage. The court would therefore accept a confession as proof of contrition only if the confessor identified the other persons present at the vile ceremonies, who would now be at large, doing the devil's bidding. The pressure was enormous not only to offer a false confession, but to validate it by false accusations that continually widened the numbers of the accused, who could save themselves only by similar confessions.

Some of those who confessed may have actually thought themselves to be witches and may have practiced the rituals that witchcraft required. But if so, they were the ones acquitted, while their imagined accomplices who refused to confess were hanged. It is under the pressure to offer a false confession with false accusations that John Proctor, in the stunning climax of the film, finds himself, finds who and what he is and what his judges are, taking us into the heart of the matter as no recital of historical facts could ever do. History can demonstrate clearly enough that the innocent were hanged for refusing to confess. What the film shows us in Proctor is an ultimate human dignity that transcends the human folly of a deluded court.

As a postscript, a statement placed on the darkened screen tells us: "After nineteen executions the Salem witch-hunt was brought to an end, as more and more accused people refused to save themselves by giving false confessions." The statement diminishes Proctor's contribution by seeming to magnify it. His refusal to confess did not serve as an example for others. Multiplication of refusals did not stop the witch-hunt. The way it ended was almost as unsavory as the trials themselves. The ministers of the colony, who properly figure as less than admirable in *The Crucible*, recognized the irregularity of the judicial procedures in the trials and should have done what they could to stop them sooner. They knew that "spectral evidence," the kind the girls offered in their supposed sighting of spirits in the shape of someone they accused, the kind offered also in some of the confessions, was legally insufficient. Early in the proceedings, as acknowledged experts in knowledge of witchcraft, they warned the court, too feebly, of its errors. Their warnings became stronger only when the circle of the accused widened to include more and more people of social prominence. The warnings then proved more convincing to the governor and his General Court because they saw the whole structure of Massachusetts society, with themselves at the top, threatened.

In October 1692, with the Salem court in temporary adjournment, they ordered an end to the prosecutions, dissolved the court, and left the disposition of the many remaining accusations to a new court that had plenty of confessions at its disposal but followed the approved rules for collecting and assessing evidence in witch trials. Under proper procedures it acquitted all but three persons, whom the governor promptly pardoned. It was not the stubborn dignity of people like John Proctor but political expediency that ended the terror. The concluding statement of the film is superfluous and ought to have been cut. We should be left with Proctor's enigmatic self-discovery as our ultimate insight into what happened at Salem. The film itself never departs far enough from historical fact to weaken its impact, and in Daniel Day-Lewis's portrayal of Proctor's ordeal it reaches the point where dramatic truth eclipses history. Shakespeare's *Richard III* has all but erased the real Richard. Arthur Miller is not Shakespeare, and he takes fewer liberties with the past than Shakespeare did, but with this film his Salem has become irresistibly our own.

January 9, 1997

Part Two

SOUTHERNERS

ARLY SOUTHERNERS offer a greater challenge to historians than New Englanders do, simply because they left behind so little evidence of what they thought and did. Virginia, home of the first English colonists and of the first Africans, is a case in point. There are more records of what happened in Virginia during the first three decades of English settlement than there are for almost all the rest of the colonial period. In those thirty years the settlers from England organized a society where landowners (planters) could reap large profits from all the labor they could lay their hands on. And they were good at laying hands on people. The first two essays are about books that reconstruct parts of the later history of that society from the surviving records and artifacts.

The crucial fact of that history was the planters' discovery of African slave labor as more profitable and more accessible than the limited labor of free men under contract. The resulting change in the laboring population was pretty complete in Virginia by the middle of the eighteenth century and was thereafter copied in all the southern colonies and states. Slaves became a major part of their population, in some places more numerous than the free. The South's dependence on their labor for the next century became the most important fact of American history, then and now.

Only in the last fifty-odd years have historians begun the daunting task of reconstructing the lives of slaves from the scant records their owners happened to make for their own purposes and from the testimony of slaves who escaped to the North and wrote or dictated memoirs. The third and fourth essays consider what has been learned about slave life by some of the most assiduous scholars. The last piece in the section concerns the special code of conduct that dictated the way slaveowners treated, not their slaves but each other.

CHAPTER EIGHT

Our Town

⟨⟩

A Place in Time: Middlesex County, Virginia, 1650–1750
Darrett B. and Anita H. Rutman

A Place in Time: Explicatus
Darrett B. and Anita H. Rutman

T HE COLONIAL period has been the proving ground in America for the new social history, which concentrates on the ordinary doings of ordinary people rather than on high culture and high politics. Unfortunately ordinary people, almost by definition, leave behind only faint traces of their existence. Until very recently most ordinary people could neither read nor write, and their lives have to be reconstituted from the way they appear in records kept by their not-so-ordinary contemporaries.

The starting point for the new history, both in Europe and America, has been the record of births, marriages, and deaths, which most literate societies preserve in one form or another. In colonial America surviving records of this kind—as of every other kind—are most abundant for New England. The southern colonists were not preoccupied with their own historical significance and mostly did not bother even to make the records of births, marriages, and deaths that they required of themselves by law. Nor did they write accounts of what they were up to for the benefit of posterity, and if they wrote and received letters they did not squirrel them away for their descendants. What is more, from 1860 to 1864 they fought a devastating war on their own ground against their record-keeping brethren to the north.

Nowhere was the devastation of that war more damaging to historical documents than in Virginia, where virtually all the central records of the colony were lost in the burning of Richmond. Historians are left only with a number of local county records and stray family papers, and whatever can be gleaned from records preserved in England and from archeological digs. On the basis of these bits and pieces, the new social history in the 1970s and early 1980s moved on Virginia. Entering by way of nearby Maryland, where the records are somewhat better, the historians began to piece together the contours of a society that contrasts dramatically not only with New England but with contemporary England as well. It has been an exacting if challenging process, requiring extrapolation from isolated bits of evidence to recover even such elementary facts as the approximate size of the population and its rate of growth, let alone the exact numbers of births, marriages, and deaths. With patience a great deal can be inferred from a few figures, in the way a paleontologist can reconstruct a dinosaur from a few bones.

As the figures accumulate, they show us a society where death was the most common fact of life. After the 1640s Virginia's population grew rapidly, to make it the largest English colony in America, but it grew at a price in human life that seems almost incredible today. One of the most remarkable discoveries of the new history about New England was that the first settlers there improved their life expectancy by as much as twenty years. Those who went to Virginia were more likely than not to die in their first year.

What sort of relationships did the survivors bear toward one another? Because they spread so widely and rapidly along the banks of tidewater rivers, they could not in any case sustain the closely knit communities that characterized early New England. But the death rate would almost seem to preclude the development of anything that could be called a community at all. Not so. Darrett and Anita Rutman have examined in loving detail a single county in Virginia during the first century of its existence. Middlesex County, on the south bank of the Rappahannock River, has better surviving records than most other

Virginia counties; but only one who has struggled through those records can appreciate the extraordinary pains that the Rutmans have taken to reconstruct from them the lives and deaths of some twelve thousand persons and the web of relationships that, despite all handicaps, bound them together in neighborhoods and the neighborhoods into communities.

The new history's computerized pursuit of numbers has sometimes had the ironic effect of dehumanizing the very people whose lives it aims at recovering. That is not the case with this work. The Rutmans give us plenty of numbers, more of them than have hitherto been available for any part of early Virginia, and the numbers themselves are eloquent. Their figures for mortality in Middlesex are even more appalling than the more general ones that have been estimated (largely on the basis of Maryland records) for the Chesapeake region in general. The life expectancy of a colonial Middlesex resident at age twenty, whether immigrant or native born, was not only much less than that of a New Englander but less than that of someone remaining in England. What is worse, while estimates for the colony as a whole have emphasized a falling off of the death rate after midcentury, in Middlesex it rose. In constructing life tables (estimates of life expectancy at a given age) for Middlesex, the Rutmans found that the models constructed for varying degrees of mortality in modern "undeveloped" countries did not even envisage rates as high as the ones in Middlesex (at age twenty a man born in Middlesex in the 1680s could expect to live no more than twenty-four years longer). Some sense of what this meant may be gained from the fact that throughout the century most native-born children in Middlesex lost one or both of their parents by their thirteenth birthday, and almost half did so by their ninth birthday. Victorian novelists with their predilection for the plight of the orphan would have found plenty of material in Middlesex.

The Rutmans are not novelists, but neither are they mere number jugglers. They have confined most of the technicalities to a separate volume, with the arch subtitle *Explicatus*. This leaves them free to con-

vey in their text something of the spirit of their community gained from
prolonged intimacy with all traces of it that they have pursued over
many years. It was a community, as must be obvious, filled with widows
and widowers, and with stepmothers, stepfathers, and stepchildren. It
was a community where, in the absence of living kin, friendship might
count for much. The fragile, transitory character of human relationships, instead of diminishing dependence on neighbors, seems to have
increased it, even though neighbors might be much more widely separated than in New or old England. And the effect of high mortality on
domestic relations may have been similar.

It had been plausibly argued by historians of the family that heavy
child mortality prevented medieval and early modern parents from
committing their affections to children who might so quickly be taken
from them. The evidence from Middlesex, admittedly fragmentary,
does not support such a view: Middlesex parents seem to have exhibited a lively affection for their children and showed their concern for
family continuity by naming children either after themselves or, more
significantly, after their own parents. Admittedly the inferences to be
drawn from the thin evidence cannot be conclusive, but in the absence
of harder data, the social historian of early America often has to be
content with probabilities.

Perhaps the most interesting and convincing data that the
Rutmans have been able to assemble is that showing the effect of slavery on their community. The Middlesex materials reveal little about
the lives of the slaves themselves, but a great deal about the way in
which the advent of slave labor affected the lives of the white settlers.
At the outset of settlement in 1650, slaves accounted for only a tiny
proportion of the labor force either in Middlesex or anywhere else in
Virginia. By 1700, they were most of it. The Virginians who experienced this transformation were remarkably silent about it, but the
Middlesex records as pieced together by the Rutmans show in concrete detail how the new labor system worked as a lottery to the benefit of the fortunate few who, literally, held the lucky numbers.

Investing in human beings was nothing new in Virginia. From the beginning tobacco planters had bought and sold white indentured servants, who worked out the cost of their passage to the New World by several years of labor. The risks to the purchaser were reflected in the fact that a servant who had survived his first deadly year or two, even though he might have only two or three more years to serve, brought a higher price than a man who had just stepped ashore. When a planter bought a newly arrived slave, at twice the cost of the most expensive indentured servant, both the risks and the possible profits were much larger. If the slave lived, he might in the course of his or her life bring a huge return on the investment and even increase the owner's capital by presenting him with children. On the other hand, death and the various afflictions of humanity might bring disaster to the small planter who invested his all or more than all in so perishable a commodity. But the large planter, who could spend enough to put the law of averages to work for him, could spread the demographic risks. Among fifty slaves there would be enough survivors to outweigh the loss. The overall return on the large investment might not be as great as that of the small planter who bet his small savings on the lives of one or two slaves and won, but the odds of the slavery game were stacked against the small-time planter and almost guaranteed a large profit to the big spender.

That was the way it worked in Middlesex. The county began with a wide gap between the largest and smallest of its independent planters, but neighborhoods and neighborly feelings could encompass both. A hundred years later both large and small householders had prospered. Inventories of the smallest households show more of the goods that suggest material comfort than had been present in comparable houses at the offset. But the gap between large and small had perceptibly widened, and the character of the community had evidently changed. Though the difference cannot be measured in the records of births and deaths and taxes and inventories, neighborhoods had lost some of their neighborliness, and the networks of human relations stretched more closely along class lines than across them.

From the fragmentary records of Middlesex the Rutmans, with

remarkable skill and meticulous care, have constructed a vivid picture
of a place in time. It is unlikely that the new social history can do more
for any place in Virginia during the time to which they have confined
themselves, between 1650 and 1750. Their very success invites reflec-
tion on the limits of the genre itself. The study of ordinary people in
their daily lives needs no justification, and there can be no doubt that
the new history has opened up vast areas of what one of its practitioners has aptly called "the world we have lost," a world lost as much to
previous historians as to everyone else. The effect has been not
directly to erase the old landmarks of the past, but to render them
seemingly insignificant. When the new history initiated its investigation of colonial New England, its practitioners did not attempt to
reassess the developments or trends, the political and intellectual crises
that had previously dictated the structure of historical accounts of the
region. They were simply uninterested in the theological controversies and political maneuverings that had occupied the attention of previous historians. It was not a question of refuting or revising earlier
interpretations but of bypassing them. It was not even a question of
replacing old landmarks with new. What are the landmarks of the history that grows from registers of births and deaths, taxes and inventories? There are occasional catastrophes: epidemics of one disease or
another, years of bad harvests—but the watersheds of the kind that
marked the old history are missing.

The Rutmans' study of Middlesex is a case in point: the opening
and closing dates are arbitrary. The first merely approximates the
gathering of substantial numbers of settlers in the county; the closing
date of 1750 is simply a hundred years later. And the arbitrary choice is
deliberate. We are not concerned here with big events. And there is an
implication, as in the New England studies, that the events that
seemed big in previous accounts were not so big when placed in proper
perspective. The period covered here saw Bacon's Rebellion of 1676,
the largest uprising against constituted authority in America before
the Revolution and the centerpiece in conventional accounts of
Virginia's colonial history. It was a revolt of Virginia's young men, who

had survived disease and years of servitude only to find themselves barred from the economic benefits of freedom by their former employers' grip on the colony's land and government. In Middlesex, so far as the Rutmans' investigation indicates, Bacon's Rebellion was no great matter, and whatever may have been the grievances that brought it about, they were not conspicuously felt by the people of Middlesex. In Middlesex it was "simply a venting of frustrations and a release of tension, precipitated by events unrelated to the county's doings and, in the end, negligible in effect." That may be a fair judgment, but it raises some interesting questions about the relationship of the new history to the old.

Is it possible that the events that seemed important in the old history have lost their significance in the new, not because they were negligible to ordinary people of the time but because the kind of sources on which the new history necessarily depends cannot disclose either their significance or their lack of it for ordinary people? Governor William Berkeley, who was first displaced by Bacon's Rebellion and then succeeded in putting it down, offered the opinion that there were no more than five hundred people in Virginia who had supported him against Nathaniel Bacon. Perhaps Berkeley was wrong, but if the great majority of Virginians were sufficiently discontented with their government to take up arms against it, it stands to reason that the evils they suffered had become insufferable. Were the people of Middlesex an exception? If not, is the new history incapable of reaching or registering the discontents that provoked the rebellion?

One is reminded of the grip that another kind of new historical method recently held on the historiography of eighteenth-century British politics. Sir Lewis Namier's brilliant study, *Structure of Politics at the Accession of George III* (1929), so dazzled a generation of British historians that they not only confined themselves to examining political structures but also followed their master in proclaiming that structure was all that mattered: the political issues that had occupied previous historians all seemed to be a sham. It is now evident, thanks to the work of a later generation of historians including John Brewer and Linda Colley, that political issues and parties disappeared from Namierist historiography because concentration on the structure of politics could not disclose them.[1] Is something analogous happening in the new social history's concentration on the kind of information to be gained by compiling and analyzing statistics? If so, it does not follow that the statistical method is at fault, but that a marriage of the new and the old might be fruitful. The new history might profit by a closer look at the landmarks of the old.

January 17, 1985

CHAPTER NINE

The Fall of the Gentry

⟨⟩⟩⟩⟩⟨⟨

The Transformation of Virginia: 1740–1790
Rhys Isaac

I T WOULD BE hard not to like *The Transformation of Virginia*. It
places familiar events in new perspectives. It uses new techniques
for making the past surrender meanings not previously available. It
gives the reader a visual experience missing in most historical works by
using illustrations as part of the argument. Not since that forgotten
classic *The Wind That Swept Mexico* by Anita Brenner and George R.
Leighton[1] have I seen illustrations so effectively combined with text.
The author's purpose is to reconstruct the society that had developed
in Virginia by 1740 and then to observe the transformation that it
underwent in the succeeding fifty years. There is, as always in historical works, an implication that this particular transformation was somehow more crucial than any that occurred in the preceding or
succeeding half century. But we have to forgive an author this sort of
myopia. The question is how well he is able to see, and make us see,
the society and social changes of his chosen time and place.

What distinguishes Isaac's vision is his insistence that relationships
among people in any society must be understood not only through the
written records of what they said about themselves (which are not in
this case voluminous) but also through mute kinds of evidence that the
historian must learn to "read" as "statements." He must extract social
relations from what people did to the landscape, from what sort of
houses they lived in, from their festivities and amusements as well as
their work. In this examination he will make large use of physical sur-

vivals—houses and house plans, for example. Although he may have to rely mainly on the written record, he will read it for what he discerns behind it, like an anthropologist trying to discover the patterns of pre-Columbian Indian society from the casual and uncomprehending remarks of the invading Europeans. The method, in fact, is borrowed from ethnographic anthropology, and the author supplies a lengthy explanation of it at the end of the book.

The Virginia of 1740 that this method reveals contains few surprises. It is composed of three elements. The first is a group of great tobacco planters, presiding over princely domains worked by groups of black slaves, who form a second element. The third is the body of independent small farmers with no slaves or very few, who also are engaged in growing tobacco for the world market. While the planters dominate the whole society and not simply their slaves, each of the component elements has its own character. For Rhys Isaac that character, as well as the changing character of the society, is to be found in greater or lesser degrees of individualism and communalism. He gives no precise definition to these terms but allows their meaning to develop from his reading of the different kinds of surviving evidence.

The prevalence of communalism or individualism in each of the three elements is most strikingly exhibited in their housing. Originally almost all Virginia houses were small and simple one-story affairs, with no more than two rooms, one of which was entered from the other. Inside them space was undifferentiated and privacy was minimal. By 1740 this was still standard for small farmers, but large planters were moving toward greater differentiation, with a central hall from which one entered separate rooms both upstairs and downstairs, and with outlying buildings symmetrically subordinated to the "great house." The only buildings not included in the formal layout of the plantation were the slave quarters, rude one-room barracks that were placed somewhere out of sight.

In these different buildings the author reads a growing individualism among the great planters, expressed in the privacy of separate rooms; a continuing communalism among the small farmers, expressed in the absence of privacy; and a more thoroughgoing communalism among the slaves, whose quarters, off by themselves, did not necessarily house family units but several families or individuals together. By virtue of their isolation and their communal housing the slaves were able to retain or develop an autonomous culture within the larger society, preserving values and social attitudes inherited from an African past. Despite their status, they were in some ways more independent culturally than the small farmers, who tended to repeat in dilute form the attitudes of their large neighbors, to whom they deferred socially as well as politically.

The author draws out the relations between and among the different groups, especially between the large planters and the small farmers, through the occasions on which they came together—at church, at the county court, at taverns, horse races, cockfights, militia musters, elections, and most revealingly at balls and dances. On all these occasions the superiority and authority of the planters as a class were exhibited and acted out, but there was also exhibited an element of contest among them and even of tension among the different classes. The formal balls of the gentry were imitated and satirized among the slaves, and the planters in turn borrowed dance forms from the slaves. Along with the regular English "country" dances at a ball there would be "jigs" in which a couple improvised pursuit and retreat, until one or another was cut out by a newcomer. Isaac sees in this not simply a symbol of courtship but "a palpable element of contest" that pervaded all the amusements of the upper class (another expression of the individualism displayed in their architecture) while the continuity of the whole society was exhibited in the fact that the form itself originated with the slaves (among whom paradoxically it must somehow have expressed communalism).

The transformation that altered this society by 1790 came from two directions. One was the quarrel with Great Britain, which produced a wide assertion of the political ideology imported from the radical Whigs of the mother country. The author does not go into the question of how this ideology came to be present at all in a colony where there had been few signs of it at the opening of the eighteenth century. Nor is he especially interested in the ideology itself, except as it affirmed a voluntary contractual basis for society and thus undermined the hegemony of the planters by extending their individualism throughout the free portion of the society.

Indeed this element of transformation commands the author's attention less than the other more complex one, which he has made his specialty: the rise of evangelical religion. After 1740 Presbyterians, Baptists, and Methodists invaded Virginia and began winning converts among the small farmers and slaves. Their whole way of life challenged that of the dominant class. Where the culture of the gentry was based on the written word, that of the evangelicals was oral. Where the gentry enjoyed contests and rivalry, the evangelicals enjoyed brotherhood. Where the gentry went to the Anglican parish church to display their grandeur, the evangelicals went to their separate meetings to be saved. Where the gentry enjoyed nothing quite so much as dancing, the evangelicals forbade it. While exhibiting communalism in their daily lives, where the gentry were banishing it, the evangelicals affirmed individualism in religion (in their insistence on rebirth) where the gentry wanted none of it. Moreover they extended their individualistic missionary efforts to slaves, a potentially subversive gesture. Without directly questioning the political dominance of the large planters, the evangelicals repudiated the symbols and rituals on which it depended.

That the large planters perceived the evangelicals as a threat is evident from the violent hostility and contempt with which they were often greeted. But the revolution against British authority dealt a blow to the established Anglican church and gave an opening to the evangelicals to win recognition. Isaac even suggests that the unanimity with which the planters embraced the Revolutionary cause may have been in part an effort to co-opt the evangelicals and reunify the whole society under their own continued domination. But if so the effort was in vain. The close of the Revolution by 1790 saw the three elements of Virginia society more widely separated, with the planters' patriarchal control destroyed or impaired and their individualism appropriated by their social inferiors. It is of course paradoxical, to say the least, that the evangelicals, stressing communal brotherhood, should also be carriers and beneficiaries of a triumphant individualism, and still more paradoxical that the individualism cherished by the great planters should be the instrument for the destruction of their dominance.

To state the thesis of the book in such bald terms is to do less than justice to the richness of the author's perceptions. But it is also to suggest the inadequacy of such fuzzy concepts as individualism and communalism for understanding what was happening in Virginia. In spite of the author's insight and imagination in interpreting the challenge presented by the evangelicals—and this challenge dominates the book—there is too much left out, too much that is unexplained in the transformation that he posits.

There is, for example, comparatively little attention to changes in the Virginia economy during the period covered. The author begins with a description of tobacco cultivation, and there can be no doubt that the special demands of that crop had much to do with the structure of the society that grew it. But the years between 1740 and 1790 saw the introduction of wheat as a major crop. How did this affect the transformation that Isaac portrays? That one did affect the other is almost certain, yet we hear nothing about it. Indeed we are told that "land usage . . . had scarcely changed." The shift to wheat was accompanied by another development that must also have affected social relations, namely a surplus of slaves who could not be profitably employed in either tobacco or wheat production. How did this change in the economic position of slavery relate to communalism and individualism?

Since the author's treatment of slavery is focused on the autonomy of slave culture, he gives little consideration either to the direct relations of slaves to masters or to the effect of racial slavery on the relations between large plantation owners and small farmers. In his "Discourse on Method" at the end of the book Isaac examines at length a set of episodes on Landon Carter's plantation that reveal something of the complexity of relations among slaves and between slaves and masters, but his analysis in this section has not visibly contributed to his portrayal of Virginia society in the body of the book. Although there was no developed concept of race as such in the period he deals with, there is more than a little evidence that the blackness of blacks and the whiteness of whites powerfully affected every kind of social relationship. It is not enough to demonstrate simply that black culture was not overwhelmed by white. Interracial attitudes by whatever name they are called deserve more attention than they receive here.

Still another missing element in the picture is the role of the Virginia gentry in the move to strengthen the central government. Isaac shows us that the establishment of a United States government in 1789 brought a reduction in the powers and importance of the state legislature and county courts as instruments of great-planter hegemony. But he does not consider how or why James Madison and his gentry friends deliberately sought that reduction or whether the national government furnished or was intended to furnish new instruments of planter dominance. This is not to say that the author should have written a political history, but he is very much concerned with the distribution of power. It is dangerous to read the signs of that distribution in architecture and rituals while ignoring the overt expressions of it.

It is dangerous because, in spite of the effort to systematize the discovery of hidden meanings in ballroom dancing or horse racing or church attendance, the meanings that emerge must depend heavily on intuitions that derive from what one expects to find. When dealing with words that have an ostensible meaning, the interpreter who thinks there is a different, hidden meaning is at least obliged to offer reasons why he dismisses the ostensible meaning. There is no such control in "reading" horse races or architecture as "statements."

We are told, for example, that the undifferentiated dwellings of early Virginia expressed and promoted communalism, while the later, more elaborate ones expressed and promoted individualism. If this is anything more than a tautology equating individualism with privacy and the absence of it with communalism, can anyone actually demon-

strate the proposition? Can anyone show that in any culture lack of
privacy has promoted power or prestige in the group as opposed to the
individuals composing it, or vice versa? One is reminded of John
Demos's different reading of the effect on the inhabitants of Plymouth
Colony of living in small one- or two-room houses. As Demos sees it,
the lack of privacy made for the temporary suppression of aggressive
impulses that later erupted in quarrels among neighbors.[2] In other
words, lack of privacy worked in the long run against communalism.
Either reading is intuitive. Probably neither is susceptible of empirical
demonstration, but they are scarcely compatible.

Or take Isaac's discussion of the conflicting tendencies within
evangelical religion toward communalism on the one hand and toward
individualism on the other. In explaining a continuing communalism
in evangelical churches, he concludes by observing: "The proximity of
a black society that was highly communal in its religion and way of life
could only reinforce the latter tendencies in white popular evangelical
forms of worship." Although he has argued that the evangelicals welcomed blacks to their meetings, thus presumably overcoming racial
prejudice, it is surely gratuitous to suppose that any group of white
Virginians in 1790 would find support for any practice in the fact that
it prevailed among blacks. The evangelicals may have overcome racial
prejudice for a time and up to a point; but their attitudes toward slavery and race were not simple, nor were they unchanging, as a study of
them in depth by James Essig demonstrates.[3]

In short, the book has blind spots. The transformation it describes
may not have been quite what we are told it was. Nevertheless, the
author did not make it up out of thin air. The evangelicals did come to
Virginia, they did change things. If they did not change them in quite
the way he says, if he neglects other changes, he has nonetheless set us
thinking about a society and its social relations during the period of
the American Revolution in ways that we never did before. That is
perhaps as much as one should ask.

January 20, 1983

CHAPTER TEN

The Big American Crime

⸺ ∞ ⸺

Many Thousands Gone: The First Two Centuries
of Slavery in North America
Ira Berlin

Slave Counterpoint: Black Culture in the
Eighteenth-Century Chesapeake and Lowcountry
Philip D. Morgan

Remembering Slavery: African Americans Talk About Their
Personal Experiences of Slavery and Emancipation
Ira Berlin, Marc Favreau, and Steven E. Miller, editors

Africans in America: America's Journey Through Slavery
Charles Johnson, Patricia Smith, and
the WGBH Series Research Team

I T HAS BEEN a long time since anyone has argued that slavery was a good thing, but just how bad it was has become a pregnant question. It is not in doubt that slaves suffered injustice and cruelty, that slave plantations, whether producing rice or tobacco, cotton or sugar, rested on systematic brutality and violence. The question is what the experience did to the people violated, especially in North America, where they were almost all black, the ancestors of present-day black Americans. Or should we say of African-Americans? The choice of a name is itself a way of taking sides, like the older one between Negro and black (or Black?), a choice between stressing national unity or ethnic diversity, between affirming racial equality or black pride. Historical investigation of what slavery did to slaves is charged with presentist implications that shadow every fact found, and consciously or unconsciously shape every interpretation.

The subject took on a new kind of sensitivity early in the twentieth century after anthropologists, under the leadership of Franz Boas, began examining the complexity and sophistication of African cultures (the plural is important). Melville Herskovits, a student of Boas, studied the cultures not only of Africans in a part of Africa (Dahomey, now the Republic of Benin) but also of descendants of Africans in Haiti, Suriname, and most significantly the United States. In *The Myth of the Negro Past* (1941)[1] he argued that much in African cultures had survived the trauma of slavery and persisted among the descendants of slaves. In Brazil and Suriname and to a somewhat lesser extent in the United States he found survivals of African music and dancing, African styles of humor and modes of address, African patterns of family relationship and social structure, African attitudes toward the elderly, toward children, toward the dead. White ignorance or denial of such cultural survivals in the United States, Herskovits argued, was "one of the principal supports of race prejudice in this country," because it left the Negro "a man without a past," unworthy of the respect that other ethnic groups inherited from identification with their progenitors.

Although it was not his intention, Herskovits seemed to imply that slavery could not have been as totally repressive as, say, the abolitionists had made it out to be. He had discovered an African past in the black communities of his own day. If remnants of African cultures had survived until then, they could not have been obliterated by slavery. Slaves must have been able to sustain a degree of cultural autonomy under the restraints of a regime that claimed the power to order their every waking hour. Of course the more power exerted over them, the greater their achievement in setting limits to it. But in any case, if Herskovits was right, slavery was not a one-way street in which slaveowners dictated every movement. The history of slavery could be understood only as an interchange between two parties, the one not as wholly subdued to the other as had been generally supposed.

The challenge for historians was to retrieve from past records the elements and extent of slave autonomy, to show what kinds of lives slave men and women had been able to carve out for themselves despite the odds against them. Historians were slow in rising to the challenge. It was not until the late 1960s and early 1970s that studies in depth of slave life began to appear, prompted perhaps by the rising consciousness of race prejudice exemplified by the civil rights movement. The roots of the civil rights movement were doubtless complex, but its objectives may have depended more on a reassessment of black history than was always evident at the time. Once the study of slave life began, it quickly became a major area of historical research and has now furnished black Americans with a past even richer in its autonomy than Herskovits had envisaged. Two books, by Philip D. Morgan (no relation to the author) and Ira Berlin, evince the maturity that the study has attained.

Berlin, who has already contributed significantly to the literature, here brings together in a magisterial synthesis much of what has now been learned about slave life during its first two centuries within the present United States. Slavery, he insists at the outset, was always a "negotiated relationship" and an "intrinsically unstable" one, the terms of which varied from time to time and from place to place. The negotiations were not conducted across a table or on anything like a level playing field. Rather they were embedded in the daily transactions between master and slave, mainly in the work place. Work was always at the center of them and "informed all other conflicts between master and slave," including conflicts of culture. Berlin sees the cultural autonomy expressed both in the continuation of African patterns of behavior (braided hair and filing teeth in the traditional manner, clandestinely performing African rites at births and burials) and the creation of new ones as deliberate and purposeful. While the contours of slave life might vary as negotiations shifted, the beliefs, attitudes, and activities that slaves nurtured among themselves always had an "oppositional content," even if concealed in the mimicry of dance or later in the metaphors of a folk tale. In places where the body of slaves had come directly from Africa, as in eighteenth-century South Carolina, they often carried so deep an attachment to old customs that "the conflict over work and over culture became one."

With the masters' determination to dominate and the slaves' resilient resistance as constants, a variety of circumstances affected the outcome of their negotiations. Were the slaves at a given time and place from one African region (and culture) or another or from many different ones? How long ago had they left Africa and what had happened to them since? Did they grow tobacco or rice or sugar or cotton in the country or did they build houses, caulk ships, or shoe horses in the city? Did their work determine a region's whole economy ("slave societies," as in most of the South) or was it merely a convenience ("societies with slaves," as in the North)? Berlin's achievement is to order the resulting variety by identifying four different regions with four different economies (the Chesapeake, the eastern tidewater from South Carolina to Florida, the Mississippi Valley, and the North) and by dividing the social developments of two centuries in each region into three periods, which he designates as the charter generations, the plantation generations, and the Revolutionary generations, stopping short of the heyday of slavery in the antebellum decades of the nineteenth century.

The contrasts of slave life in different places and at different times can be appreciated in Berlin's depiction of the two regions that held most of the country's slaves before the nineteenth century, the regions studied in greater detail by Morgan, on whose previous research Berlin frequently relies (the two have collaborated in earlier works). The Chesapeake enjoyed the relatively favorable conditions of the charter generations from the beginning of slavery there in 1619 until the last two decades of the century. Before then the Virginia labor force was mainly white, and Africans joining it enjoyed more rights and had a better chance of becoming free than those who came after them in much greater numbers. Most of the charter generations had left Africa some time earlier. Many were what Berlin calls "Atlantic creoles," slaves who had been born and raised in the great trading

centers of the Atlantic, in Spain, Portugal, West Africa, and the
Caribbean. They were often of mixed European and African descent,
already familiar with European cultures, and thus "did not arrive as
deracinated chattel, stripped of their past and without resources to
meet the future." In consequence they blended into the existing society, sometimes gained freedom, and developed only a thin autonomous
culture of their own.

But they were not assimilated or fully accepted as equals, and a
flood of coerced immigrants from Africa in the half century after 1680
coincided, not accidentally, with a legal elimination of whatever privi-
leges they had originally enjoyed. Race and slavery were deliberately
identified. Yet the Africanization of the Chesapeake labor force apparently did not create a durable African culture. By the middle of the
eighteenth century, the fertility of the black population produced a
majority of Chesapeake slaves who had never seen Africa: "Slaves with
teeth filed, hair plaited, or skin scarred in the ritual manner disappeared from the countryside." By the time of the American Revolution,
with tobacco fields exhausted, Chesapeake planters found themselves
with a surplus of slaves, mostly nativeborn. That fact, along with the
ideology of freedom that accompanied the Revolution, produced
an increasing number of manumissions and regained for Chesapeake slaves, at least temporarily, some of the benefits of the charter
generation.

The history of South Carolina slave society is one of both greater
oppression and greater autonomy. The colony began with a charter
generation of Atlantic creoles who worked beside their masters in
mixed agriculture and stock raising. Slaves mistreated could easily take
to the woods. Swamps deep in the interior harbored "maroon" settle-
ments of successful runaways, whose continuing presence furnished a
refuge, for those who dared risk it, from the rigors that arrived with
rice culture at the end of the seventeenth century. Rice required heavy,
unhealthful, and exhausting labor. The death rate among slaves was so
high that the labor force could be maintained only by a continuous
influx of new slaves, especially as rice cultivation generated ever larger

plantations. The result, combined with the possibility of escape to the maroons and the absence of any close relationship with masters (who frequently preferred the comforts of Charleston to the steaming heat of the plantation), was the creation of an African culture more autonomous than any other in North America. Slaves were able to negotiate a task system of labor whereby instead of working as a gang, everyone was given a specific task for the day, a number of plants to plant or rows to hoe, however long it took. With their daily stint completed, slaves could work for themselves, even growing their own crops of rice on patches of land assigned them.

Since they came from different regions of Africa, often with different languages, it was their common plight and a recognition of their common origins in another continent that brought them together. Consequently, as Berlin notes, with implications for the present that are hard to assess, "The construction of an African identity proceeded on the western, not the eastern, side of the Atlantic." At the same time, South Carolina planters, who became familiar with the character of the peoples from different parts of Africa, sometimes gathered their forces from a particular region, so that it became possible for "specific African cultures to reconstitute themselves within the plantation setting."

One would like to know more about the African identity constructed in America and about the content of African cultures reconstituted here. How was their oppositional character manifested? Admittedly the distinguishing marks of different slave cultures, varying so widely, are difficult to retrieve from the existing sources. The words and acts of slaves in the seventeenth and eighteenth centuries survive mainly in the unsympathetic and uncomprehending notation of them in the diaries, letters, and travel accounts of whites, and in testimony by and about slaves and free blacks on the rare occasions when their activities came under notice of the courts. It is perhaps a little too easy to ascribe African origins or oppositional purposes to actions or customs about which we still know so little. The great virtue of Berlin's work is to furnish a frame and vocabulary for more detailed studies of the different slave cultures that he identifies.

Philip Morgan's work is confined to eighteenth-century slavery in the two regions just noticed. Morgan's closer examination, the closest yet made of slave life anywhere before the nineteenth century, yields not only more of the content of slave cultures but a somewhat different interpretation of them. It is difficult to convey here the complexity and subtlety of his analysis. In general, like Berlin, Morgan finds the relationship of masters and slaves in the Chesapeake to have been less harsh, less adversarial than in the low country of South Carolina and Georgia. Slaves in the Chesapeake not only enjoyed more material comforts in food, clothing, and housing, but also more intimate daily contact with their masters. Chesapeake slavery was more paternalistic and grew increasingly so during the century.

In South Carolina, he agrees, the isolation of slaves from their masters on much larger plantations than in the Chesapeake made possible the much greater development of independent slave cultures: "Material conditions and communal autonomy appear to have been inversely related." But Morgan sees few signs of direct African influence as a source of autonomy, even in the low country. African familiarity with rice cultivation, which earlier historians have credited with introducing the crop, seems actually to have had little effect on the way it was produced in South Carolina or on the lives of those who produced it. The task system, which Morgan was the first to describe and which helped to make Carolina slaves more autonomous than their Chesapeake counterparts, developed independently of African influence.

Morgan finds the oppositional content of slave cultures in both regions to lie not in any specific elements but rather in the very existence of these cultures. Divisions among slaves, readily exploited by whites, made the creation of autonomous cultures among them the more difficult: Igbos were arrayed against Angolans, Creoles against "salt-water Africans," Africans against Indians, slaves of one master against those of another. The cultures they created in overcoming these divisions have to be understood more as a triumph of humanity than as survivals of an African past. Morgan traces the distinctive features of family life, language, music, dance, humor, and religion in both regions, stressing the imaginative creativity found in them. For example, no single African language survived, but slaves in different regions put together distinctive adaptations of English, varying in phonology, grammar, and vocabulary, sometimes unintelligible to masters but used in speaking to one another. Forbidden to use drums (which whites feared for their emotional effect and signalling capacity), they substituted hand-clapping and developed the banjo from an original African instrument into a new American one. Supplied with the plainest rough clothing, they dyed it with the bark of local trees and decorated it and themselves with ornaments and fancy hair styles and headgear, so that the very drabness imposed on them "helped create a people keenly interested in fashion, intensely aware of personal style, and fervently committed to expressiveness in their everyday life." Morgan's account is exhaustive, and sometimes exhausting, in its detail, but it is more than a recovery of hard-to-find facts. It is informed throughout by Morgan's recognition that slavery, as an extreme form of domination, resonates with the ambiguities present in all human relations. He wisely resists the temptation to draw out the implications for present-day race relations, for the implications are uncertain and unpredictable.

The recognition of a Negro past that Herskovits called for as a prerequisite for eliminating prejudice is abundantly documented in these two books and in many others. But it is not quite the African past Herskovits envisaged, and its impact on racial prejudice may not be quite what he expected. While Berlin sees a larger element of African survival than Morgan, both would probably agree that the significance of slave cultures for race relations at the time lay more in their affirmation of autonomy than in their origins. And here begin the ambiguities. Where slavery was less oppressive and race relations the more "pliable" (Morgan's term), as in the Chesapeake, slaves were unable to develop a healthy culture of their own as a base from which to carry on the negotiations that Berlin sees as determining their status. Yet, superficially at least, their status in the Chesapeake was better than in the low country. Where slavery was more oppressive, as in South Carolina, slave culture was stronger, more African, more autonomous, more oppositional. But, as Morgan points out, while the formation of their own culture was in itself "*the* most significant act of resistance" by slaves, yet "by creating an autonomous culture, slaves also eased the torments of slavery, and, in that respect, their cultural creativity created accommodation." Autonomy could thus help to perpetuate the torments of subjection.

The implications for the present carry a similar ambiguity. It does not impeach the scholarly integrity of these and other deeply researched studies of slave culture to recognize that they do send messages to the present of which the authors can scarcely have been unaware. The effect, and surely in some measure the intention, of all these studies must be to induce a greater respect by whites for the "Negro Past" and a greater pride in it on the part of blacks. Herskovits, while continually emphasizing the scientific character of his anthropological study, had made plain at the beginning that his scientific rigor was aimed against race prejudice. Historians, including Berlin and Morgan, generally leave such an intention implicit. But if slave culture was a mode of opposing slavery, the study of it is surely a mode of opposing racism.

Race prejudice, however, is a protean animal, not necessarily vulnerable to demonstrations of scientific or historical fact—even without the muddying of the waters by critical racial studies and the "postmodern" refusal to distinguish fact from fiction. The result of serious historical reconstruction of slave culture, whatever the intent of the authors, may be a greater feeling of guilt on the part of whites for what their ancestors did to so creative and independent a people. And the posthumous assumption of ancestral guilt can paradoxically offer support to present-day racism, just as the severity of slavery did to slavery's persistence. George Rawick, in a pioneering study of slave culture, recognized the danger and warned that "only those who feel themselves innately superior can feel such guilt about the conditions of others."[2] Whites who assume ancestral guilt to themselves cannot dissociate it entirely from the ancestral assumption of racial superiority that produced whatever there is to feel guilty about. Moreover, what neither white nor black historians seem to understand and none of our authors addresses is the nature of the guilt feeling that supports white racism. Slavery now seems too horrendous a crime to fasten wholly on its beneficiaries. Whatever guilt we may feel for slavery stops short of repudiating our national heroes because of their role in oppressing a whole race. Their sins have to be attributed to a system in which everybody was involved, including the slaves, whose necessary participation was an embarrassment to men like Washington and Jefferson. Guilt feelings are a continuation of that embarrassment, and racism is a way of exorcising it by blaming the victims and their descendants.

This may seem a perverse line of reasoning. Surely the blame ought to go in the other direction. But "ought to" has not governed the history of oppression. Oppressors commonly blame the oppressed, and if they or their descendants feel guilt they blame that too on the oppressed. Benjamin Franklin, who understood human relations as well as anyone ever has, recognized the phenomenon not in the tyranny of master over slave but in the lesser tyranny of Britain over the American colonists. He thought that Britain, by not giving the colonists the same rights as Englishmen and by trying to subdue them by force, was truly oppressing them, indeed threatening them, with the same slavery they themselves exercised on their rice and sugar plantations. By the time the colonists declared independence, the breach with Britain was beyond repair, he said, because "Great Britain has injured us too much ever to forgive us." He explained himself more fully in answer to an overture for reconciliation. Even if it were possible, he said, for Americans to forget and forgive what the British had done to them, "it is not possible for *you* (I mean the British Nation) to forgive the People you have so heavily injured; you can never confide again in those as Fellow Subjects, and permit them to enjoy equal Freedom, to whom you know you have given such just Cause of lasting Enmity."[3] As no good deed goes unpunished, bad ones are seldom forgotten or forgiven by those responsible for them.

Franklin's reasoning was close to that of Thomas Jefferson in thinking that whites could never admit blacks to freedom and equality in the United States. Not merely "Deep-rooted prejudices entertained by the whites," and not merely the racial differences he believed to be real, but "ten thousand recollections, by the blacks, of the injuries they have sustained" would "produce convulsions which will probably never end but in the extermination of one or the other race."[4] Jefferson's observation was not as acute as Franklin's, for he did not admit the difficulty he and his friends would have as oppressors in "forgiving" the people they oppressed. But he himself exemplified the difficulty by his belief in white superiority and by his conviction that emancipation could be acceptable only if the freed slaves went somewhere else. Jefferson's feelings of guilt for slavery went hand in hand with a contempt for its victims and a fear of them that made forgiveness impossible. Franklin's observation about Britain was never put to the test. The Americans, of course, did not rejoin the British Empire and so did not have to look for equal freedom under British rule. But the slaves who were freed in 1865 and their children and their children's children remained in the United States. The convulsions that Jefferson feared have not materialized, but neither side has fully forgiven the other. Blacks have been given equality under the law. But they have never quite been confided in as fellow subjects, have never quite been forgiven for the embarrassment of their ancestors' sufferings.

Those sufferings, like the admittedly much lesser ones that the British dealt the American colonists, were accompanied by a profound contempt and would have been unthinkable without it. Franklin had personally endured British contempt at the hands of officials whom he had tried unsuccessfully to dissuade from the measures that alienated his countrymen. Slaves endured a more withering contempt every day of their lives from masters who considered them barely human, their ideas and customs beneath notice, fit only to be driven like cattle. The resuscitation of slave culture by anthropologists and historians should ultimately gain its exponents the respect that slaveowners could not grant. But that respect requires the sophisticated understanding that only books like Morgan's and Berlin's can supply. Understanding requires a recognition, not easily admitted, that slavery was a negotiated relationship and that both masters and slaves remained human beings throughout the negotiations. It is much easier to view them as tyrants and victims, and to displace contempt by a condescending feeling of guilt that secretly blames the victims. Victims often earn pity and inspire feelings of guilt for what was done to them, but seldom respect.

George Rawick, whose strictures on guilt we have already quoted, reminds us continually that the existence and continuance of slave culture is itself proof that American slavery was a workable and durable human relationship, continued from generation to generation, and to be studied as such regardless of its horrors. Rawick's own understanding of slave culture (and now the singular is important) rested on a unique source: interviews with former slaves conducted in the 1920s and 1930s, mainly by the Federal Writers Project. The slaves interviewed were all in their eighties or older. The culture they remembered from their childhood in the decade or two before the Civil War was an amalgam of earlier cultures, homogenized by two powerful forces: cotton and Christianity. Rice and tobacco had given way to cotton throughout the South in the nineteenth century as plantations spread westward; and slaves had found in evangelical Christianity a religion that could be molded to contain their different beliefs, unify their different cultures, and lend support in and against their adversity, which did not diminish with the switch to cotton.

Rawick published the interviews on which he drew in forty-one volumes.[5] Readers can now find a sample of them in *Remembering Slavery*, which Berlin has selected and edited with two colleagues. They are arranged in five chapters to focus on the former slaves' memories of their masters, their work, their family ties, their culture (music, dance, religion), and their emancipation. Any reader can extract from these rambling recollections a good deal of what is now known about slave culture in its final form. Unfortunately what people who had been free for sixty or seventy years remembered most vividly

about slavery was not the degree of autonomy they were able to negotiate. What stands out in all these interviews in grim monotony is the
unrelenting dominance of masters, maintained by regular whipping
and torture, sometimes by exemplary murder.

What former slaves remembered about their work after so many
years was the lash that set the pace for it: "Dey did'n cah how ole o'
how young yo' wah, yo' nebbah too big t'git de lash." What they
remembered about their family structure was the whippings they had
to watch one another endure: "Many a day my ole mama has stood by
an' watched massa beat her chillin 'till dey bled an' she couldn' open
her mouf. Dey didn' only beat us, but they useta strap my mama to a
bench or box an' beat her wid a wooden paddle while she was naked."
What they remembered about their prayer meetings was the need to
keep them secret from their masters, because if they were caught, the
patrols hired to catch blacks who strayed would "whip all caught in
attendance." Readers in search of a guilt trip will have no trouble finding it here, abetted by the scrupulous attempt to reproduce in print the
pronunciation and dialect of the speakers. The very quaintness of the
language in which we hear of unspeakable tortures, casually related as
they were casually given, serves to aggravate the horror. It is hard to
read this book without anger, shame, pity—or guilt. Such feelings are
even more keenly induced by an audiocassette broadcast accompanying the book, which aired on public radio in 1998, in which a few rare
voice recordings made at the time of the interviews have been
enhanced by modern technology, while others are read aloud skillfully
and movingly by well-known black actors and actresses reproducing
the old dialect.

Only toward the end are we brought to our senses, and to an
awareness of the racist connotations of guilt, by the extraordinary
words of one ex-slave, not recorded in any interview but recalled by
John Henry Faulk, who conducted many of the interviews. He
remembered chatting with an ancient man to whom he had been
explaining his own view that blacks were entitled to more rights than
they currently enjoyed:

And uh, I remember him looking at me, very sadly and kind of sweetly, and condescendingly and saying, "You know, you still got the disease, honey. I know you think you're cured, but you're not cured. You talking now you sitting there talking and I know it's nice and I know you a good man. Talking about giving me this and giving me that right. You talking about giving me something I was born with just like you was born with it. You can't give me the right to be a human being. I was born with that right. Now you can keep me from having that if you've got all the policemen and all the jobs on your side you can deprive me of it, but you can't give it to me, cause I was born with it just like you was."

That quotation redeems the book and carries us back from guilt to simple respect. And if we can read the interviews themselves the way Rawick did, with a consciousness that the people who wielded the lash as well as those who felt it were engaged in a continuing human relationship, we may gain a better perspective on the significance of slave cultures. That slaves were able to build lives of their own may show that slavery was not quite as bad as it theoretically could have been, but the survivors tell us that it was actually as bad as a human relationship can get. As slaveowners pushed that relationship to its limits and beyond, slaves could sustain it only by developing the countercultures in which they accommodated to the horrors and at the same time resisted them. The interviews are a testimony not only of human endurance but of the endurance of humanity under conditions that tested the limits of both.

How difficult it is to see slavery as a negotiated relationship was apparent to viewers of a PBS series, *Africans in America: America's Journey Through Slavery*, which also debuted in 1998. The series, in four ninety-minute episodes, followed the history of slavery in America from its tentative beginnings in seventeenth-century Virginia to its abolition during the Civil War. As the horrors of the institution dominated the later recollections of those freed from it, they overshadow everything else in this depiction of early American history as the history of slavery. The small triumphs of autonomous slave cultures pale here beside the ruthless subjection of slave to master. Patterns of speech and dress, of music and dance, play no role in the long fight for freedom and its ultimate success. The story is not one of what slaves did as slaves but of what was done to them, until the violence of civil war overcame the violence of slavery.

The series faced the same problems as other attempts to bring the past to the screen through visual images that have to be either static or irrelevant. We have shots of plantation mansions, slave quarters, prison bars, portraits, engravings, cartoons, and documents, animated only by the camera's roving lens. These are interspersed among action shots of ships at sea, rivers flowing, trees against the sky, birds flying (usually egrets), bare feet shuffling (a favorite), and a few reenactments in dim light and dim focus, the faces obscure, of people tormented and struggling. What drives the series and holds it together is not sight but sound, a spoken narrative to which the images are no more than background, like the subdued music that accompanies them. It is an eloquent narrative, recited in voice-over, but continually shifting to pertinent and incisive quotations, in different voices, from people of the time: slave traders, freed slaves, planters, sailors, abolitionists, statesmen. The most effective quotations are passages from the autobiographies of a few slaves who made it to freedom and left a record of their experiences. In a couple of episodes they figure as protagonists, their lives lending drama to the record of human misery.

Taken by itself, the narrative is a grim and accurate piece of historical instruction. The grimness is relieved a little by the pictorial accompaniment but more surprisingly by the explanatory commentaries from a large battery of talking heads, who bring more life to the screen than historical artifacts and scenic vistas can. They are mostly historians, including too briefly John Hope Franklin, the dean of black historians. One of the few non-historians is Colin Powell, who appears for a brief discussion of Jefferson and again in a perceptive comment on the way service in the Continental Army (reluctantly allowed by Washington) gave new dimensions to the lives of blacks who enlisted.

All in all it is fair to say that the talking heads save the show. None of them has a good word to say for slavery, and none of them talks about slave culture. But they give an interpretive depth to the series that makes it much more than a recital of horrors. They are particularly good at placing slavery within the larger context of American history. Without indulging in the righteous indignation that the subject invites, they do their best to make the actions of both slaves and slaveholders intelligible as part of national history. It is unfortunate and a little surprising that neither they nor the show's designers thought that the autonomy of slave culture was worth the kind of attention that other historians and anthropologists have given it, for that culture's later transformations are the one positive heritage of slavery. But the commentators, by their obvious respect for their subject, do give direction to the show and save it from being simply an exercise in pity or guilt.

How much they do for it is obvious when one reads the book prepared as a "companion" to the series by Patricia Smith and Charles Johnson. Johnson's contribution is a set of fictional vignettes, not used in the series, that take us imaginatively inside the minds of slaves and slave owners, including Martha Washington. They break into the narrative written by Smith as human interest episodes, but they are completely independent of it. While quite moving in themselves, they do not serve the explanatory function that the commentators did in the series. Instead they magnify the feeling of outrage that the book seems designed to induce. Smith's narrative follows the script of the series closely, employing the same quotations and giving the same facts, often in the same words, but with an interpretive slant that is more polemical than instructive.

It does not take much to turn a straight history of slavery into a polemic. Smith does not distort the facts, but without the independent commentaries of the series the facts become a bill of indictment. In the series Washington appears always as a slaveholder with little else to his credit, but the picture of him is placed in context when his biographer, John Ferling, explains that "his parents owned slaves, his grandparents were slave owners, his older brothers were slave owners. Slaveowning was common in the Northern Neck of Virginia where Washington grew up. It was just an accustomed part of life." Well, it was not really just that, and it only requires a few words from Smith to twist the knife. While she never implies that slavery was not an accustomed part of life for the Washingtons, she leaves us with a damning, if justifiable, view of the first president when she says that he "had decided to live comfortably, and he could not continue to live that way without his slaves."

Jefferson appears as often as Washington in the series, and in an equally unflattering light. The contradiction between his declaration of human equality and his lifelong dependence on slave labor has often been pointed out before, as it is again here. Colin Powell states it plainly: "Thomas Jefferson kept slaves but Thomas Jefferson nevertheless wrote those remarkable words and he understood the inconsistency." Smith, too, stresses the contradiction, but for her the remarkable words do not weigh much in the balance against the facts of slaveholding: Jefferson's "egalitarian veneer barely disguised the spirit of a Negrophobic southern planter whose solution to the country's most pressing problem was avoidance."

That is certainly a defensible judgment. Smith states the facts of American history as a history of slaveholding, and she states them simply and unequivocally. We learn how white Americans created their union at the expense of blacks. They did, in the protections for slavery in the Constitution, without which the South would not have accepted it. We learn how the Missouri Compromise of 1820 preserved the Union "but did nothing to resolve the problem of an immoral system in a society that stressed its morality." Can anyone deny it?

In a history of Africans in America before the Civil War, there is some justice in emphasizing the immorality, injustice, and hypocrisy of the slaveholders who dominated the government as they dominated their slaves. Where masters are unmitigated tyrants, slaves have to be victims. But the relentless simplicity of this theme, when unrelieved by the complexities that emerge from the series commentators, is symptomatic of a crippling condescension that afflicts both the book and the series. They both victimize the slaves. Smith depicts white abolitionists as patronizing their black co-workers. But this history of slavery patronizes the slaves.

The study of slave culture, from Herskovits's discovery of the Negro Past to Berlin's insistence on a negotiated relationship, rests on a recognition that slavery could not have been quite as repressive as the abolitionists believed it to be and as slaveholders may have wished it to be. In ignoring that recognition and depicting slavery only as an evil that is now safely past, both the book, and to a lesser extent the series, fit slaves into a stereotype and devalue the humanity whose expression in slave culture has occupied a generation of historians and anthropologists. The commentators saved the program from the worst effects of this condescension, but both the book and the program produced less understanding than pity, less respect for slaves than guilt. If the study of slave culture can help to erode racism, the story of slavery crushing its victims can only make us congratulate ourselves that it's over. We may feel shame that it was not over sooner, but it *is* over. And since it is over, polemics against it are exercises in sentimentality.

What is not over is racism, and what is also not over is the cultural heritage whose beginnings Morgan and Berlin have delineated so well. It is a heritage that slaves bequeathed not only to their offspring but to the nation which slaves and slaveowners built together. Respect for that heritage can be as powerful an antidote to racism as slave culture was to slavery itself. As Berlin has noted in another context, "We continue to benefit from the language, cuisine, folklore, music and religion that slaves created. It is difficult to imagine how impoverished American culture would be without this legacy."[6] When black and white Americans can both acknowledge the legacy at full value, they may be able to forgive each other for what the founding fathers did to the other founding fathers and mothers they held in bondage.

December 3, 1998

CHAPTER ELEVEN

Plantation Blues

———— ❧ ————

Runaway Slaves: Rebels on the Plantation
John Hope Franklin and Loren Schweninger

Rituals of Blood: Consequences of Slavery in Two American Centuries
Orlando Patterson

JOHN HOPE FRANKLIN and Loren Schweninger announce at the outset of their study of runaway slaves that "even today important aspects of the history of slavery remain shrouded in myth and legend." The myths and legends are not only those that still romanticize the old plantation but also the contrary ones that demonize it. Like other myths they have only a remote resemblance to fact, but historians who seek to dispel them, an enterprise that has engaged some of the best of them in the past fifty years, have found that in the study of slavery myth clings stubbornly to fact. Every exposition of what actually happened on the plantation carries implications, frequently unintended, that echo the myths. And this is particularly the case with attempts to recover the facts of what slavery did to slaves, where a long tail of implication sometimes seems to wag the dog.

Stanley Elkins argued in a seminal work in 1959 that slavery reduced its victims to mindless "sambos," comparable to the brainwashed inmates of concentration camps.[1] This indictment carried the unintended implication that slaves lacked the character or strength of mind to resist the destruction of their self-respect by heartless masters. The implication gathered new significance in a 1965 Department of Labor report by Daniel Patrick Moynihan, which drew on Elkins to argue that "the slave household often developed a fatherless matrifocal (mother-centered) pattern," a pattern which continued into the twentieth century with disastrous consequences.[2]

Moynihan's report, aimed toward a national effort to break that continuity, made its appearance just at the time when many black leaders of the civil rights movement were tending toward a separatism in which they cherished a positive continuity with slave culture and resented any deficiencies that whites might find in blacks, slave or free. In 1974, in a work ostensibly designed to reveal "the record of black achievement under adversity," Robert Fogel and Stanley Engerman used a statistical economic analysis to portray the plantation as an enlightened business enterprise: under masters guided by cost-effectiveness, slaves enjoyed somewhat better conditions of life than free workers, and lived in nuclear families headed by husbands.[3] This went way beyond any refutation of Elkins or Moynihan, and other historians immediately challenged it, not only in its benign statistics but in its seeming "return to a very old-fashioned concept of the acquiescent slave, and to all of its potentially racist implications."[4] A large number of more detailed studies, avoiding any such implications, have explored the slave culture of resistance, and portrayed the building of nuclear families within it as acts of defiance rather than compliance.[5] Orlando Patterson, in *Rituals of Blood*, returns to the view of the Moynihan Report in dismissing such families as not families at all but mere "reproductive units," at the service of their masters.

That serious scholars could arrive at such conflicting conclusions testifies to the inconclusiveness and malleability of the multitude of surviving sources—ledgers, laws, letters, diaries, newspapers, books— all written by the free for the free. There are a few autobiographical narratives by escaped slaves and some recollections by survivors, gathered sixty or seventy years after emancipation by the Federal Writers Project. But for the most part what slaves thought or felt has to be extracted almost entirely from what other people did to them or said about them. That is not an insuperable barrier, for historians commonly have to cull facts from testimony not necessarily designed to disclose them. But the exercise is a nice one when the facts all derive from controversy and can fuel further controversy. Franklin and Schweninger have been able to reduce the inherent bias of their sources by confining themselves to two kinds of documents where "it was in the interests of individuals to state their case as clearly and truthfully as possible": descriptions of runaways in advertisements for their capture and petitions to legislatures and county courts in cases involving runaways. While these sources give us only fleeting glimpses of what life on the run was like for those with the daring or desperation to undertake it, they do make possible the first comprehensive analysis of slave resistance during the seventy years prior to emancipation. The analysis neither romanticizes nor demonizes the plantation and dispels some legends, but it too carries implications that the authors may not have intended.

Violent rebellion was never a possible option for Afro-American slaves because they were outnumbered everywhere in the United States by Euro-Americans (not the case in the successful rebellion in Haiti in 1801). Running away, on the other hand, was not directed toward the goal of overthrowing the slave system. Rather, as becomes apparent in Franklin and Schweninger's study, flight served, perhaps not deliberately or consciously, as a way of limiting and defining the operation of the system. Running away kept slavery within bearable limits both for those who ran and for those they left behind, even though in the short run it usually meant trouble for both. The book's aim is simply to demonstrate with abundant evidence that slaves did not acquiesce quietly in their enslavement. They could be kept at the job of producing a profit for their owners only by the whip or the threat of the whip. And the threat was made thoroughly plausible by the continual realization of it. Slaves who ran were usually caught in the end and suffered for it, knew they would suffer, but were ready to pay in pain for a brief spell of freedom. A few made it to the free states of the North or to Canada. A few remained hidden for years or even a lifetime, in the "maroon" camps of the swamps and forests or in the anonymity of cities like New Orleans or Charleston. But most of them were quickly captured or forced by cold and hunger or some internal compulsion to return. Many of them repeated the process again and again, gaining a reputation as "runners," thereby incidentally lowering their market value and also disrupting production sufficiently to give planters a motive for making life on the plantation more attractive than life on the run.

Because runaways were seldom advertised unless they had been gone as much as a month, the total can never be known. The authors estimate that they may have averaged fifty thousand a year or more. The number advertised from 1790 to 1860 was only about 8,400, but the authors argue that "while runaways constituted a small minority of the slave population, they were of enormous significance in the plantation universe." That significance may have lain, as the authors say, "in their defiance of the system," but it was not the defiance itself that mattered so much as its effect on the planter's profits. Analysis of age and sex, where known, supports such a judgment. Over 80 percent of runaways were male, and of these three out of four were under thirty. In other words, those most likely to run were also those most capable of hard work. But slaves of all ages and both sexes ran away as opportunities presented themselves. Eternal vigilance, to change the metaphor, was the price of slaveowning.

It was a price that slaveholders gladly paid. While Franklin and Schweninger emphasize the universal resistance of slaves to their subjection, the implication that emerges unmistakably if unintentionally from the evidence offered is the failure of that resistance to seriously impair the success of the slave system. Those who went on the run generally struck out alone. Though couples or entire families sometimes made the attempt, there seem to have been no examples of concerted or mass desertions. Running away became a regular and accepted thing for masters to put up with, "a matter of course," contained within dimensions that never challenged the viability of the system itself. Analysis of the different occasions that prompted or enabled slaves to run shows them to have coincided with irregular situations and events in their lives as slaves, such as a change of masters or overseers, sale or the threat of sale, forced separation from wives or husbands, children or parents, quarrels between a master and his wife that disrupted discipline, being hired out on loan to other masters.

Cases of enticement by whites who promised freedom were relatively rare, though continually feared. Runaways seldom headed north toward freedom, because the odds against making it were too great. Most of them stayed in the South, often in the immediate neighborhood, where they were assisted with provisions by fellow slaves and sometimes gathered in gangs until caught. The occasion or opportunity for running might come at any season of the year, but the only season when the recorded numbers dropped was during the autumn harvest. Presumably the decrease was due to closer surveillance at a time when labor was most needed, but again it shows the ability of masters to limit the impact of this kind of resistance. Because owners counted on regularly losing a certain amount of labor from runaways anyhow, they also counted on making up the difference by driving those who remained that much harder while their companions were gone. As Franklin and Schweninger observe, "Since those who went out were usually brought back within the fortnight, they did not represent a serious economic loss nor did the temporary loss of hands mean the work could not be transferred to those who remained behind."

The success of masters in keeping all resistance within bounds is evinced even by their corresponding success in persuading themselves that they were playing the role of benevolent fathers to children who owed them not only labor but gratitude. Prompted perhaps by verbal assaults from the North, they learned to speak of their "peculiar institution" as one of "domestic" slavery and increasingly referred to their slaves as part of their "family." "Again and again," Franklin and Schweninger note, "slaveowners used the same word to describe runaways: ungrateful." Their departure always seemed "without any cause," a betrayal of their paternal keepers.

To dismiss such habitual designations as hypocrisy (which the authors do not do) would be to miss the significance of the fact that running away, however common, could be treated as abnormal, deviant behavior. One New Orleans physician diagnosed it as "drapetomania, or the disease causing Negroes to run away." It was, he insisted, "as much a disease of the mind as any other species of mental alienation." The norm was happy childlike Negroes who loved their masters and deserved punishment if they failed to do what they were told. Whippings that left a man or woman scarred or maimed for life could be considered without regret as applications of the old adage about sparing the rod. It required no more than the usual human capacity for self-deception to sustain this delusion.

Measures to limit running away were not difficult to devise, because freedom and slavery were so closely tied to color in a society where miscegenation was common that the market value of a slave depended in some degree on complexion: any light-colored slave lost value by virtue of the fact that he or she could too easily escape and pass for free. The proportion of mulattoes among runaways was three to four times their proportion in the slave population, because it was easier for them to get away with it. Most runaways of whatever shade returned of their own accord in a short time, because the forces arrayed against them were so many: the slaveowners of a region kept up a network of correspondence in which they alerted one another to escapes; tracking runaways became a profession for a small class of men, who made use of dogs trained for the purpose; patrols rode up and down the roads night and day, requiring every person of color to explain his or her presence away from a plantation.

Free black persons away from home (where a neighboring white could vouch for them) would likely wind up in jail as presumed runaways and perhaps be auctioned off as slaves before their status could be verified. One free son of a white woman and a colored man escaped such a fate while traveling in Virginia only because no one would buy him: he was "too white." Trackers sometimes bought at bargain prices any runaways who had evaded capture long enough to make owners decide to cut their losses rather than bank on their recapture. When and if the tracker succeeded in running down the fugitives, he could sell them for whatever the market would bear. And the continually rising price of slaves made the possible profits worth the risk. On the other hand, the expected return of most runaways kept any rewards offered for their capture at a surprisingly low figure, averaging no more than 5 percent of what a slave would sell for. Franklin and Schweninger have demonstrated conclusively that slaves resisted their subjection by running from it despite the obstacles that normally made their escape shortlived and painful. What they have also demonstrated, whether intentionally or not, is that this form of resistance posed no serious threat to the system. It does not follow that the resistance was futile. The authors do not draw that conclusion, but neither do they give us a direct assessment of what runaways did achieve, apart from requiring slave owners to organize effective measures to thwart them.

The constant pressure of runaways on the system can be seen as one indication of the determining role played by slaves in setting practical limits to a coercion that was only theoretically absolute. For slavery to be cost-effective, as it clearly was, running away had to be made normally less attractive than submission. The costs and the modes of deterring it must not exceed or cancel the rewards. Measures severe enough to make it impossible might have debilitated or demoralized the labor force and defeated the purpose. Slavery, as Ira Berlin has argued, was a negotiated relationship, varying from time to time and from place to place.[6] The threat of running away was one of the few bargaining chips that slaves could always bring to the negotiations; and Franklin and Schweninger record a few instances in which slaves actually "left with the intention of lying out for a few days, or weeks, and then negotiating to gain concessions."

But the larger significance of running away lay in the silent negotiation that defined the system itself. Just as the threat of punishment accompanied by frequent exercise of it was sufficient to prevent most slaves from running most of the time, the threat of running away accompanied by continual examples of it was sufficient to keep the exercise of owners' powers within limits acceptable to the owned. By showing that they could be pushed just so far and not farther, slaves won what amounted to rights that could be violated only by endangering the relationship: the right to grow a small crop of their own, to buy and sell property of their own, and especially the right to have a family of their own.

Although John Hope Franklin is currently presiding over a national "dialogue" on race relations, he avoids making any connections here between runaway slaves and present-day relations between or within ethnic or racial groups. His and Schweninger's findings nevertheless point to the strength of the slave family ties that have figured so largely in recent studies of slave culture: separation from "loved ones" by a sale was one of the common occasions for running away. Orlando Patterson would scarcely challenge such a connection or the possibility of genuine affection in slave unions. But in *Rituals of Blood* he deploys his characteristic superlatives to denounce the resurrection of the idea of the stable slave family in studies that he considers "not just an academic absurdity" but "an intellectual disgrace, the single greatest disservice that the American historical profession has ever done to those who turn to it for guidance about the past and the etiology of present problems." The historical profession may perhaps take comfort in the fact that Patterson also finds the whole history of Christianity before Martin Luther King, Jr., "one of the greatest distortions and misappropriations in the history of the world."

Despite his addiction to hyperbole, Patterson's is a voice that should be taken seriously in any national dialogue on race, a term which he customarily places in quotation marks as something that exists only in mistaken minds. He speaks as a sociologist, historian, and philosopher, not to say prophet. And as a historian his specialty has been the effect of slavery on slaves. He began in 1967, two years after the Moynihan Report, with a sociological analysis of slavery in his native Jamaica. In it he observed that "the nuclear family could hardly exist within the context of slavery. . . . Furthermore, even where such families did develop, the male head could not assert his authority as a husband or as a father. His 'wife' was the property of another."[7] Patterson went on to a study of slavery in every part of the world from the beginning of recorded history to the present. He found that

Jamaica had been no exception: "In all slaveholding societies slave couples could be and were forcibly separated and the consensual 'wives' of slaves were obliged to submit sexually to their masters; slaves had no custodial claims or powers over their children, and children inherited no claims or obligations to their parents."

Patterson admitted that in the American South "stable unions and households were encouraged, sometimes even required, by the master class." But what he calls "natal alienation" was one of the distinguishing marks of slavery in the United States and everywhere else. Slaves, by definition, were "socially dead." They might have informal social relations among themselves but no legal relationship to anyone, living or dead, except their masters. They could have sexual unions but not marriages or families that their master or anyone else was bound to recognize.[8] Patterson has continued to study "the structures and culture of domination in human life" but with more attention to the relations of Euro-Americans and Afro-Americans (terms he insists on in place of "white" and "black") in the United States after the end of slavery. In 1997 he offered one of the most judicious assessments we have yet seen of affirmative action in *The Ordeal of Integration.*[9] This was billed as the first volume of a trilogy. *Rituals of Blood* is the second volume, consisting of three long essays on disparate phenomena in American life, related only by a sometimes tenuous connection to the slave past of Afro-Americans.

The first and longest essay, "Broken Bloodlines," examines the similarities and differences between Euro-American and Afro-American families on the basis largely of opinion polls and statistics collected by government agencies and private foundations. The opinions are detailed and the statistics derived with a precision that sometimes boggles the mind, for example the opinions about whether a single mother can successfully raise a son. We find that the majority of Americans as a whole think she can, but "being married diminishes the odds of concurring by 43 percent," while "those who have never been married are 2.75 times more likely" to concur and "the divorced and separated 63 percent more likely." There are scores of statistics like

this, with tables and graphs to match. They all point in one way or
another to Patterson's main concern, the isolation of Afro-Americans,
which he attributes in large measure to the failure of fatherhood
among them:

> *Afro-Americans are the most unpartnered and isolated group of people in
> America and quite possibly in the world. Unlike any other group of
> Americans, most of them will go through most of their adult lives without
> any deep and sustained attachment to a non-kin companion. Sixty percent
> of Afro-American children are now being brought up without the emo-
> tional or material support of a father. This is so because the great majority
> of Afro-American mothers have been seduced, deceived, betrayed, and
> abandoned by the men to whom they gave their love and trust.*

Patterson's analysis of how this situation came about is nowhere
directed toward excusing "the men who so wantonly impregnate these
mothers, then abandon them and their children." He finds it "hard to
imagine a more execrable form of immorality and irresponsible behavior" and heaps scorn on the "cool-pose culture" that endorses it among
the underclass of Afro-Americans in urban ghettos. But he has no
doubt that the explanation of such behavior lies in an unbroken chain
leading back to the plantation. After studying slavery in the rest of the
world he needed no deep immersion in the slave culture of the
American South to confirm the "natal alienation" of its slaves and particularly of males who had to surrender every right of a husband and
father to their owners. Slave motherhood "had legal status [in the
slaveowner's legal right to the offspring, whoever the father] and was
jealously guarded by the slaveholder"; slave men, on the other hand,
compensated for their emasculation by abusing their partners and
indulging themselves in heedless promiscuity.

The historians whom Patterson denounces for giving a sustaining
role to families in slave culture earn another rebuke for cherishing the
continuation of African customs and kinship relations as a source of
support. Patterson points out that slavery was well established in West

African societies with the usual effect of social death for slaves: "Slaves had children and relatives but no legitimate kin." As a result, enslavement and transportation to a strange land had a traumatically isolating effect on those who suffered it. Deprived of the customary restraints and obligations of fatherhood and bound by no new ones, male slaves adopted a stark Darwinian strategy: "Bringing a child into the world became a virtual obligation of manhood and of ethnic survival that did not entail any consideration of the means whereby one would support it." The modern consequence is that "male descendants of slaves firmly believe that 'birth control is a plot to kill the Negro race.'"

Patterson is evidently not one of the majority of Americans who think that a single mother, at least in the situation of Afro-American women in the ghetto, can successfully bring up a son. The abuse such women and their partners suffered in childhood begets the abuse of their own children, and their children's children, "all leading back to that most heinous form of abusive socialization: the slave plantation, which let it not be forgotten, is less than three generations away. Many of the grandparents who brought up the parents of today's underclass children were themselves brought up by ex-slaves." The social death of slaves has been carried forward, not only in the broken families of the Afro-American underclass but in other kinds of isolation of Afro-Americans from one another and from the rest of the world. They are less willing, in proportion to their numbers, to intermarry with Euro-Americans than the other way around. Their networks of friends and associates generally include fewer kin than is the case with Euro-Americans, and are more "dense," that is, their friends all tend to know each other and do not intersect or overlap with other social networks. The total effect is that Afro-Americans are shut off or shut themselves off from social and economic opportunities of all kinds and also lack the security and support of kinsmen that Euro-American groups enjoy.

Patterson rests his portrayal of Afro-American isolation on the array of statistics he has derived from the U.S. Bureau of the Census, from the National Health and Social Life Survey conducted by University of Chicago sociologists in 1991, from a 1997 survey of gender roles sponsored by Harvard's School of Public Health, *The Washington Post*, and the Kaiser Family Foundation, and finally from the annual General Social Survey of the University of Chicago. He makes full use of earlier studies of gender relations among Afro-Americans and considers a multitude of variables affecting the way the sexes treat each other and the differences in attitudes, opinions, and sexual relations among Euro-Americans as well as Afro-Americans of all ages. He considers the effects of external factors such as economic opportunity and the much greater upward mobility of Afro-American women than of Afro-American men.

But in the end he traces the ultimate source of Afro-American isolation to attitudes induced by slavery and perpetuated from generation to generation, first in the neoslavery of sharecropping and then in the ghetto. Like Moynihan before him, he wants to break that continuity, and he has nothing good to say about the black separatism that serves to perpetuate it. Studies that confer stability on slave families can be seen as offering support to separatism, coming as they did in conjunction with black separatist reactions to Moynihan. That conjunction, it would seem, has dictated Patterson's heated denunciation of them and their authors.

It would be hard to disagree with his strictures on separatism, but his rejection of slave families rests less on historical research than on a projection of the attitudes of current underclass Afro-Americans back onto their slave ancestors, another case of the long tail of implication wagging the dog. Patterson's earlier study of slavery throughout the world developed a definition of the institution that fits it for the role he here assigns it but left no room for the negotiated relationship which subsequent historians have found in the American South. It requires a doctrinaire sort of assurance to dismiss out of hand the evidence for such a relationship, for its variation from place to place and from time to time, and for the existence of nuclear slave families in defiance of the legal imperatives of slavery. If slavery had been as controlling as Patterson's view requires, any book on runaway slaves would have to have been much shorter than the one Franklin and

Schweninger have given us. It does not diminish Patterson's diagnosis of the current situation, or the urgency of addressing it, to question his attribution of its origin.

It may well be that relations between men and women are at the heart of the problem and that therefore, as Patterson concludes, the only solution is ultimately to be found in "a radical recommitment to stable gender, marital, and parental attitudes and behavior" on the part of Afro-American men. But if the unfortunate attitudes and behavior that need replacing have been generated by more proximate causes than slavery, they may be more susceptible to present remedies. In the first volume of his trilogy, *The Ordeal of Integration*, Patterson hailed the success of government action in integrating schools and expanding economic opportunity. Here he suggests some short-term steps government might take to curb child abuse and to enforce laws against deadbeat fathers. But the long-term goal of overcoming the cool-pose culture of the ghetto can scarcely be brought closer by giving it a respectable ancestry it does not have. The slave culture that is delineated in recent studies has never been seen as supporting the Darwinian strategy of heedless procreation that Patterson ascribes to male slaves. If nuclear families played the sustaining role historians have assigned them in slave culture, a respect for them could also help to sustain Afro-American families in the radical recommitment (should it not in his view be a new commitment?) that Patterson calls for. In his dismissal of such families among slaves, in favor of an a priori assertion of their impossibility, he deprives Afro-Americans of a highly usable past. If that past never existed, it should not be invented, but if it did exist, and the best evidence says that it did, it is worth cherishing.

Rituals of Blood might well have concluded with this first essay. One might say better have concluded there. The other two essays have little relation to its message. They are tours de force, in which Patterson's creative imagination discovers cosmic meanings in two mass phenomena of post-slavery Euro-American culture. "Feast of Blood" treats lynchings as rituals of human sacrifice, dictated by the cannibalistic imperatives of a Christianity that went wrong with Saint

Paul and has not recovered. In counterpoint, "American Dionysus" treats the surprising popular idolization of black sports heroes like Michael Jordan as Dionysian symbolism, crossing and at the same time dissolving boundaries of color and sex. In it we learn that Dennis Rodman, formerly of the Chicago Bulls, is "possibly the most authentic epiphany of Dionysus since the fall of ancient culture." Patterson has a lot of fun with this fantasy, and many readers will too. This reader didn't quite get it. The first essay is not much fun, and neither is its subject, but it deserves the attention that the other two should not be allowed to obscure.

June 10, 1999

CHAPTER TWELVE

The Price of Honor

≆

The Shaping of Southern Culture: Honor, Grace, and War, 1760s–1880s
Bertram Wyatt-Brown

Southern Honor: Ethics and Behavior in the Old South
Bertram Wyatt-Brown

Honor and Slavery
Kenneth S. Greenberg

F EW WORDS in any language carry such a load of meaning as "honor." It is an old word, unchanged even in its spelling from classical Latin to modern English. Spoken or written it does not seem to require much explanation; most people think they know what it means. But why have Latin scholars suggested that it derives from *onus*, meaning "burden," a concept not usually associated with it? Why do dictionaries need so much space for it? The *Oxford English Dictionary* in 1901 listed eight meanings, *Webster's* in 1996 fifteen. The *Encyclopedia of Social Sciences* in 1931 devoted a little more than three columns to it, the *International Encyclopedia of Social Sciences* in 1966 gave it fifteen. And in the past twenty or thirty years the number of books exploring its application to different things at different times and places and in different situations has grown exponentially.

Those examined here on the American South have to be seen as part of a larger development in the study of social relations that has placed honor in a central position. It seems to have begun quietly in 1950 with a little book by Marcel Mauss called, as translated from the French, *The Gift: The Form and Reason for Exchange in Archaic Societies.*[1]

In brief, the book argued that there has never been a free lunch. In archaic or premodern societies what appeared to be free gifts were never quite that. Every gift, though it might have seemed to be offered freely, indeed had to seem so, always had strings attached, always required reciprocation. The honor of both parties depended on the exchange. Failure to answer one gift or favor with an equal or better one was a badge of dishonor. In some cases, Mauss says, "the punishment for failure to reciprocate is slavery for debt."

Gifts were, in fact, the principal mode of exchange in societies that had not, or had not yet, developed market economies. In these societies the sacredness of honor served the purpose that the legal obligation of contracts serves in modern ones. In response to Mauss, anthropologists began to see the force of honor not merely in the economies but in practically all the social transactions of undeveloped societies from Melanesia to Alaska. More particularly, led especially by Julian Pitt-Rivers, they began to examine the role of honor in social enclaves close to home, especially around the Mediterranean, in Sicily, Spain, Morocco, Greece.[2] As they did so, the complexities of the concept grew. Honor was the opposite of shame but could also accrue to the shameless. It was at once the reward of virtue and of violence, of hospitality and hostility, of acquiring property and of giving it away. It was one thing in an upper class and another in their dependents, one thing in men and another in women, one thing in Greece and another in Cyprus.

But it retained a solid core. Wherever it could be found, in whatever situation, it defined and limited behavior, for it marked the intersection of a person's view of himself and the estimation of his peers. As Pitt-Rivers put it in 1966, "Honour is the value of a person in his own eyes, but also in the eyes of his society. . . . Honour, therefore, provides a nexus between the ideals of a society and their reproduction in the individual through his aspiration to personify them."[3] That does not mark much of a change from the definition that the political philosopher T. V. Smith offered in 1932 before the proliferation of studies began: "Honor is an open acknowledgment of external demand but an acknowledgment which through pride has become enthroned in the very citadel of the self."[4]

HONOR HAS operated in all its permutations as a form of social control. In archaic societies it may be the only form, while in modern ones it has to do its work alongside written codes of law, laid down by governments that have all the means of compulsion at their command. Honor too has its codes, but they are not, like laws, the product of an assembly's deliberations or a sovereign's dictate. They are unwritten and exist only in the public opinion of the societies or social groups where they are recognized. They cannot ordinarily be enforced by the courts that enforce laws and may even prescribe behavior contrary to law. Honor violated requires direct personal action, sometimes violent, for its recovery, as in a duel. But in the ordinary course of things honor guides social behavior outside the reach of law, ordering daily life by the force of reputation, a force that few resist.

European historians readily took up the challenge that anthropologists presented them with to search out the development, decline, and persistence of honor in the transformation of gift economies of the past into the market economies and legal systems of the present. American historians were slower to rise to the task. Bertram Wyatt-Brown seems to have been the first. Impressed by Pitt-Rivers's redaction of Mauss, he perceived that the American South before the Civil War could be seen as a distinct enclave like those that anthropologists had discovered in Mediterranean countries. In the South honor had retained its force outside the law (and sometimes even in the law's own courts) much longer than in the North. In *Southern Honor: Ethics and Behavior in the Old South* (1982), he surveyed the manifestations of honor among white southerners in a wide range of social customs, showing how they reflected ancient Celtic and Germanic practices. By contrast, in contemporary New England evangelical religion and contract law eroded the authority of the older code. For example, he found that white southerners honored aggressive male behavior and therefore encouraged it in their young sons to the point where "boyish battles were the effective Southern substitute for the religious revival experience" (which he posits, I think gratuitously, as a rite of passage in New England). Southerners attached honor to large landholdings and preserved them in arranged marriages, frequently between cousins, more often than northerners did. Family ties were stronger, women more subordinate, gambling, hunting, dueling, and debt more common and more honorable than in the North.

In *Southern Honor*, Wyatt-Brown deliberately omitted consideration of the role of honor in two aspects of southern life, each of which might have required a book in itself: politics and slavery. He gave some consideration to the opportunities for miscegenation that slavery provided and the extent to which it violated honor (not much for white males, provided sexual relations were with one's own female slaves and not someone else's). But slaves, being non-persons, could not ordinarily be admitted to have anything to do with the honor of whites except as possessions, like land. Wyatt-Brown was familiar with Jefferson's famous diatribe against the influence of slavery on the character of southern children who were "nursed, educated, and daily exercised in tyranny." But he dismissed that influence as of less consequence than the general parental encouragement of male aggressiveness. "White Southerners," he acknowledged, "seldom forgot the presence of blacks; nevertheless, what mattered most to them was the interchanges of whites among themselves."

Such interchanges, heavily charged with issues of honor, lay at the heart of southern politics, in which slavery and honor joined in a marriage that could be broken only in war. Wyatt-Brown allowed that if southerners "had been able to separate it [honor] from slavery, there would have been no Civil War." But he did not dwell on the complexities of the connection. Nor did he attempt to follow the role of honor in the politics leading to the war that separated the two. He envisaged his next volume, already in preparation, as a discussion of "honor, race, and slavery."

The Shaping of Southern Culture: Honor, Grace, and War, 1760s–1880s cannot be that volume. It is directed neither to the politics of slavery nor to any further consideration of the way slavery or race affected the day-to-day relations described in *Southern Honor*. This book is a collection of discursive essays, most of them previously published as articles in professional journals. They offer a number of new perspectives on honor, but they are only tenuously connected with one another: one on slave life and the limited validity of Stanley Elkins's comparison of it to life in Nazi concentration camps,[5] one on honor as a factor in the American Revolution; one on Andrew Jackson as an exemplification of southern honor; four on the growth of churches and evangelical religion in the nineteenth-century South and the challenge they posed to the existing code of honor among whites; and five on the coming of the Civil War and its aftermath. The most original essay in the book is the one on the American Revolution. In recent years study of what the revolutionaries wanted has made much of their devotion to republican virtue in the face of British monarchical corruption; but little attention has been given to the "sacred Honor" that they so resoundingly committed to their cause in Jefferson's Declaration. Wyatt-Brown emphasizes the violation of honor that Americans detected in the parliamentary measures directed against them in the 1760s and 1770s.

Particularly striking is his explanation of their view that submission to parliamentary taxation would be dishonorable. Americans asserted again and again in formal resolutions that taxes were supposed to be considered as "free gifts," and as such could be offered only by the elected representatives of those who possessed the property thus given. In the light of the new understanding of gifts, the assertions take on added meaning, for in the code of honor derived from gift exchange, "taxation and honor have always been incompatible. Coerced payment signifies abject disgrace." It signifies that the people who unwillingly make the payment are inferior to those who collect it. It was not that the Americans received nothing in exchange for their taxes: they received the protection of the British army and navy. But the exchange could not be honorable unless both sides gave voluntarily. In depriving them of the sole right to tax themselves, the right to offer whatever they gave in taxes as a free gift to their king, Parliament deprived them of honor.

What can one say of the other essays? The four on religion, grouped under the heading "Grace: Southern Religion in Transition," pursue disparate aspects of a subject that several historians have treated more systematically and in greater detail. The five concluding essays have more coherence. They recount the resort to secession as the ultimate answer of southern whites to northern insults and then describe the despair and depression, psychological as much as economic, that followed defeat. Despite Northern soldiers' willingness to minimize the outward symbols of dishonor in surrender, despite the laments that "all is lost save honor," honor was in fact lost. It could only be redeemed, as was so often the case, by violence. It was not coincidental that the state governments that ended Reconstruction and prepared the way for the degradation of former slaves came to be called "Redeemer" governments.

Southern whites recovered a degree of honor by putting blacks in something like their former place, not only by law but also by the violence that honor demanded outside the law, in the Ku Klux Klan and in lynchings conducted as grisly ceremonies. In these concluding essays Wyatt-Brown makes good use of letters and diaries to show what it meant in human terms to lose. But this is not a new story. Nor is it quite what we had hoped for from the historian whose work has been the starting point for all subsequent treatments of "Southern honor." Slavery remains ominously in the background, as it did in the first book. That was a pathbreaking work of cultural history, defining a field. And it was a tour de force to portray social relations among southern whites in detail while looking away, as they themselves may have wished to do, from the people under their feet. But Wyatt-Brown knew that slavery lay at the center of southern history and that southern honor could not really be separated from it. He was and is better qualified to examine the connection than anyone else. He has chosen not to do it and instead has given us miscellaneous essays on southern history that any number of historians could have written.

It remains, then, a task for others to fathom the way southern honor was shaped by its attachment to slavery and then by slavery's destruction. Kenneth S. Greenberg, in *Honor and Slavery*, began the task by returning to Mauss's seminal exposition of gift exchanges. "Southern men of honor loved to give gifts," Greenberg tells us, and "gift exchanges flourished because they were so intimately connected to the values and behaviors associated with the language of honor and slavery." Southern slaveowners continually demonstrated their own honorable status and the corresponding dishonor of their slaves by treating as gifts everything they provided simply to keep slaves alive and productive. Slaves could not reciprocate even with their labor, because the master already owned both them and their labor, which in any case they did not offer voluntarily.

Since gifts carried the association of mastery over slaves, "every gift given to a Southern man of honor *was* a potential insult." It had to be given with care to imply, though not to state, the expectation of reciprocity that gifts between equals required. Greenberg extends the meaning of gifts to the point where virtually all transactions between men of honor in the South could be seen as part of "a *system* of gift exchange" that defined communities and extended families. Southern hospitality was part of the system. It did not apply to strangers, who might be refused or charged for an overnight stay. Only kinfolk and other known persons of honor could expect a welcome for visits of weeks at a time or longer, which they must be ready to return whenever called upon to do so. Borrowing and lending followed the same rules. Even duels were "an extreme form of gift exchange": trading pistol shots was a way "to reaffirm the equality [and honor] of the principals after it had been disrupted by an insult."

The principles of gift exchange applied to the gift of freedom when benevolent masters bestowed it on a slave. There came to be substantial numbers of such beneficiaries in the South, but they remained in the position of disgrace occupied by all recipients of an unreciprocated gift. Orlando Patterson in his comparative study of slave societies throughout the world (published in the same year as

Wyatt-Brown's *Southern Honor*) found the same prescriptions to prevail in some way in virtually all of them.[6] Gift exchange affected not only the relationship of masters and slaves but also the manumissions by which masters might give slaves freedom. In slave societies, ancient and modern, the emancipated generally retained in freedom a subservient client relationship to their former masters. In the American South before the Civil War, however, manumitted slaves enjoyed no such relationship. The gift conferred a dishonor, aggravated by racist fears, that consigned them to a lower status than their counterparts in other slave societies. They became what Ira Berlin has designated as "slaves without masters" in his book of that title.[7] Greenberg explains: "Because one of the distinguishing characteristics of a master was the ability to give gifts, and one of the distinguishing characteristics of a slave was the inability to give gifts, an emancipation that assumed the form of a gift paradoxically reconfirmed the master-slave relationship." Consequently the "images of Abraham Lincoln and Northern soldiers as great emancipators—as bringers of the gift of freedom to the downtrodden—actually worked both to liberate and to degrade newly freed slaves."

Greenberg does not expand this insight, and it is not easy to assess the extent to which the degradation of southern blacks in the century following emancipation can be attributed to the surviving prescriptions of gift exchange. Substantial numbers of northerners, especially among former abolitionists, would have reversed the application of those prescriptions: the belated gift of freedom was scarcely an adequate return for its long denial. And many northerners recognized also that blacks had played too significant a part in the war to consider them as mere recipients of a free gift. Moreover, racism or racial prejudice may have been sufficient in itself to account for what happened. Prejudice had already assigned free blacks an inferior position, in both North and South, into which the dominant whites on both sides could comfortably fit the large new numbers after emancipation. But the common, if unspoken, identification of emancipation as an unreciprocated gift may have served to reinforce that placement.

•   •   •

IT WOULD BE a mistake to underestimate the surviving prescriptions of gift exchange as a force in human relations even today, but they can operate in unexpected ways. Gift exchange can become a contest that borders on the violence so often associated with honor. A deliberately paltry gift can be used to dishonor the receiver, perhaps resulting in the return of an even more demeaning gift and leading eventually to blows (as Shakespeare portrayed in the French dauphin's gift of tennis balls to Henry V, avenged at Agincourt). Among the Kwakiutl Indians of British Columbia the contest took the opposite form of progressively extravagant exchanges that could wind up by reducing to abject poverty the persons who won the greatest honor.

The maintenance of honor has been the driving force of gift exchange and can still affect exchanges dictated by law, where it may not seem to be involved at all. Affirmative action has been seen in its application to black Americans as a recompense to the descendants of slaves for the forced labor of their ancestors. Conversely it has been seen, like emancipation, as a free gift that both rewards and degrades the recipients. Mauss himself suggested that modern social security systems should be viewed as a form of gift exchange in compensating labor that the economic marketplace did not adequately reward. Other anthropologists have rejected such an interpretation because the compensation is enjoined by law rather than honor. That objection should not apply to a modern form of gift that would seem to be fully free: the anonymous donation of blood, destined for utter strangers, through a blood bank. There is certainly a degree of honor attached to such a seemingly selfless act. But an extensive study of blood donation and of participation in medical experiments where there is no expectation of personal benefit has found that "There is in all these transactions an assumption of some form of gift-reciprocity; that those who give as members of a society to strangers will themselves (or their families) eventually benefit as members of that society."[8]

If we consider emancipation as a gift, there is a curious parallel. It too was a gift to strangers with the expectation that the donors or their

families would eventually benefit as members of the society that prescribed the gift. The expectation has been fulfilled in the immeasur-
able political and cultural benefits that slaves and their descendants
have brought to the society that embraced them. If affirmative action
is a gift, it too is made with an expectation of benefit to society, and
that expectation too has been fulfilled in the discovery of talents that
would otherwise have been left undeveloped and unhonored. Honor
flows in many directions, sometimes in opposing streams, in the world
of the free market. But it can still be discerned, however obscured by
the cash nexus, moving back and forth along the pathways that Marcel
Mauss marked out fifty years ago.

May 31, 2001

Part Three

REVOLUTIONARIES

STUDIES OF the Revolution have proliferated in the past half century, and, as befits a revolution, they frequently disagree. As inhabitants of the United States and thus beneficiaries of the Revolution, most Americans have to start with the assumption that it was a good thing. But good for whom? Good for the people who ran it, but did it benefit common people? When did it start? When did it end? Is the Constitution of 1787 the embodiment of the Revolution or a reaction against it? The founding fathers, like the Revolution itself, have to be looked on with approval. But do they deserve it?

Fortunately the answers to these questions, disputed in so many books, have been accompanied by the greatest editorial enterprises in American history, the collecting, editing, and publication of the debates over the Constitution, together with the complete papers of the founding fathers. My own reaction to some of these collections in essay #19, entitled "The Great Political Fiction," resulted some years later in a book, *Inventing the People* (1978). My view of two founding fathers gave the title to one of the essays and to this book.

CHAPTER THIRTEEN

How the French Lost America

———— ∞∞∞ ————

*The Crucible of War: The Seven Years' War and the
Fate of Empire in British North America, 1754–1766*
Fred Anderson

*The most important event to occur in eighteenth-century North America, the
Seven Years' War (or as the colonists called it, the French and Indian War)
figures in most Americans' consciousness of the past as a kind of hazy backdrop
to the Revolution.*

Thus Fred Anderson begins his account of the war that
began (two years early) in America when young George
Washington rashly opened fire on a detachment of French troops in
western Pennsylvania in 1754 and that ended with the elimination of
French power on the continent in 1763. But for the war, Anderson
argues, the American Revolution would not have occurred when it did,
if at all, or "for that matter, the Wars of Napoléon, Latin America's
first independence movements, the transcontinental juggernaut that
Americans call 'westward expansion,' and the hegemony of English-
derived institutions and the English language north of the Rio
Grande. . . . Why, then," he asks, "have Americans seen the Seven
Years' War as little more than a footnote?"

He blames the neglect on the mistaken assumption, prevailing
even among professional historians, that it was the Revolution, rather
than the preceding war, which "determined both the shape of our
national institutions and all the significant outcomes of our national
development before the Civil War." His book is an effort to correct

this misconception by narrating the events of the war and their effect on the participants. It is a large book, he says, because the story it tells "is, in fact, epic in scope and consequence." And it was indeed the first truly global war in history, fought not only in North America and Europe but also, by land and sea, in the Caribbean, India, Africa, and the Pacific.

Anderson is not the first historian to treat the Seven Years' War in epic terms. In 1884 Francis Parkman published two volumes, entitled *Montcalm and Wolfe*, as the culmination of his monumental study of the French in America. Parkman begins with a complaint similar to Anderson's: "It is the nature of great events to obscure the great events that came before them. The Seven Years' War in Europe is seen but dimly through revolutionary convulsions and Napoleonic tempests; and the same contest in America is half lost to sight behind the storm-cloud of the War of Independence." And he points out, in the characteristic idiom of the nineteenth century, that if the war had not evicted France from its American possessions, "then a barrier would have been set to the spread of the English-speaking races; there would have been no Revolutionary War; and for a long time, at least, no independence."[1]

Similarly, in 1946, Lawrence Gipson, in the first of three volumes on what he called *The Great War for the Empire* (in a fourteen-volume series on *The British Empire Before the American Revolution*), complains that "American national tradition treats this war as a mere interlude in the resistless westward march of the American pioneers." In contrast to the traditional view, he says, "stands the simple fact that the war was destined to have the most momentous consequences to the American people of any war in which they have been engaged down to our own day. . . . For it was to determine for centuries to come, if not for all time, what civilization—what governmental institutions, what social and economic patterns—would be paramount in North America."[2]

Despite these extravagant pronouncements, none of the three authors tries to establish lines of continuity between the Seven Years' War and what followed in succeeding centuries. Parkman carries his account in two more volumes through 1764, Gipson in five more through 1776, and Anderson in his single volume through 1766. They all agree that the war was a contest in which the future existence of the United States and much else hung in the balance. But what concerns them all, at least in these volumes, is neither the causes nor the immense consequences but the contest itself. We are left to ask, then, what Anderson can tell us about it that Parkman (over a century ago) and Gipson (half a century ago) missed and also what he leaves out that they thought worth telling.

The answer lies as much in style as in content. Parkman had his eye on the drama of the conflict and made the American wilderness, which he knew at first hand, into a backdrop for theatrical encounters. Gipson and Anderson have neither the talent nor the taste for theatrics. Parkman made great reading in his time and still does, but he has to be read as a period piece. His introduction of the exploits of the American rangers under the celebrated frontiersman Robert Rogers will suggest what Anderson could not have written and could not have got published if he had:

> Summer and winter, day and night, were alike to them. Embarked in whaleboats or birch canoes, they glided under the silent moon or in the languid glare of a breathless August day, when islands floated in dreamy haze, and the hot air was thick with odors of the pine; or in the bright October, when the jay screamed from the woods, squirrels gathered their winter hoard, and congregated blackbirds chattered farewell to their summer haunts; when gay mountains basked in light, maples dropped leaves of rustling gold, sumachs glowed like rubies under the dark green of the unchanging spruce, and mossed rocks with all their painted plumage lay double in the watery mirror: that festal evening of the year, when jocund Nature disrobes herself, to wake again refreshed in the joy of her undying spring. Or, in the tomb-like silence of the winter forest, with breath frozen on his beard, the ranger strode on snow-shoes over the spotless drifts; and, like Dürer's knight, a ghastly death stalked ever at his side. There were those among them for whom this stern life had a fascination that made all other existence tame.[3]

Gipson allows that the rangers played a significant role in North American warfare but has little to say about it. Anderson gives them short shrift as relatively unskilled substitutes for the Indian allies that the English usually had to do without. Rogers himself, Anderson says, "tried indefatigably to perfect the rangers' skills in woodlands warfare, yet never entirely succeeded in doing so. . . . What Rogers lacked as an irregular, however, he made up as a self-publicist. His *Journals*, published in London in 1765, secured his reputation as the very model of the frontier guerrilla leader."

Another index of the difference between Anderson and his predecessors lies in the treatment of the Acadians, the five thousand or more French settlers who were wrenched from their homeland in Canada and scattered through the American colonies in 1755, winding up in greatest numbers in Louisiana as the well-known Cajuns of today. Longfellow's *Evangeline* (1847) had given the exiles the status of martyrs to British cruelty. Parkman, having cast the French as the villains of his story, has to admit that deportation was "too harsh and indiscriminate to be wholly justified." But he devotes two chapters to "explain and palliate" the uprooting in vivid descriptions of the "entire heartlessness" of the French government's treatment of the Acadians in the years before the war.[4] Gipson goes further in three chapters, concluding that "great as was the blow that fell upon the inhabitants of old Acadia, their dispersion constituted, it should be emphasized, an even greater blow to the imperial ambitions of France in the New World."[5] By contrast, Anderson gives the whole episode only a little more than a page, in which he invokes the chilling resemblance to "ethnic cleansing," a resemblance intensified by his suggestion that the "real intention was less to . . . neutralize any Acadian military threat than to make the farms of the Acadians available to recolonization by New Englanders and other Protestant immigrants."

Parkman and Gipson both felt the need to apologize for the treatment of the Acadians because for the one it sullied the triumph of the "English-speaking races" while for the other it raised questions about the enlightenment of British imperial policy, which was the theme of

Gipson's whole series. Anderson takes no sides. But Gipson's imperial perspective, which made the American Revolution a little difficult to explain—if the empire was so benevolent, why did the colonies reject it?—gains new life in Anderson's insistence on the colonists' consciousness of themselves as British, without any vision of future glory in independence. Anderson relies on Gipson's reconstruction of events, but without adopting his reverential attitude toward the British. Anderson writes in the context of the cultural relativism that became the academic creed of the late twentieth century. What he brings to the story that neither Parkman nor Gipson could have or would have is a recognition of the multicultural interaction that shaped the course of the war.

Where Parkman and Gipson saw only an obvious jealousy between colonial troops and regulars on both sides, as well as difficulty on both sides in securing and controlling Indian allies, Anderson sees an interplay of five different cultures: French, French colonial, English, English colonial, and Indian. The Indians, strictly speaking, did not constitute a single culture, and the aggressiveness of the Iroquois Confederacy toward other tribes had a profound effect on the efforts of both English and French to win native allies. Success and failure in Indian diplomacy depended on recognition of Indian cultural norms, which among all tribes required a great many formal speeches of undying love and friendship, a great many presents of English or French manufactured goods, as well as a knowledge of existing intertribal relations. Anderson brings together in a brilliant synthesis what a host of recent studies of Indian cultures have now disclosed. In the half century preceding the war the Iroquois Confederacy in upstate New York had reduced adjoining tribes like the Delaware, Shawnee, and Mingos to clients and through them extended Iroquois influence, if not dominance, as far south as the Ohio Valley. The French, assisted by Jesuit missionaries, had countered by cementing an alliance with various Algonquian tribes to the north and west in which the French successfully assumed the benevolent role of "father" to them all. When the French and English began to contend for the interior of the continent, the Iroquois maintained a diminishing power by a policy of armed neutrality, playing one side against the other, offering protection or assistance in warfare in return for gifts.

Because of their skills in woodcraft, Indian assistance was extraordinarily valuable in wilderness warfare. But Indians at war followed cultural conventions that eighteenth-century Europeans could not, at least openly, condone. Indians gave no quarter and did not expect any. On their own they usually struck only in small parties; but when they were enticed into the large-scale actions of British and French military operations, they still carried the expectation that victory meant the right to do what they wished with prisoners of whatever age or sex. What they wished was to torture and kill some of them, maybe eat a few, and to adopt some of the rest into their own depleted ranks, procedures that continued to horrify and mystify Europeans. To regular British and French officers alike, Indians were dubious, if necessary, allies, not only because of their indiscriminate butchery, but also because they were too hard to control in organized sieges and battles.

Troops recruited from the two countries' respective colonists seemed little better to the noble lords sent to command them. They were all unreliable and untrained in the maneuvers that centuries of European warfare had standardized. Anderson explains convincingly the problem that the colonials presented to the British. The regular troops of the British army were drawn from men who lived on the margins of British society, where desperation and hunger were common. Without many alternatives they accepted a relatively permanent status in the army under upper-class officers whose commands they dared not question. The colonies had few such men. Colonial troops had to be drawn from householders, who were willing to offer their services when dangers threatened their families or homesteads, but only for the duration of the danger and only on a contractual basis. Military service for them was more a temporary change of occupation than of status, and certainly not a way of life. They were horrified by the despotism of officers who could deal out lashes by the hundred for any kind of disobedience to their arbitrary commands.[6]

Canadians recruited for French forces were more accustomed to absolute authority in civil as well as military government. But since the French Canadian population was small, French officers had to rely much more heavily than the English on Indians to do their scouting and fighting. And the successful use of Indians required treating them as allies rather than subjects. The future of the war was foretold in the aftermath of the French capture of Fort William Henry on Lake George by the Marquis de Montcalm in 1757. General Daniel Webb, the ineffectual English officer at nearby Fort Edward, with plenty of troops under his command, delayed reinforcing William Henry while sending out frantic messages for help from New England militias. Montcalm, supported by a force that included nearly two thousand northern Indians, laid siege to the fort and in less than a week had his big guns trained on it at point-blank range. He accepted the capitulation of the outnumbered and outgunned English under terms that guaranteed safe passage to British lines of the garrison, which included substantial numbers of sick and wounded soldiers as well as women and children and civilian laborers. Unfortunately, he had failed to consult his Indian allies, whom he regarded as troops subject to his orders. The Indians felt betrayed by his denial of their hard-earned human perquisites. Anderson comments:

> The only rewards that the Indians—whether Christian or heathen—had expected were plunder, trophies to prove their prowess in battle, and captives to adopt or sacrifice as replacements for dead warriors or perhaps hold for ransom. When it became clear that the man whom they had called "Father" intended to do what no real father would and deprive them of the reward they had earned, most of the warriors decided merely to take what they had come for, and then to leave.

The immediate result was "the massacre of Fort William Henry," familiar to all readers of James Fenimore Cooper's *The Last of the Mohicans*. Despite all efforts to restrain them, Montcalm's Indians killed close to two hundred of the garrison, troops and civilians alike, and carried off more than three hundred captives, at least one of whom was ritually boiled and eaten just outside Montreal. The general and his regulars were aghast, and they did their best to prevent the Indians from taking any more prisoners than they did. But the breach of Montcalm's terms of surrender meant that the British and British colonials would never again trust his word and "would be disinclined to behave generously toward any French garrison in the future." At the same time, Montcalm's interference with the Indians' enjoyment of their spoils meant that he lost their trust as well: "Never again would Indian allies flock to the French colors as they had in 1757."

Yet another lesson of the episode, not appreciated at the time, was the success of General Webb's hysterical calls to the New England militias. They arrived too late to induce the timid general to reinforce Fort William Henry. But within three days of the surrender, more than four thousand colonial troops arrived at Fort Edward, with more on the way. The northern colonies, Anderson says, "had demonstrated a capacity to respond to a military emergency without parallel in the English-speaking world." It is not recorded that British generals in America recognized that capacity until it overwhelmed them eighteen years later. The men who responded to General Webb's call were irregulars, who quickly returned to their homes. British generals needed troops who would stay in the field, and they retained a low opinion of the colonials who had hitherto joined their ranks only in small numbers.

In the years that followed, as William Pitt, late in 1756, took over the conduct of government in England, he was able to reverse the fortunes of war in America by a policy that included what Anderson describes as treating the colonies like allies. As Anderson explains, Pitt saw North America as the crucial place to destroy French power. He funneled money to Frederick the Great of Prussia to hold the line in Europe, sent small forces to seize lightly defended French outposts in Africa and India, and directed the main body of British troops and ships to America. At the same time he persuaded the colonists to raise unprecedented numbers of supporting troops. He did it by promising the colonial assemblies to reimburse the expense and by giving colonial officers what they had never before enjoyed, a superiority to any British regulars below them in rank. Within a month, the various assemblies made provision for 23,000 men under arms, in addition to thousands more in auxiliary civilian roles, all animated by pride in an empire that recognized them as equals.

The Iroquois now saw in alliance with the British the only way to recover the ascendancy they had been steadily losing over the tribes of the Ohio Valley. Thus a concatenation of diverse cultural forces gave the British a military superiority that determined the outcome of the war and left them in seeming control over the whole of North America east of the Mississippi. That it was only a seeming control became apparent with the coming of peace when Britain ceased to treat either the Indians or the colonists as allies and began treating them in earnest as subjects. The Indians responded with armed resistance that the British regulars narrowly succeeded in putting down by 1764. The colonies responded with armed resistance that the British regulars proved unable to put down.

In detailing the history of the Seven Years' War, Anderson has taken pains never to look over his shoulder at the coming American Revolution. Throughout he emphasizes the contingencies that determined the outcome of every battle and the final victory. Only in closing does he return briefly to whatever consequences may be attributed to the outcome. The consequences may have been as far-reaching as he and Gipson and Parkman aver, but it is not easy to assess them. In speculating about them, Anderson takes as a starting point the fragility of imperial control under which the British Empire in America "had grown into an economically robust, if institutionally anemic, state system sustained by the cooperation and loyalty of the colonial elites, the members of which exercised local control." He reflects on what might have occurred if the British had continued after the war to rely on cooperation, loyalty, and local control, instead of insisting on sovereignty. The result, he concludes, might have been the same dominance of English language and institutions across North America, north of the Rio Grande, perhaps with a bloodless assertion of independence by the relentlessly growing Americans. But independence in fact followed almost at once, after a decade in which the British acted on the illusion of a supremacy that the colonists denied. During that decade they developed "the concepts of equality, rights, and freedom" that became the guiding principles of the new American republic. If the war had momentous consequences, they were not what the people who fought it had expected.

There can be no doubt that the Seven Years' War was, as Parkman says, a great event. It involved so many people in both Europe and America and changed the relations among them so radically that it has to be more than a footnote in American history. But as with many great events in history, it is easier to guess at how different the future would have been without it than to connect it directly with what happened next. The American Revolution happened next, but like the war that Anderson describes, its progression was the product of so many contingencies, so many decisions that might have been made differently, that it is difficult to establish any direct causal connection between it and the war that preceded it. The war drove the French from America, but fifteen years later the new United States allied with them, invited them back, and but for the dissent of an older and wiser Washington might have restored them to power in Canada, undoing the principal achievement of the Seven Years' War.

All the great events attributed to the Seven Years' War might conceivably have happened without it, and none of them need have happened simply because of it. The greatness of an event is sufficient reason for trying to understand it, and what makes us consider it great also makes understanding it a challenge. Anderson has met the challenge with a new understanding of the war that enables us to experience its complexity as never before and to see our colonial predecessors as they saw themselves. If the war remains a backdrop to the Revolution, it will no longer be hazy to any reader of these pages.

May 11, 2000

CHAPTER FOURTEEN

A Loyal Un-American

———∞∞∞———

The Ordeal of Thomas Hutchinson
Bernard Bailyn

A S THE BICENTENNIAL of the American Revolution approached, historians were in no mood to celebrate. On the left, they were busy seeking out the role of the inarticulate masses who were somehow forgotten or betrayed by the gentlemen who ran the show. On the right, historians who survived the activities of would-be campus revolutionaries in the 1960s had difficulty seeing the merits of the Boston Tea Party. And the hard-core liberals who made up most of the academic establishment, if they honored the wisdom of the founding fathers, wished to dissociate them as far as possible from the morally bankrupt government that claimed its descent from them.

On both right and left and even in much of the middle there was a greater sympathy with the losers in the American game, whether of the 1970s or the 1770s. Studies of the loyalists had multiplied in recent years, and one of the few serious scholarly projects generated by the bicentennial was a large-scale effort to collect and publish the papers of loyalists. Here we are given a sympathetic and penetrating study of the most important, and perhaps the most hated, loyalist of all, Governor Thomas Hutchinson of Massachusetts. And it is presented by a historian who had already written with similar penetration and sympathy on the ideas that moved the other side. Indeed it grew out of and in a sense completes the author's previous work.

Sympathy with the loyalists on the part of historians of the Revolution was not a new thing. When Charles Beard argued that the

founding fathers were motivated by class interests rather than patriotism, the result was to make the men whom they drove into exile
appear less wicked. When Carl Becker argued that the American
Revolution in New York was a contest about who should rule at home,
he too made the winners seem less heroic and the losers more attractive. At the same time a group of scholarly historians had been examining the old British Empire and finding it to be a pretty good thing
and thus, by implication at least, deserving of the loyalty that the loyalists gave it. By the 1930s the Revolution had begun to look like a
mere struggle for power, in which the losers, whether the English or
the loyalist Americans, became the victims of artful propaganda, put
over on the people at large by a handful of self-serving demagogues.

After the World War II a number of us who looked again at the
record began to argue that it did not support this interpretation, that
the revolutionists not only meant what they said but that it was worth
saying. The special contribution of Bernard Bailyn to this perception
was an analysis of the pervasive influence among Americans of the
ideas of the English republican thinkers who have become known as
The Eighteenth-Century Commonwealthmen (from the book of that title
in which Caroline Robbins described them). Although historians of
the Revolution had hitherto given little attention to the writings of
these men, the American revolutionists, as Bailyn demonstrated, had
studied them assiduously. Their ideas furnished the rationale behind
the indignant protests with which Americans greeted British efforts to
tax them. The development of American political thought not only in
the dozen years before 1776 but in the dozen years that followed can
best be understood as an outgrowth from their writings.

After thus examining *The Ideological Origins of the American
Revolution* (1967), Bailyn carried his investigation to an earlier period
and found the same ideas affecting *The Origins of American Politics* in
the half century or more before the Revolution. A basic tenet of the
commonwealthmen was the need for eternal vigilance against the
efforts of the executive branch of government to effect a tyrannical
control. In England the commonwealthmen cried out incessantly

against the corruption of Parliament by the king's ministry, but gained little attention, perhaps because the powers of the monarch had been so effectively curbed in England at the beginning of the century. But in the colonies the royal governors had powers that seemed to exceed by far those of the king in England; for the governor not only continued to exercise a veto power over legislation but generally controlled the composition of his council, which in a colonial government doubled as the upper house of the legislature.

This seeming concentration of power in the hands of one man was belied by the actual weakness of the governor. For a governor, unlike the king, had no independent source of revenue and almost no patronage to dispense. As a result he was in fact more dependent on the lower, representative house of his legislature than the king was. In this disparity between the nominal and actual power of the royal governor, Bailyn found a key to the paranoid character of colonial politics, in which colonists detected in every move of the executive to exercise his nominal powers a conspiracy to deprive them of their liberties. It was this fear of a conspiracy against liberty that later animated colonial resistance to England and eventuated in the Revolution. It had been latent in colonial politics for half a century.

What Bailyn gave us in 1974 was a careful, meticulously researched biography of the principal American victim of the revolutionary paranoia. And the study reveals an implication of Bailyn's previous work that we, and perhaps he, had not previously fully recognized. Thomas Hutchinson's only real faults were qualities of character that would have served him well in most times and did serve to earn him a small fortune by colonial standards, before he became caught up in a web of malevolence that grew stronger by every effort of his to break from it. Hutchinson's most conspicuous quality was prudence. He never acted from passion or pique. He never did anything impetuously and always weighed the consequence of any decision. He was keenly sensitive to the scale of deference that governed human relations in the colonies as in England and never misjudged his own place in the scale. When already governor of Massachusetts, for example, he politely dissuaded the son of an earl from seeking the hand of his daughter, saying it was an honor too high for him and his family, and it would be criminal in him to encourage the young man in so unequal a match. With his equals and inferiors he knew how to stand firm, as was his right. With his superiors he was always cautious of presuming. It was Hutchinson's prudence and his sense of propriety that prevented him from expressing openly, or even privately except to his confidants, his own bitter opposition to the English measures that alienated the colonies. Before the Stamp Act of 1765 was passed, he wrote a pamphlet against parliamentary taxation and sent it to an English friend, but refrained from publishing it. He was so careful not to indicate his views to the wrong people that he was popularly charged with being the secret author of the Stamp Act, and as a result his house was all but leveled by an angry mob in the worst riot of Boston's history. He similarly opposed the changes that his predecessor, Francis Bernard, had proposed for the Massachusetts government. But when the changes were made, in the Massachusetts Government Act of 1774, he was blamed for them.

As portrayed here, Hutchinson was a Burkean conservative, who wanted to make the system work by avoiding confrontations on matters of principle. But step by step he was drawn into one confrontation after another with men who had become convinced that he was trying to betray colonial liberties. Each time, because he thought it his duty to defend the system, he emerged looking more than ever the champion of arbitrary power. His prudence only served to feed the suspicions of his enemies, and it was in any case no avail against the theft of his private letters, which Benjamin Franklin obtained and sent to the Massachusetts assembly. Despite Franklin's injunction that they were not to be published, the people of Boston were shortly reading them in the newspapers, placed out of context, with editorial comments to assure the worst possible interpretation. And when Hutchinson finally fled to England, hoping to work out a reconciliation between mother country and colonies, he was blamed for every hostile measure that followed. By the time he died in 1780 in the midst of the Revolution,

Englishmen and Americans alike were blaming him for the whole thing.

Were they all wrong, then? Bailyn's answer seems to be yes. And what is more, they were wrong not simply from ignorance but almost by necessity. Given the nature of the revolutionists' position, as depicted in the author's earlier studies, if Hutchinson had not existed they would have had to invent him, for "the need to find hidden malevolence was part of the very structure of opposition thought." In effect, Hutchinson's enemies did invent him, in the shape of a villain who never existed. They imposed the image on the man and thwarted his every effort to cast it off.

In the concluding pages of the book Bailyn points out that Hutchinson never understood the forces that destroyed him, never understood "the moral indignation and the meliorist aspirations that lay behind the protests of the Revolutionary leaders." And in the opening pages he tells us that his own instinctive sympathies remain with the revolutionists, that he is simply showing us how it was possible for a good man to take the other side. But in between the opening and closing pages he succeeds so well that he leaves the American Revolution looking a pretty shabby affair. After we read of what it did to Hutchinson, our own moral indignation is likely to be reserved for the rebel politicians who could destroy a decent man for things he did not do, while congratulating themselves on their own righteousness. What kind of morality is it, we ask, that can subject a man to such persecution on grounds that can now be proved totally false? What kind of meliorist aspirations require the sacrifice of an innocent scapegoat? We are almost led to conclude that the United States was born in a fit of paranoid self-righteousness.

But one learns to be wary of calling a whole nation insane. Hutchinson's worst enemies included some otherwise sane and sober people. If we ponder more closely the extraordinary hostility he attracted, we may find in his career more than colonial paranoia to illuminate the meaning of the revolution. Few other loyalists had to endure such continuous vilification. The fact that he did not deserve it only compounds the puzzle.

A clue may lie in his closeness to the men who persecuted him. His bitterest years were the last, after he was obliged in 1774 to leave for in exile in a strange land that he could not learn to love. He yearned for New England, and his greatest agony was his rejection by New Englanders. He was one of them and not simply in the fact of having grown up with them, a descendant of the founding generation of settlers: his ideas of right and wrong were not far different from theirs. He could not like England partly for the same reasons that moved his countrymen to independence. Life in England was too riddled with luxury and corruption for him to feel comfortable there. This same hostility to English corruption was one of the potent forces that pulled Americans together in the movement for independence. Their governments had been comparatively free of the patronage and sinecures that lubricated the cumbersome machinery of politics in England. As they resisted the efforts of England to tax them, they were resisting involvement in a system to which they knew all governments and all men were highly susceptible and which they associated with tyranny. In the last stages of resistance, they began to think of independence as a means of escaping contamination. Thus Patrick Henry at the Continental Congress warned against Joseph Galloway's plan of conciliation through an intercolonial legislature that would stand between the colonies and Parliament. "We shall liberate our Constituents," he argued, "from a corrupt House of Commons, but throw them into the arms of an American Legislature that may be bribed by that Nation which avows in the face of the world, that bribery is a part of their system of government." Better to stand clear.

Self-righteousness is never attractive, and there was a great deal of self-righteousness in the incipient American nationalism. Yet no one supposed Americans to be immune to corruption. Precisely because they knew themselves to be as susceptible as other men they needed to affirm their resistance to corruption at every opportunity; they sought their national identity in rejecting the evils that had overtaken England. They therefore denounced with particular vehemence those in their midst who seemed to have succumbed to English temptations.

Thomas Hutchinson seemed to have succumbed. And guiltless as he may have been of most of the charges against him, he was not wholly guiltless of the one that bothered his enemies the most. He had built a network of political influence in Massachusetts of which family connections were the principal common denominator. John Adams tallied up the score in 1765. "Has he not grasped," asked Adams,

> *four of the most important offices in the Province into his own hands? Has not his brother in law Oliver another of the greatest places in government [Secretary of the Province]? Is not a brother of the Secretary a judge of the Superior Court? Has not that brother a son in the House [of Representatives]? Has not the Secretary a son in the House, who is also a judge in one of the counties? Did not that son marry the daughter of another of the judges of the Superior Court? Has not the Lieutenant Governor [Hutchinson] a brother, a judge of the pleas in Boston? and a namesake and near relation who is another judge? Has not the Lieutenant Governor a near relation who is Register of his own Court of Probate, and Deputy Secretary? Has he not another near relation who is Clerk of the House of Representatives? Is not this amazing ascendancy of one family foundation sufficient on which to erect a tyranny?*

To other Americans Hutchinson seemed to be an agent of the same insidious forces that he himself encountered and disapproved in England. And if his enemies had known all the facts now uncovered, they would have found him no less guilty of this. Indeed, even as he frowned on Englishmen who thought of the state "as a great plum pudding," he was already trying to scrape up a few more crumbs for his friends and relatives, including his son, whose health and character made it unlikely that he could ever earn a living of his own. There was nothing illegal about his efforts. They were less than what many Englishmen in his position would have done. But they had become un-American.

The word was not in use at the time, but it conveys what Hutchinson's enemies felt about him. It is a word that has seldom been used in this country to mean what it seems to say: it does not designate a foreigner by birth. It has been reserved for Americans who fail to conform to the norms that the national consciousness prescribes. And it has been used, perhaps more often than not, to hurt men who are innocent of any crime. The ordeal of Thomas Hutchinson was the first of its kind, but far from the last.

But to leave it at that is to reduce the Revolution to the level of a witch-hunt. And although that is the level where nationalism, here and abroad, sometimes operates, it seems only fair to acknowledge, a little more explicitly than I think Bailyn does here, that Hutchinson's enemies were not wrong about the dangers that he represented. It was not mere malice that moved John Adams to see in Hutchinson's political activities a threat to freedom. Hutchinson's position, as portrayed by Bailyn, was that the British Parliament ought not to tax the colonies, that prudence and good policy forbade it, but that the authority of Parliament to tax could not be limited. The position of the revolutionists was that men cannot be trusted with more power than you expect them to exercise. To acknowledge absolute authority in a body over which you had no control and to rely on the good sense of the men in it was to take up the relationship of slave to master.

Hutchinson insisted that this was and had always been the colonists' relationship to Parliament, though he vigorously denied that it deserved the name of slavery. His enemies disagreed. At the beginning of the contest they were not altogether clear about where the limits of Parliament's authority lay, but they never doubted that there were limits and that those limits stopped short of the authority to tax the colonies. The attempt to tax them demonstrated, if any demonstration was needed, that the good sense of men in power is not a sufficient security for liberty. It was in fact to the interest of every Englishman to extract as much in taxes from the colonists as possible. Every shilling that Parliament obtained from them meant a shilling less to be obtained from the members of Parliament and their constituents. It might be bad policy to tax them, but greed has often proved more potent than prudence.

Had Parliament shown the good sense that Hutchinson expected of it, his ordeal would never have occurred. But if Parliament and the ministry had not failed him, if he had been able to make the system work in his own time, he would have left the colonists more vulnerable to later lapses of good sense on the part of their masters. As it was, though they may have been moved in part by "a need to find hidden malevolence" among men in power, they were not deluded in perceiving the shape of tyranny behind the submission that Hutchinson sought from them. His position was not only un-American but in the long run anti-American. It does not follow that he deserved the treatment he received. But in mourning his fate we may still reserve a share of sympathy for the men who saw farther than he did.

May 21, 1974

CHAPTER FIFTEEN

The Oedipal Revolution

———⚉———

American Patriots and the Rituals of Revolution
Peter Shaw

A*merican Patriots and the Rituals of Revolution* was inevitable. Someone was bound to write it sooner or later, and better sooner than later. Peter Shaw brings together a series of disparate psychological, anthropological, and historical insights and perspectives and develops them into a new interpretation of the American Revolution, an interpretation that some readers will see as a work of synthetic genius and others as a projection of credible scholarship into incredible flights of fantasy.

The primary ingredient is the suggestive study of ritual by the anthropologist Victor Turner, who has shown the ambiguous character of folk rituals, especially festivals that seem to challenge the social and political order of a society at the same time as they serve to support it.[1] The reversal of roles common in these rituals (where the servant becomes the master, the peasant becomes the lord, and a fool is king for a day) overtly defies the social order and thereby defines it, but the defiance may sometimes overcome the definition and turn into social protest.

A second ingredient is also anthropological: the rite of passage, which in various societies accompanies or brings about the transition from adolescence into manhood, another slightly ambiguous ceremony, in which young males are humbled and abused before being raised to adulthood. This is a concept that can be all too easily applied to a whole society rather than to the individuals within it. The third element in Shaw's interpretation is straight out of Freud's *Totem and Taboo*, the killing of the father by a band of brothers, which becomes the basis for later ritual enactments of the killing of a king and the succession of another.

Historians have found all three phenomena suggestive, but Turner's delineation of rituals has been the most fruitful. Such scholars as Le Roy Ladurie, Natalie Davis, and E. P. Thompson have shown that festivals and folk rituals in France and England could be made to carry a burden of social protest and might even spark rebellions. Although folk rituals in early America were much less common than in England and France (or at any rate have left fewer traces), they have recently begun to interest American social historians. Pope's Day, the anniversary of Guy Fawkes's attempt to blow up the Houses of Parliament on November 5, 1605, was celebrated in eighteenth-century Boston by parades, with effigies of the pope, the devil, and the "guy" carried about the streets and later hanged and burned. May Day, the king's birthday, coronations, and various other occasions were also celebrated from time to time in various places, though the elaborate rituals that accompanied the seasonal festivals of Catholic Europe were missing.

Shaw has built his interpretation of the American Revolution on these popular ceremonies. He relies most heavily on the celebration of Pope's Day in Boston. The Bostonians, to be sure, did not choose November 5 as the time to rise against the British, but no matter that. What does matter, according to Shaw, is that they adapted the Pope's Day display of parades and effigies to carry out protests at other times. And the importance of these protests lies more in the symbolic rituals they enacted than in the grievances they expressed or the violence they sometimes bred. For instance, when the Stamp Act was passed in 1765, a Boston mob in August destroyed the stamp distributor's office, but this act of real destruction was actually less significant than the symbolic destruction the mob enacted in ceremonially burning the effigies of the distributor and of several other persons who were thought to have contributed to the passage of the act. Shaw sees these rituals in

Boston, which were imitated in several other colonies, as necessary "rehearsals of revolution." The message of his book is that such ceremonies did not simply help to make the American Revolution possible but were essential to its fulfillment. The effigies destroyed were surrogates not merely for the persons represented but for the king, the father who had to be overthrown by the children who were coming of age. The Revolution was a rite of passage, a youth movement: not only did children, especially boys, play a large role in ritual protests, but they were joined by adults "who had adopted the spirit of youth initiation." Young or old, they could not kill the king until they had prepared themselves by killing other father figures in effigy, ritually. The ritual, we are told, enabled people to express their true inner feelings, to direct "at substitutes like Thomas Hutchinson what they actually felt toward the king."

Actually there seems to have been no substitute quite like Hutchinson. He figures in the book as almost indispensable to the Revolution. He was not only the target of popular anger, expressed in the destruction of his house by a mob, but the surrogate father against whom patriots worked out their Oedipal antagonisms. Shaw's rituals of revolution include not merely ceremonies adapted from folk holidays but also a pattern of subconscious adolescent rebellion that he finds rife during the pre-Revolutionary years among persons whom he calls "conscience patriots." A major portion of the book is devoted to biographical analysis of four of these—James Otis, John Adams, Joseph Hawley, and Josiah Quincy—who suffered inner turmoil because of their symbolic patricide. Each of them transferred his antagonism against his father to Hutchinson and ultimately from Hutchinson to the king. And each of them in doing so suffered periodic feelings of guilt and "revolutionary remorse." For example, as late as 1798, John Adams's acceptance of the Alien and Sedition Acts is to be seen as a final gesture of expiation for his youthful hostility to Hutchinson.

The actual relationship of each man to his father seems not to have been crucial to the development of his Oedipal politics. James Otis had an overbearing father whom he attacked by seeming to defend him against Hutchinson. Adams's father was not overbearing, so Adams attacked Hutchinson as an exemplification of evils his father had warned him against. Hawley was angry with his father for committing suicide and displaced his anger first on to Jonathan Edwards, his minister, and only later made the transference to Hutchinson and then to the king. It was not the actual parental relationship that mattered but a "widespread psychic strain" induced by a national coming of age and evident in nosebleeds, tuberculosis, and broken windows as well as in the rituals of revolution.

What makes this improbable diagnosis enticing is that it seems to offer a kind of climax to three quite different interpretations of the Revolution. Lawrence Henry Gipson in fifteen large volumes on *The British Empire Before the American Revolution* painted so rosy a picture of the empire that it was difficult to see why anyone should have rebelled against it. After describing the churlish behavior of the ungrateful colonists, Gipson fell back on metaphor. The colonists, he said, had arrived at maturity. They therefore resented and resisted the control of the mother country, even though that control was exercised in their best interests. Gipson did not explain what maturity was in a society as opposed to an individual. Neither, for that matter, does Shaw, but Shaw has dressed the metaphor in anthropological and psychological terms that many will find appealing. A rite of passage, as applied to colonial mob actions, is still a metaphor and nothing more, but it sounds like more.

Rites of passage also add a new twist to the work of another group of historians (this author among them), who have given their attention to the colonists' avowed objections to the British measures that brought on the Revolution. Bernard Bailyn in particular has stressed the suspicion of corruption in government that American pamphleteers derived from English radical thinkers. From the time of the Stamp Act there developed in America a suspicion that there was a conspiracy among evil-minded English statesmen to deprive Americans of their liberties. In a later work Bailyn traced the way in which this suspicion worked among the people of Massachusetts to place Thomas Hutchinson at the center of the conspiracy. Since Hutchinson had done little to deserve the hatred and suspicion that fell upon him, the men who attacked him, including those whom Shaw has singled out for attention, appeared in Bailyn's work as little short of paranoid. Now we have another explanation: they were undergoing a private rite of passage, using Hutchinson as surrogate father in order to prepare for the killing of the king that would bring them to the political manhood they yearned for.

Finally, Shaw's interpretation offers to make sense out of the crowd actions that have fascinated historians on the left. Every effort to see the American Revolution as a rising of the masses against an upper class has foundered on the facts. Mobs or crowds, whichever we call them, were conspicuous in the early stages of the Revolution, and historians have been trying for years to endow them with purposes distinct from those of upper-class leaders of the Revolution. None of the attempts has been persuasive. Shaw's interpretation does not quite fill the bill, but it does give new dimensions to the actions of the inarticulate. It discovers "extra-political" motives, albeit unconscious ones, for revolutionary crowds, and throughout it emphasizes the "insurrectionary potential" of rituals.

Because the book addresses so many of the themes that appear in recent accounts of the Revolution, it has to be taken seriously. It is the first book to consider the ritualistic character of the crowd actions of the Revolution, and it deserves credit for doing so. One can predict that historians will give much more attention to this subject in the future and ought to do so. It is nevertheless troublesome to have insights presented as fact and isolated events extrapolated into a systematic interpretation of phenomena that may be totally unrelated. It will be noticed, for example, that the American Revolution, as it appears in this book, took place almost entirely in Massachusetts. We get only passing reference to rituals outside of Boston. And we don't hear about the surrogate fathers of Patrick Henry or George Washington or Thomas Jefferson or Benjamin Franklin. We don't know if they had any, though it will not be beyond the ingenuity of assiduous searchers to find some. Well, all right. The author is giving us illustrative examples, not proof. What he has to say is not really susceptible of empirical demonstration anyhow. If it works for Massachusetts, maybe that is enough. But does it work even there?

The most disturbing thing about the book is the basic assumption upon which the author proceeds, namely that the Americans had unconsciously or subconsciously decided on independence by 1765 and needed only to repeat a set of rituals in order to recognize their decision. If that is the case, then all the objections they offered for resisting British taxation were just so much talk: the causes of the Revolution are to be found in the Americans' collective psychic development, not in whatever reasons they may have offered for their rebellious behavior. Indeed their rituals proceeded without close relation to the grievances that ostensibly occasioned them, for the persons picked for symbolic punishment as surrogate fathers, particularly Hutchinson, had not actually had much to do with the measures that the colonists professed to be protesting. The choice of victims was incidental, because it was only the ritual itself, the symbolic act of killing the king or his surrogate, not any actual grievance, that was needed to propel them toward the independence they already unconsciously grasped. What this amounts to is psychological determinism, comparable to the economic determinism that was fashionable among the Progressive historians in the early part of this century. For them too the substance of what the colonists said in objection to British measures was not worthy of serious consideration. Everyone was supposed to be moved by economic motives, hidden behind the window dressing of political and constitutional argument. Shaw does not give us economic motives. He does not give us motives at all. The measures to which the colonists objected are for him mere occasions for the performance of rituals; it is the rituals themselves that must be considered as "operative."

The scope of their operation is, of course, limited. They only bring to conscious realization a subconscious decision of many years standing. It is in keeping with his assumption that Shaw refers to the victims of riots in 1765 as "loyalists," as though their opponents had already rejected the king. And indeed, by Shaw's assumption, they had. They had arrived at the stage in the psychic life cycle of their society where it was necessary to undergo a rite of passage. The Stamp Act crowds with their effigies were undertaking "the imagining of revolution in symbolic terms years before any conscious decision to repudiate submission to the king." But the unconscious decision had already been made. Where a diarist in 1765 speaks of the Boston "Liberty Tree" (where effigies were hung) as "the Royal Elm," Shaw sees it as a revealing slip of the pen: "It indicated that the tree represented a transfer of sovereignty from king to people several years before one took place politically."

In other words, the Revolution had already taken place in the minds and hearts of the people before they knew it, as John Adams suggested in 1818. But John Adams was speaking with hindsight, and so is Peter Shaw. Hindsight is the one advantage that a historian has over the people he studies. But if not used with great caution it can be a trap. I think Mr. Shaw has fallen into the trap.

April 16, 1981

CHAPTER SIXTEEN

Secrets of Benjamin Franklin

⸙

Benjamin Franklin's Science
Bernard Cohen

Le Sceptre et la foudre: Franklin à Paris, 1776–1785
Claude-Anne Lopez

Mon Cher Papa: Franklin and the Ladies of Paris
Claude-Anne Lopez

Becoming Benjamin Franklin: The Autobiography and the Life
Ormond Seavey

The Papers of Benjamin Franklin, Vols. 1–14
Leonard W. Labaree, editor

The Papers of Benjamin Franklin, Vols. 15–26
William B. Wilcox, editor

The Papers of Benjamin Franklin, Vol. 27
Claude A. Lopez, editor

The Papers of Benjamin Franklin, Vols. 28–35
Barbara B. Oberg, editor

Benjamin Franklin: His Life As He Wrote It
Esmond Wright, editor

Writings
Benjamin Franklin

WHEN BENJAMIN FRANKLIN died on April 17, 1790, over two hundred years ago, the first Congress of the United States under its new Constitution was busy addressing the problems of a young republic in a world of monarchies. Franklin was eighty-four years old, had been ill for some time, and his death could scarcely have come as a surprise, Still, apart from the republic's new president, Franklin was the best known of the founding fathers. His death could not go without some sort of official notice. The House of Representatives, after listening to a brief tribute by James Madison, voted to wear badges of mourning for two months and then got on with business.

In France, the reaction was more dramatic. There the new National Assembly was in session in June when the comte de Mirabeau, who had just received the news, rose and announced simply, "*Franklin est mort.*" There was a stunned silence before Mirabeau proceeded to an eloquent eulogy, giving Franklin credit not only for American independence and the framing of the United States Constitution but also for gaining recognition of the rights of man throughout the world. The Assembly voted by acclamation to join the United States Congress in mourning. That evening the Commune of Paris commissioned another eulogy, which was delivered to an audience of three thousand on July 21, a little over a year after the storming of the Bastille.

Something more, or less, than mourning lay behind these proceedings in both France and America. Enlisting dead heroes in live causes has always been a stock in trade of politics. In France, where Franklin lived from 1776 to 1785, he had won an extraordinary place in the public mind. The French had lionized him to the point of absurdity—or so at least his colleagues in the American mission thought. John Adams, who joined the mission in 1778, remembered years later that "His name was familiar to government and people, to kings, courtiers, nobility, clergy, and philosophers, as well as plebeians, to such a degree that there was scarcely a peasant or a citizen, a *valet de chambre*, coachman or footman, a lady's chambermaid or a scullion in a kitchen who was not familiar with it and who did not consider him as a friend to human kind." Franklin himself was surprised to find his image everywhere, in medallions, portraits, busts, and prints. He could hear his name linked regularly with those of Voltaire and Rousseau in the galaxy of Enlightenment heroes. He could view the three of them in waxworks at the fair of Saint-Germain, standing together beside the king, queen, and dauphin. The adulation reached the point where the king himself found it a bit much and is said to have presented one overenthusiastic admirer of Franklin with a Sèvres porcelain chamber pot carrying the philosopher's portrait.

In 1790 Franklin was remembered in France as "that great man, who will be ever the object of the admiration of succeeding ages."[1] Mirabeau's motion for mourning in the National Assembly was probably motivated not simply by grief but by the desire to associate "that great man" with the liberal monarchical constitution which Mirabeau was promoting. Although no one ventured to speak against mourning, those who opposed the new constitution abstained from the vote. In America, the politics of mourning were more complex than the vote in the House of Representatives would suggest.[2] Here Franklin was not only a more controversial figure but one now associated with a controversial country: many Americans were beginning to have doubts about the French Revolution. After the House of Representatives passed Madison's resolution of mourning, Charles Carroll introduced a similar resolution in the Senate. The motion was opposed before it could be seconded and was quickly withdrawn. A vote for Franklin, it seems, would have been a vote for the French Revolution, even though Franklin's career in France had been under the *ancien régime*. And when the official notice of the French Assembly's action arrived in December, the various branches of government tossed it back and forth like a hot potato until they could draft a suitably noncommittal reply.

Franklin was certainly not without honor in his own country, but from that day to this the honor has been a little mixed with mockery, from John Adams to Mark Twain, not to mention D. H. Lawrence, whose *Studies in Classic American Literature* gave a twentieth-century twist to the contempt of eighteenth-century English statesmen for an uppity colonist. Modern scholars have found much to admire in the man, but they have also found puzzles in his writings that often make him seem contriving, to be not quite what he wants people to think he is. Carl Becker's brilliant sketch of Franklin in the *Dictionary of American Biography* may have been the inadvertent source. Becker was actually remarking on the depth of Franklin's genius when he wrote: "In all of Franklin's dealings with men and affairs, genuine, sincere, loyal as he surely was, one feels that he is nevertheless not wholly committed; some thought remains uncommunicated; some penetrating observation is held in reserve."

Subsequent scholars have gone beyond Becker's insight to emphasize the poses that Franklin assumed in his voluminous pseudonymous writing for newspapers and almanacs as Silence Dogood, the Busy-Body, and a host of other names, including above all Poor Richard. Was any of these the real Franklin? And was the *Autobiography*, with its depiction of a thrifty, industrious young tradesman, a true portrait of the man who retired from business at the age of forty-two, prepared from then on to spend what he had got rather than accumulate more? For his remaining forty-two years (he happened to divide his lifetime neatly in half) he had no need to think about making or saving money. Although he kept a government office as postmaster until 1774 and turned it into a considerable source of profit, he could afford to leave the actual work of his printing business to others. As he himself remarked in *The Way to Wealth*, "money can beget money," and he had made enough of it to beget an income of almost £2,000 a year, more than the governor of Pennsylvania enjoyed. He did not use it frivolously. But was it not a little disingenuous of him to keep on, as he did, singing the praises of frugality and affecting a simplicity of dress that belied the comfortable style of living he treated himself to, whether in Philadelphia, London, or Paris? Does the real Franklin lie hidden behind a mask or masks? The question is worth asking, but it is a good deal less searching than the attention given it would suggest, and it would scarcely be worth the trouble if there were not so much of Franklin that is not hidden at all, so much that brought him conspicuously in view of the whole world. The real Franklin, I would argue, is not all that hard to know, and concentration on any discrepancy between what he was and what he seemed distracts from the message he sent not only in his writings but in the whole shape of his public life.

Franklin lived the better part of his life in the public eye. He was the only one of the founding fathers who had achieved international renown before the American Revolution and achieved it as an intellectual peer of the eighteenth century's foremost figures. When he arrived in France in 1776, the French made such a fuss over him not simply because of his winning ways but because his reputation had preceded him by many years. Bernard Cohen long ago explained why in two major works (*Benjamin Franklin's Experiments*, 1941; and *Franklin and Newton*, 1956) and repeats the explanation in *Benjamin Franklin's Science*, a collection of earlier essays revised and reprinted. The essays are mainly about Franklin's contributions to electricity and electrical theory, but they all sustain Cohen's main point; that Franklin was no mere tinkerer, that he was moved by the same intellectual curiosity that has driven pure science in every age. Franklin did like to tinker, to devise gadgets that would make life easier for himself and everyone else. But his tinkering, Cohen shows, was an afterthought, the result, not the cause, of his scientific explorations. He won worldwide recognition in his own time and a secure place in the history of science ever since, not by his invention of the lightning rod but by his discovery that electricity, like gravity, was one of the basic forces of nature. Before Franklin electricity was a curiosity, something known through the amusing parlor tricks that could be played with the Leyden jar. Franklin devised the experiments, first carried out in France under his written instructions, that demonstrated lightning to be electric. And it was Franklin, experimenting with the Leyden jar, who formulated the general hypotheses that guided future electrical research. Some of them, such as the concept of plus and minus current, still prevail.

Franklin had finished his crucial work with electricity by 1750, and thereafter he was showered with honors for it at home and abroad: honorary degrees from Harvard, Yale, William and Mary, and St. Andrews in Scotland; election to the English Society of Arts, the Royal Society of London, the Batavian Society of Experimental Science (Rotterdam), and perhaps most significantly the Académie Royale des Sciences (Paris). When Franklin arrived in France in 1776 as America's representative, Cohen reminds us, "he was already a public figure, well known to the French court and to the French public at large in a sense that would have been true of no other American in the political diplomatic arena, and this was so because of his stature as a scientist and because of the spectacular nature of his work on lightning."

Franklin did not make a life work of electricity. He showed no proprietary interest in his discoveries and no evangelical urge to propagate his theories. Happy to encourage and give credit to other investigators, he declined to enter into the usual controversies that follow breakthroughs in science and that inevitably followed his. Instead, he let his fruitful curiosity range off to other natural phenomena—heat, sound, fluid dynamics. So much was unknown and discovery so rapid that he sometimes wished he could have been born two centuries later when more of the answers would have become available. He made his own answers available to anyone who was interested, not only to his intellectual peers in the various academies but also in casual letters to friends. He might explain his ideas about tides and river currents to his London landlady's daughter (in a five-page letter) with as much care as in a paper for the Royal Society. When his ideas led to useful devices like the lightning rod or the Franklin stove, he did not attempt to profit from them, preferring to let the public receive any benefit they might bring. If he withheld any part of himself from public gaze, it was certainly not in his pursuit of science or in the discoveries it produced.

BUT SCIENCE WAS, of course, not Franklin's only pursuit or even a major one. Although his contemporaries often likened him to Isaac Newton, his priorities differed from Newton's. As he explained in a letter to a fellow scientist, "Had Newton been Pilot but of a single common Ship, the finest of his Discoveries would scarce have excused or atoned for his abandoning the Helm one Hour in Time of Danger; how much less if she had carried the Fate of the Commonwealth." When he was appointed Minister to France by the Continental Congress, Franklin did carry the fate of the Commonwealth.

It has to be allowed that he seemed to carry it lightly. During the years from 1776 to 1778 when he shared the burden with Silas Deane, John Adams, Arthur Lee, and Ralph Izard, all but Deane thought he carried it much too lightly. John Adams, consumed with jealousy of Franklin's reputation, complained that

> *The Life of Dr. Franklin was a Scene of continuall discipation. . . . It was late when he breakfasted, and as soon as Breakfast was over, a crowd of Carriages came to his Levee or if you like the term better to his Lodgings, with all Sorts of People; some Phylosophers, Accademicians and Economists . . . but by far the greater part were Women and Children, come to have the honour to see the great Franklin, and to have the pleasure of telling Stories about his Simplicity, his bald head and scattering strait hairs. . . . 3*

They came to him and he came to them, enjoying every minute of it, dinner party after dinner party. If Franklin arrived in France already trailing clouds of glory, the French found the man even more entrancing than the philosopher, wise, wordly, and witty. Claude-Anne Lopez has captured the scene in her two studies of Franklin in Paris. *Le Sceptre et la foudre: Franklin à Paris*, published in France, is an abridgement, revision, and in parts an expansion, of *Mon Cher Papa: Franklin and the Ladies of Paris*. From a lifetime spent in the editing of Franklin's papers at Yale, Lopez knows intimately, as no other biographer has, the man whom the French encountered. Whether writing in French or in English, she gives us a sharper appreciation of his mature humanity than can be found anywhere else.

Lopez's portrayal is made possible by the habit of the time for friends and neighbors to bombard each other with little notes, invitations to dinner, thank-you notes, begging notes, scolding notes, and notes for no reason at all. Many of those that Franklin received were from men, on serious issues of science and politics and philosophy: from Turgot, the famous economist, from the duc de la Rochefoucauld, from the great Lavoisier, father of modern chemistry. Lavoisier became a close friend, as did his wife, who painted Franklin's portrait and made a duplicate for herself. And indeed it was mainly the women who kept up the barrage of social correspondence.

Franklin's relations with them have long been a subject of sly speculation, for the letters, not to mention John Adams's direct observations, suggest that Franklin in his seventies had become the Don Juan of diplomacy. The letters are filled with references to hugging and kissing, sitting on laps and holding hands, together with professions of undying love and demands, on his part, for greater intimacies with what would seem to be a whole harem of passionate and beautiful women. He liked to tell them that "love thy neighbor" should be coupled with the injunction to increase and multiply; he liked to confess his failure to obey the prohibition against coveting thy neighbor's wife. This kind of half-joking, half-serious badinage delighted the French, who responded in kind. Lopez allows us to enjoy the spectacle in all its richness but also lets us see just how far it went and where it stopped. Franklin may complain to Madame Helvétius, with whom he says he has spent "so many of his days," because "she seems very ungrateful in never giving him one of her nights." But when a lady actually yields to such entreaties, he asks for a delay "until the nights were longer."

Franklin, it is clear, enjoyed the company of women, and chastity was low in his scale of virtues. He had had one illegitimate son and he spent much of his (common-law) married life away from his wife. His friendship with a series of other women in America, England, and France was not without a large element of sexual attraction. Read out of context, passages in his letters sound like what today would be called propositions, if not proposals, but Lopez shows us that Franklin's seeming affairs were all what the French call "amitiés amoureuses." They were "more than close friendship," but they stopped short of any consummation of physical passion. It could be argued that these relationships show Franklin once again assuming a persona, wearing the mask of a passion he did not feel. To be sure, some of the ladies he courted so happily were women of influence, and their fondness for him could have assisted him in his official mission. But whatever benefit he may have received in that way was wholly incidental, indirect, and almost certainly uncalculated. Franklin was having a good time. He had always liked to flirt, and the French had raised flirtation to a fine art. The letters, which sound a little shocking today, were part of a game that everyone, in France at least, understood, a game that could be played hard and might conceivably slip out of control but in Franklin's case never did. Most of the women who played it with him had husbands who watched it as a spectator sport (when they were not similarly engaged themselves) and enjoyed Franklin's skill at it. *Le Sceptre et la foudre* and *Mon Cher Papa* give us a chance to watch with them.

That Franklin's social connections interfered with his diplomatic mission, as John Adams believed, is as doubtful as it is to suggest that they were undertaken on behalf of it. Franklin's diplomatic style was certainly disorderly and casual, a cross for the methodical Adams to bear. But Franklin was the key man in the mission. He had secured the French alliance before Adams arrived on the scene, and he had done it by dealing with the French court more openly and cordially than Adams thought advisable. Franklin as a diplomat did not play his cards close to his chest. Following his own too much misunderstood aphorism that "honesty is the best policy," he believed that in American relations with France, "an Expression of Gratitude is not only our Duty, but our Interest."

Adams, as Franklin reported to his superiors, thought the United States could get more out of the French by "a little apparent Stoutness, and greater air of Independence and Boldness in our Demands." But Adams in France succeeded only in offending the French foreign minister, and Franklin breathed a sigh of relief when Congress dismissed Adams from the mission and left Franklin to deal with the French in his own way. In that way he succeeded in getting the continued financial and military assistance that made American victory possible. If Franklin's public stance differed from his private one, it was not in diplomacy, where one might expect to find it. In truth the variance that scholars find between the public and private Franklin lies not between the positions he took in public and in private on public policy or on philosophical and scientific questions but rather in his literary creativity. Nature may imitate art and art nature, but they are never quite the same. And Franklin's creative writing was clearly artful.

We can easily dismiss most of the early pieces he wrote for newspapers. The story is familiar of his precocious success in secretly submitting the "Silence Dogood" letters to his brother's Boston paper, *The New England Courant*. When he himself acquired the *Pennsylvania Gazette* at the age of twenty-three, he continued to fill it with facetious, pseudonymous essays on the model of Addison's *Spectator*, mildly satirizing the follies of the day. These were the standard fare of eighteenth-century newspapers, and most of Franklin's were no better than the standard. They are all so derivative and imitative that the only real Franklin to be found in them is the clever young printer on the make. The best that can be said for them is that they were exercises in which Franklin learned something about writing. But somewhere, somehow he learned a lot more than is evident in any of them. The *Autobiography*, though written at three widely separated intervals, is an enduring work of art in a recognized genre.

Franklin called it his "memoirs," for the word "autobiography" did not come into use until the nineteenth century. But the genre existed long before the modern name for it, and like other autobiographies Franklin's is selective and studied. The selection is dictated in part by the fact that it was originally addressed to his son and in the process of writing became a cautionary tale for other younger persons. As such it has a hortatory tone that readers often find irritating. What makes it fascinating for those seeking some elusive real Franklin is that it is the work of an older and wiser man reconstructing a youth that he wants to make instructive. He does it with a literary skill that is all the more artful for its artless appearance. The book invites literary analysis and has received it in large measure. Some of the best is to be found in Ormond Seavey's *Becoming Benjamin Franklin: The Autobiography and the Life*.

Seavey guides us through the *Autobiography* as an expression of Franklin's identity as finally achieved in maturity and then through Franklin's life on the way to achieving it. As is often the case in such analyses, Seavey tends to attribute to Franklin motives derived from concepts that had to be unknown to him. But the fact that Franklin would not himself have seen his career in terms of finding an identity does not necessarily vitiate the analysis. It makes Franklin's development seem more deliberate than it probably was, but it does show us how his restless movement from Boston to Philadelphia to London and back again reflected the young man's ambition to gain a place in a larger world than local circumstances offered him. He courted the friendship of men in power, and he made his way easily into local politics, but he had his eye on a world beyond Massachusetts or Pennsylvania or even, as it turned out, England, a world that did not quite exist at the time, a world with America at its center. As Seavey shrewdly comments, "Politically he was an American before it was really possible to be one."

Seavey's most arresting insights are those in which he examines Franklin's sense of audience: beginning the *Autobiography* after he had already spent a dozen years in England, he writes as everyman, addressing himself to posterity, to young men who could be either in England or America. Franklin had in mind an enduring imperial society that was actually, as Seavey puts it, a "particularly fragile construct" at the time (1771) when he started writing. As the fragile construct began to destruct, he stopped writing and did not take up the manuscript again until after the Revolution, when his vision of a rising American empire restored his confidence in his own career as a model for the young.

YET THE *Autobiography*, however worthy of study as a work of art in its own right, has become something of a red herring for the study of

Franklin himself and of his place in history. It does not get beyond his arrival in England as agent of the Pennsylvania Assembly in 1757. By that time he was fifty-one, had won his reputation as a scientist, had become a prominent figure in Pennsylvania politics, and had already formulated some prescient views about the British Empire. But his most brilliant years in London and Paris were just beginning, and the materials for following him through those years are more abundantly available today than ever before. They are being published in scrupulously accurate form in the *Papers* of Benjamin Franklin, reaching to the thirty-seventh volume with perhaps another ten to come. The period covered by the *Autobiography* lasts only to the middle of the seventh volume. If there is a real Franklin different from the one on display in the *Autobiography*, he is to be found in the letters and memoranda and essays of these volumes, especially in the later ones. In them Franklin devotes his literary skill to stating his views both on the ephemera of everyday life and on the manifold public issues of his day. Since Franklin was closely involved in the events that led to the creation of the United States and conscious of what he was doing at every step, his developing opinions as the events unfolded are as instructive for adults as the *Autobiography* was supposed to be for the young. To read any one of these volumes is to be thrust into a part of the past that still bears heavily on the present.

For anyone daunted by such full participation in one man's life, there are a couple of samplings. The newest, *Benjamin Franklin: His Life As He Wrote It*, edited by Esmond Wright, gives selections from the *Autobiography* interspersed with other writings, followed by more of these for the years after 1757. Wright has chosen passages that reveal Franklin's daily life and public career, his wit and wisdom, and Wright gives continuity to them with brief introductions and comments. The whole is all too brief, much shorter than Wright's own widely read biography, *Franklin of Philadelphia*.[4] Unfortunately the transcription and editing of the selections leave something to be desired. The editor tells us that he has attached to each extract its source and date and that omissions within each selection are marked with ellipses. But in too many cases the source or date is missing, and whole pages, paragraphs, and phrases have been dropped without indication. For a quick taste of Franklin the collection nevertheless serves reasonably well.

A much larger selection and one adhering meticulously to high editorial standards is J. A. Leo Lemay's volume in the Library of America series, 1,605 pages, including 134 pages of notes, chronology, and index. Lemay has identified as Franklin's a number of newspaper pieces not hitherto attributed to him and includes them in the edition along with many more of Franklin's early newspaper writings. He devotes 491 pages to the period covered by the *Autobiography* as well as giving the entire *Autobiography* itself and all of *Poor Richard's Almanack*. This is more than most of us would want for the copybook exercises of the young printer. But it still leaves 687 pages for the later years in London and Paris and the final five years in Philadelphia. The items selected are given in full. The annotation is sparse, and for one accustomed to the assistance that the editors of the *Papers* provide in their volumes it is sometimes annoying not to know the context (the *Papers* include the letters Franklin received) and not to have obscure allusions and references explained. But more of this would have meant less of Franklin: in this splendid volume, one quickly ceases to worry about any variance between Franklin as he was and Franklin as he makes himself appear. No one reveals all of himself in his writing, but there is less apparent reserve in Franklin than in most public figures, Jefferson and Washington for example. With Franklin, as with John Adams, what you see is what you get.

What you get, in Lemay's volume as in the *Papers*, is a man who offers his opinions freely to anyone who asks for them and often gives vent to them in print when they are not asked. Franklin's opinions are still worth listening to, not simply for the wit and the literary grace with which he delivered them, but for the example they offer of what Emerson called "man thinking." Franklin thinking is especially worth listening to because what he thought about most was not his persona but the configuration of social forces that had begun to shape the modern world. Franklin was present at the creation, in London during the crucial years when Britain secured its hold on North America and then lost it, in Paris when Americans won their place in the world of nations, in Philadelphia when the United States gained its present government. At every stage he perceived what was going on more clearly than any other participant who has left us his thoughts about it.

Franklin was one of the first British colonists to think, as Alexander Hamilton later put it, continentally, to think as an American and of America as a factor in world power. Traveling probably contributed to his perspective. By the time he was twenty, Franklin had already lived in Boston, Philadelphia, and for a year and a half in London. Over the next two decades, as printer of a newspaper, postmaster, and a tireless correspondent, he kept in touch with what was going on in the other colonies and in England. After he retired from the printing business he began to think more and more about America and its place in the British Empire.

Franklin loved and honored the mother country and wanted to think of America as part of the whole, but he recognized early on that America was the most dynamic part of the empire and that its growth posed a challenge which statesmen in London were proving slow to recognize. British imperial policy in the eighteenth century was directed more by pressure groups in England than by any larger vision. In 1750 Parliament passed the Iron Act, prohibiting the growth of iron manufacturing in America in order to benefit English producers. Franklin responded with a small treatise, never mentioning the Iron Act, that analyzed the social dynamics of empire. He took it as given that the wealth of any country lay in the numbers of its people, and proceeded to show (before Malthus was born) that the growth of population was governed by economic opportunity, that economic opportunity in America would for a long time be almost unlimited because of the unique abundance of land, that population in America increased accordingly, by natural propagation, far more rapidly than population in England and more rapidly than English manufacturers would be able to supply. It was therefore unnecessary and unwise to restrain

American manufacturing, unwise to do anything to discourage economic opportunity and growth within the empire. American growth could itself contribute to English growth by furnishing an ever larger market for English producers. But the important thing was to see America itself as the place where the English could grow. As Tocqueville in the next century saw America as the future of Europe, Franklin saw the American colonies as the future of England.

Behind these observations lay an imperial ethnic pride. Franklin was not pleased by the immigration of Germans or other foreigners to Pennsylvania or of African slaves to the southern colonies (though he himself owned slaves), for he wanted America to be peopled by the English. He was proud of being English, he wanted the English to prosper, and he was sure that North America was where they could prosper most rapidly. It distressed him that the English in England did not recognize where their future lay. The English in North America, he observed, simply by natural increase, "will in another Century be more than the People of *England*, and the greatest Number of *Englishmen* will be on this Side the Water. . . . We have been here but little more than 100 Years, and yet the Force of our Privateers in the late War [the War of the Austrian Succession], united, was greater, both in Men and Guns, than that of the whole *British* Navy in Queen *Elizabeth's* Time."

There is perhaps just a hint here that it might be well for an English government not to alienate a growing body of Englishmen who could already mount a naval force larger than England had been able to send against the Spanish Armada. Franklin dispatched these "Observations concerning the Increase of Mankind, Peopling of Countries, etc." privately to friends in England, and they were not published until 1754. He was not so gentle or so cautious in another admonition. In 1751 he published in his own newspaper a letter, which he appropriately signed "Americanus," directed against the British government's veto of colonial laws that forbade the importation of convicts, a veto justified on the ground that excluding convicts would interfere with the peopling of the colonies. Americanus urged the colonists to show their appreciation by shipping in exchange a regular cargo of rattlesnakes to England. There they might teach "the honest rough British Gentry . . . to *creep*, and to *insinuate*, and to *slaver*, and to *wriggle* into Place (and perhaps to *poison* such as stand in their Way) Qualities of no small Advantage to Courtiers!" Franklin was not only giving a direct rebuke to British policy makers but also taking a jibe at the corruption in the British government that reformers had been denouncing for half a century. He was reluctant to believe that things could be quite as bad as the critics made out. But, as he told his friend Peter Collinson in 1753, if the degeneration of England came to the worst, "the good among you" might take refuge in America. "O let not Britain seek to oppress us," he wrote, "but like an affectionate parent endeavour to secure freedom to her children; they may be able one day to assist her in defending her own."

In the fifteen years he spent in England after 1757 Franklin was able to observe at firsthand the narrowness of vision and the politics of place-hunting that prevented the government from facing facts or even getting close enough to recognize them. He enjoyed England and the people he met there, enjoyed them so much that he found it hard to leave them. "Of all the enviable Things England has," he wrote to a friend, "I envy it most its People." Why, he asked himself, "should that little Island, enjoy in almost every Neighbourhood, more sensible, virtuous and elegant Minds, than we can collect in ranging 100 Leagues of our vast Forests?" In every neighborhood, it seemed, but Whitehall. There Franklin encountered the complacency, the incompetence, the corruption, and the insularity that were proof against all his efforts to direct imperial policy away from self-destruction.

Franklin, serving at one time as the agent of four different colonies (Massachusetts, New Jersey, Pennsylvania, and Georgia), lobbied incessantly against the succession of measures from 1764 to 1775 that alienated Americans beyond recovery, against the Stamp Act of 1765, against the Townshend Acts of 1767, against the Tea Act of 1773, against the Coercive Acts of 1774. Although he had secured a place for his son as royal governor of New Jersey, he continually warned the government that the reports reaching England from royal governors were not reliable indicators of American opinion, that American dissidence was not the product of a few agitators but deep-seated, justified, and very English. He did not confine himself to pleading with officials. He wrote pamphlets and filled the newspapers with letters and articles in which he pointed out the folly of treating Americans as though they were not English. He wheedled, he cajoled, and he stung. In 1773, for example, he dedicated to a Secretary of State for the Colonies a brief history of the government's actions during the preceding decade. The title said it all: *Rules by Which a Great Empire May Be Reduced to a Small One.*

Franklin still believed, as he had told Lord Kames in 1760, "that the Foundations of the future Grandeur and Stability of the British Empire, lie in America." But by 1766 he was convinced that the British Parliament could not be trusted to preserve or direct the empire. The only way to preserve the empire was to acknowledge the exclusive legislative authority of each colonial government within its own borders. This was too radical a suggestion to be taken seriously in England at the time, and historians, equally limited in vision, have generally agreed. Franklin's espousal of it, before anyone in America had taken such a position, invites us to ask whether he was radical or profoundly conservative.

WHAT FRANKLIN wanted was to preserve the empire. He did not despair of doing so, but he was the only one of the future founding fathers who had dealt face-to-face with the people who ran the British government. He was also more of a pragmatist than other colonial leaders, without much interest in political ideas as such. All he asked of Britain's leaders was that they stop doing demonstrably foolish things. Despite Mirabeau's tribute to his defense of the rights of man, Franklin did not often talk the language of rights. Like Edmund Burke he thought that when people began to talk that language, it was a sure symptom of an ill-conducted government. His American friends had begun to talk it, and he knew much better than they did just how ill-conducted the British government was. He was willing to go on trying to improve its conduct, hoping against hope, counseling patience to his outraged constituents. The persistent blundering of the British ministry convinced him as early as 1771 that it would probably come to war in the end and that the Americans would probably win such a war. But, as he told the Massachusetts House of Representatives, he wanted to be sure that "whenever this catastrophe shall happen, it may appear to all mankind, that the fault has not been ours."

By the time he left England in March 1775, he was sure that nothing more could be done. His last weeks had been spent in negotiations initiated by Lord Richard Howe, a well-wisher who, like other Englishmen, continued to underestimate the seriousness of American demands and the consequences of meeting them with force. When Franklin boarded ship for Philadelphia he knew that the point of no return had passed. A little over a year later Lord Howe and his brother were in America, in command respectively of British naval and military operations for reduction of the colonies to obedience. As a last resort Howe sent Franklin another offer to pardon the colonists if they would submit. Franklin's reply displays once again his cool perception of realities, quite beyond the rhetoric of rights. War had been in progress for more than a year. The English had burned American towns, he reminded Howe, and were even now enlisting mercenaries and savages to fight against people whom they claimed as fellow subjects. It would be difficult at best for Americans to forget such injuries. "But were it possible for *us* to forget and forgive them," he told Howe, "it is not possible for *you* (I mean the British Nation) to forgive the People you have so heavily injured." No single statement of Franklin's reveals so sharply his insight into human relations. He went on to explain:

> *You can never confide in those as Fellow Subjects, and permit them to enjoy equal Freedom, to whom you know you have given such just Cause of lasting Enmity. And this must impel you, were we again under your Government, to endeavour the breaking our Spirit by the severest Tyranny, and obstructing by every means in your Power our growing Strength and Prosperity.*

For a quarter of a century Franklin had been reminding the British of growing American strength. His conservatism had kept him trying to constrain the growth within the confines of "that fine and noble China Vase the British Empire." But when British arms shattered the vase he knew it could not be put together again.

Throughout his years in England, as he became a citizen of the world, he had never ceased to be an American. He knew where his loyalties lay, as his son, the governor of New Jersey, in Franklin's view did not. William Franklin opposed the Revolution, and Franklin never forgave him. Once the point of no return had passed, Franklin devoted himself wholeheartedly to building the American empire he had originally envisaged as an extension of England. He had formulated a union of the colonies under Britain in 1754 at the Albany Congress only to see it rejected by both Britain and the several colonies. He urged it again in 1773 as a means of bringing the British to their senses. When he arrived home in May 1775 the Second Continental Congress was about to assemble, and he was immediately elected to it. The other delegates soon discovered that he was ahead of them in his thinking. "He . . . seems to think us too irresolute and backward," John Adams observed, "He thinks, that We have the Power of preserving ourselves, and that even if We should be driven to the disagreeable Necessity of assuming a total Independency, and set up a separate State, We could maintain it."

A separate state was precisely what Franklin had in mind, and he found out how far in front he was when, a year before the Declaration of Independence, he drafted articles of confederation that provided for a perpetual union among the colonies. In his plan the central congress would have had power to make ordinances "necessary to the General Welfare" that the legislative assemblies of the separate states "cannot be competent to." Without dissolving the existing colony or state governments, this would in effect have created a single sovereign American government. The other delegates, more attached than Franklin to their local governments and more reluctant than he to turn their backs on old times, would not even put his proposal to a vote.

Franklin was quite willing to wait for them to catch up. They never quite did. After finally declaring independence, when they came to discuss confederation, they could not accept the degree of centralization that Franklin advocated. He was a little too American.

By 1776 Franklin had spent fifteen of the preceding twenty years abroad. He would spend nine of his remaining years in France, winning time for Americans to build their own empire. He did not get everything he wanted for them, for he did not get Canada, which he had first attempted on a fruitless mission in 1776 to persuade the Canadians to join in the Revolution. He tried again unsuccessfully in the peace negotiations to get Britain to cede the region. Franklin always thought continentally. He wanted not only Canada but the Mississippi Valley as well. When he heard rumors in 1780 that Spain might try to exclude the United States from the Mississippi as a price for help in the Revolutionary War, he wrote to John Jay, the American envoy to Spain, that "Poor as we are, yet as I know we shall be rich, I would rather agree with them to buy at a great price the whole of their right on the Mississippi, than sell a drop of its waters. A neighbor might as well ask me to sell my street door."

When Franklin returned home for the last time in 1785, after his nine-year love affair with the French, he was still too "American" for most of his countrymen, still too continental in his thinking. Attending the Constitutional Convention of 1787, he argued for a single national legislative chamber, with representation distributed entirely according to population. The other delegates listened politely, but they had no intention of going that far in overriding the authority of the separate states. Characteristically it did not bother him. Forms of government were not a crucial matter, and he supported the Constitution without hesitation because it was the best you could get a majority to agree to.

Franklin devoted his remaining years to the abolition of slavery. It was a cause to which he had come only late in life and without the religious zeal that spurred many of its advocates, but once again he was too far ahead. The reluctance of the United States Senate to indulge in mourning for his death may have been prompted not simply by his association with France but by the fact that he had just sponsored a memorial to Congress calling for an end to slavery in the whole United States. Congress had been embarrassed.

Was Franklin too "radical" or too "conservative" for his countrymen? It is easy to make a case that he was too radical. Although he never stopped extolling industry and frugality, he had no reverence for the sanctity of private property. Everyone, he believed, had a right to the property needed to keep alive and propagate the species. "But all Property superfluous to such purpose is the Property of the Publick, who, by their Laws, have created it, and who may therefore by other Laws dispose of it, whenever the Welfare of the Publick shall demand such Disposition." When he helped draft a constitution for Pennsylvania in 1776, it provided for the most democratic government of any state then in existence, but Franklin would have made it more so with a clause to limit large holdings of property. Nor did Franklin, the friend of so many aristocrats, have much use for aristocracy. When the officers of Washington's army formed the Society of the Cincinnati after the war, with a provision for hereditary membership, Franklin mocked the idea. Hereditary honors, he said, would much better be made to ascend to parents rather than descend to children.

Nevertheless, a case can be made for Franklin as a conservative, provided we use a broader definition of conservatism than most American conservatives today would accept. Conservatism in America has been for the most part an intellectual desert. It has been too often a rear-guard, somewhat desperate and indiscriminate struggle against change, its spokesmen more stubborn than rational. For intellectual support it has had to resort to the likes of John Caldwell Calhoun with his absurd and doctrinaire formulas for preserving the status quo, whatever it might be. For more respectable philosophical foundations American conservatives have had to look abroad to Edmund Burke.

Burke was Franklin's contemporary and a kindred spirit. They had both tried to save the British Empire, and their prescriptions for saving it were much the same (stop treating the colonists as aliens). They both recognized that once broken it could not be put back together. The two shared an impatience with the doctrinaire. Franklin liked to fix things, to make them more workable, but along with Burke he shunned the urge to fix what was working (the British Empire had been working until statesmen began to fix it). Where he perhaps went a little beyond Burke was in his quickness to recognize when a political or social change was irreversible, when constructive political activity must lie in making the most of the change. Or perhaps this is only to say that Franklin was an American. When he was convinced, before most of his countrymen, that Americans were irretrievably out of the empire, he devoted himself to making the most of America. The most, as he saw it, included immediate independence and a real national government. It also included, as he saw at the end, putting a stop to slavery, for which his reasons may have been as much ethnic or racist as humanitarian.

Was he radical or conservative? Was it radical or conservative to deny the authority of Parliament over the colonies in 1766? Was it radical or conservative to want a more consolidated national government in 1787? Was it radical or conservative to oppose slavery in 1790? Can a conservative be ahead of his time?

January 31, 1991

CHAPTER SEVENTEEN

Don't Tread On Us

───∞∞∞───

A Struggle for Power: The American Revolution
Theodore Draper

THIS MASTERFUL NARRATIVE by one of our most acute political analysts can be enjoyed simply as a lucid account and explanation of the quarrel between England and its colonies that eventuated in American independence in 1776. The story has often been told before; but while Draper has few new details to add, he brings to it an instinct for the jugular and a worldly perspective that make the Revolution more intelligible in human terms than it has often appeared to be in other scholarly discussions. Draper's Revolution, as the title suggests, was first and foremost a struggle for power.

Draper is something of an expert on struggles for power, for he has dealt with several in his previous work: struggles within the left wing of the American labor movement out of which came the American Communist Party, struggles in Cuba through which Fidel Castro was able to take over the country, struggles within the staff of the National Security Council that accompanied the Iran and Contra affairs, struggles within the Allied command in World War II. In these earlier studies part of the problem was to identify the participants and the (often hidden) issues and ideas dividing them. Here the participants are obvious, and the burden of Draper's argument is to show that what divided them was not issues or ideas but mainly the desire for power. He tells the story in vivid detail, with many quotations from the participants, to show how each side viewed the other and how each grew toward a strength that threatened the other, until there was no way out but war.

Draper's insistence that this was primarily a struggle over power implies that others have found something more or less than power involved in the contest, which is indeed the case. Although Draper is too good a scholar to stray into polemics, his book can be read—and I think he intends it to be read—not merely as the gripping story that it is but also as a corrective to an intellectual interpretation of the Revolution that has prevailed among most scholars for the past thirty or forty years.

That interpretation, though with many variants, has emphasized the political and constitutional rights the colonists claimed for themselves as British subjects, rights which they thought a corrupt administration, bent on tyranny, was attempting to deny them and would ultimately deny to their countrymen in Britain as well. The premise of the interpretation has been that the colonists' objections to Parliamentary taxation were genuine and decisive, that they believed and acted on what they said and based their beliefs on a widely held, though disputed and perhaps outmoded, understanding of the British Constitution. It is admitted that they were not wholly consistent, that they objected at first only to taxation by a Parliament in which they were not represented, and then moved to denying such a Parliament any authority over them at all, before finally declaring total independence of British authority. But the emphasis of this view is on what Bernard Bailyn called, in his seminal *Ideological Origins of the American Revolution*, an emphasis on political and constitutional ideas as motivating forces.

Draper is not the first to challenge the key role of ideology in the Revolution. Neo-Marxist scholars have done their best to discount the importance of ideas expressed in pamphlets and newspapers and speeches by upper-class leaders of the Revolution and emphasized a posited discontent among the inarticulate lower class. Draper gives short shrift to this kind of challenge. He acknowledges the existence of an "anonymous mass of the poor to the middle stratum" whose support of the Revolution "generally expressed itself in destructive local violence, which suddenly flared up and just as suddenly subsided." But whatever discontent may have moved the lower classes, it was "mainly expressed against the British rather than their own elite." "In the end," he says, "the elite managed to hold on to its leadership and to direct the Revolution where it wanted it to go."

Where the leaders wanted it to go, however, is not to be found, he asserts, in what they told themselves they wanted or imagined they wanted in the years before 1776. He does not suggest that they were hypocrites, mouthing talk about rights that was mere camouflage for tax-dodging, a view commonly implied if not expressed by the so-called Progressive historians of the 1930s, like Charles Beard. Rather, he thinks that the colonists did not quite know at first what they wanted, namely the removal of all the restraints that membership in the British Empire imposed on them. It took them ten years or more to recognize that their quarrel with the British Parliament, once started, was irreconcilable. They could not have been satisfied with anything short of total independence, nor could the British have been satisfied with anything short of total subjection; because each side wanted a power that the other could not allow.

Draper gives a detailed account of the course of the political and constitutional arguments on both sides, as the colonists worked their way toward recognition of what they really wanted. He does so to show "the intellectual struggle that preceded the outbreak of hostilities." But he is convinced that "something of longer range and deeper significance [than the arguments indicated] was driving the Americans to an ever more extreme resolution of the conflict." As he sees it, the ideological interpretation makes too much of the colonists' adherence to the English Commonwealth tradition of Milton and Sidney, perpetuated by the "eighteenth-century Commonwealth-men" who mounted a vocal but unavailing opposition to the Whig oligarchy in England. Preoccupation with that tradition has led historians to emphasize constitutional issues and to neglect a longer line of English thinking about colonies that stressed the likelihood of their seeking independence as they grew in size and strength and therefore in power. Draper demonstrates with a host of quotations that the English already in the seventeenth and early eighteenth centuries had mixed feelings about their colonies. Colonies might be useful as sources of raw materials for the country that founded them and as captive markets for its manufactures; but as colonies grew, they could become competitors rather than servitors, and in the end would throw off all subordination. If colonies were not kept under strict control, Charles Davenant warned in 1698, they would be "like offensive Arms, wrested from a Nation, to be turn'd against it, as occasion shall serve." And David Hume in his *History of England* (1754–62) complained that the colonies would surely go off on their own "after draining the mother country of inhabitants." This line of reasoning was as old as colonization. Indeed, even in the sixteenth century, before England had any colonies, the chief proponent for founding them, Richard Hakluyt, conceded that they might ultimately "aspire to government of themselves" and attain it.[1]

The likelihood of such an outcome was magnified by the fact that when the English launched their colonies, they did it, as Draper observes, "on the cheap." English colonies were the product of private enterprise, authorized by the king at a time when the king was truly sovereign, but they were paid for by corporations and individuals who hoped to profit from them. Although they remained legally subject to royal control, usually through a royally appointed governor, the actual colonists were expected, both by the king and by their backers, to pay for their own government and defense, taxing themselves through their own representative legislative assemblies. The governors appointed by the king usually had to rely on those assemblies to pay all the expenses of government, even the governors' own salaries. As a result the assemblies attained a power that posed an increasing threat to imperial control.

By the opening of the eighteenth century the governors were deluging the king's ministers in England with complaints of their helplessness to carry out the instructions sent them. Draper cites the case of Robert Hunter, who after two years of fruitless struggling with the New York Assembly, wrote to his superiors in 1711 that "without a speedy and effectual remedy her Majesty can make no state of any government in this place, and in a little time the disease may prove too strong for the cure." Eleven years later, he tells us, Governor Samuel Shute reported from Massachusetts that "the people here pay little attention or no defference to any opinion or orders that I receive from the Ministry at Home." But this was the era when British policy toward the colonies was one of "salutary neglect," and Draper shows that the governors' pleas for a show of power from home went unheeded. By the middle of the century, neglect was beginning to look not so salutary. The colonies were growing in population at a rate unheard of in Europe, doubling every twenty-five years. It was apparent that in less than another century they would overtake the mother country. Predictions of ultimate independence now took on a more immediate relevance. Already the colonies comprised so large a portion of the market for English manufactures that England's economy was more dependent on them than they were on England. And as they grew, their very growth undermined their usefulness, for their original scarcity of labor no longer inhibited their engaging in manufactures competing with England's.

Draper argues that the English government failed to confront the implications of this growth until the 1760s, when the conquest of Canada from the French doubled the national debt and brought the overseas empire suddenly to national attention. If new colonies in America were worth acquiring or defending at such a price, it was time for Parliament to take a hand in the way all the colonies were governed. Parliament had long since gained a dominant position over the king in the government of England. Neither its members nor the king himself ever doubted that its supremacy extended to the colonies, though it was a supremacy hitherto exercised only in the regulation of colonial trade, with local government left to the colonial representative assemblies and the royal governors. The assemblies, exercising the same power of the purse that had driven parliamentary ascendancy over the king, had come to regard that power, within their boundaries, as their exclusive right, and they had used it to gain their own superiority over the royal governors. They did so, Draper explains, by delay-

ing or withholding funds for crucial government activities and by dol-
ing out the governors' salaries only on a year-to-year basis. Parliament
assumed too easily that it could ignore the assemblies: by levying its
own taxes directly on the colonists, it could preempt whatever power
of the purse the assemblies might have supposed they had. It could
even legislate directly for the colonies if it chose to do so. Parliament
and the colonial assemblies were thus on a collision course which
would become apparent as soon as Parliament attempted to exercise its
presumed supremacy.

When Parliament made the attempt with the program of direct
taxation that began with the Sugar Act of 1764 and the Stamp Act of
1765, it was already too late. The colonists had already grown to the
degree of strength needed to sustain a bid for independence. Draper
insists that the British understood this before the colonists did. In
resisting parliamentary measures, the colonists tried for a decade to
draw a line between their own powers and those of Parliament within
a British Empire toward which they retained an ever diminishing pride
and loyalty. The English, schooled in the expectation of an eventual
colonial independence, saw every colonial denial of total parliamentary supremacy in the light of that expectation and acted to thwart its
fulfillment for as long as possible. In effect, Draper is saying that the
British were right. The colonists may not have thought that they were
headed for independence, may have sincerely denied any such intention, but once they challenged the supremacy that Parliament would
not relinquish, they could not have stopped short of the independence
that the English knew all along they really wanted.

The story as Draper tells it is fascinating. After all, it did happen.
The Americans did go for independence in the end. They could not
find a durable line between Parliament's authority and their own that
would enable them to stay within the empire. It may have been as
much the arrogance of Parliament as colonial growth that made compromise impossible, but it did prove impossible. Without the conquest
of Canada and the new attention it brought to the colonies, the confrontation might not have come when it did. But it did come, and the

expectation of it may well have contributed to its coming when it did. The prophecies may have been irresistibly self-fulfilling.

Draper is careful not to treat the events he narrates as inevitable, but the working out of the old predictions seems to demonstrate an inescapable sequence: political power will ultimately conform to changes in economic power. Draper repeatedly cites a prediction by James Harrington that when the colonies came of age they would "wean themselves." He might appropriately have cited Harrington's main contention that economic power begets political power, that the shift in economic power in sixteenth- and seventeenth-century England from the king to the gentry had required the shift in political power from king to Parliament, a shift that also involved a struggle, and culminated in the English Civil War. Draper is offering a Harringtonian analysis, affirming that the colonists, even before they realized it, were grasping for the political power that their growth had already given them. The analysis may also remind us that ideology generally conforms to political power, even as political power conforms to economic power.

But in reducing the Revolution to nothing more than a struggle for power, Draper departs from Harrington, who he thinks "was only useful [to the Americans] to stress that when the colonies had come of age they would have a right to their own place in the sun." That assessment neglects the fact that Harrington was a commonwealth-man, indeed a republican, imprisoned by Charles II as a threat to the restored monarchy and admired by the Americans not so much for his predictions of their independence as for his proposed limitation of government by a written constitution, in order to make the executive subordinate to the legislature and to keep both subordinate to the people by frequent elections, secret ballots, and rotation in office. By contrast, Draper seems to be arguing that the struggle over posses-sion of power in the Revolution had little to do with whatever politi-cal or constitutional restrictions people may have wished to attach to it. Apart from the growth of colonial population and economic power, he says, "it would have mattered little who was right or wrong in the ideological, constitutional, and political arguments of the years after the Stamp Act."

We may agree that such arguments might have mattered little in the ultimate outcome of a struggle for power, once it came to a trial of strength on the field of battle (though that, too, is debatable). But the struggle Draper recounts took place before the trial. It was marked only occasionally by violence and was conducted largely in words, in pamphlets, newspapers, and speeches, as well as in acts of Parliament and resolutions of colonial assemblies. The verbal struggle was ideological, constitutional, and political, and it had as much to do with the legitimation and limitation of power as with its location.

The colonists may have been mistaken in thinking that they could achieve a curtailment of governmental power within the empire, but they embraced the necessity of independence only after Parliament had demonstrated that it would not be bound by its previous restraint in leaving them to make their own laws and levy their own taxes through their own representative assemblies. They believed that restraint to be a matter of right, embedded along with other rights, such as trial by jury, in the unwritten British Constitution. As British subjects they had been proud of those rights and had never doubted that they were entitled to them. They struck for independence when the British government refused to recognize their entitlement. They wanted not merely power but power defined and limited as they believed the British Constitution defined and limited it. Since the British government had been able to violate limits not expressly set down in black and white, they took pains to supply the deficiency at once in their own new constitutions, specifying not only what powers their governments should have but also what powers they did not and should not have. Without such a specification (such as Harrington had favored a century earlier) they could no longer trust anyone, themselves included, not to abuse power as Parliament had done.

In discounting the colonists' constitutional arguments (which, incidentally, many constitutional historians now regard as historically valid) Draper seems to imply that constitutions are something other than instruments for the distribution and control of power. Constitutional arguments seem to take place for him on some plane isolated from the actual use of power. "In form," he allows,

> *this debate was "constitutional." It was superficially a controversy over the jurisdiction of Parliament over America. Yet the term "constitutional" hardly conveys what was really at stake. It was whether and to what extent Parliament's power extended as far as the colonies. If Parliament did not have such power or if it was restricted to only as much power as the colonists were willing to consent to, the implication was that the colonies were declaring themselves to be de facto independent. This in any case was how the British saw it. The Americans were long loath to admit even to themselves that this was what they were aiming at.*

The extension of Parliament's power over the colonies was indeed at stake, but the question of its extension was nothing if not a constitutional one. Questions of governmental power in Anglo-American history have generally been constitutional questions, and constitutional limitations of governmental power have often come into existence after and as a result of, not to say the objective of, a struggle for power.

The distinction is not merely semantic. When the colonists maintained that they could be taxed only by their own consent given through their representatives, they believed they were affirming a constitutional limitation of government already established in the seventeenth-century struggle for power in England that they so often cited for precedents. Their outrage at England's attempt to tax them arose from their dismay at Parliament's provincial interpretation of representation to mean only what took place at Westminster, where they were said to be represented by stretching the concept to a meaningless length. (It could as plausibly be said that the whole world was represented there.) Parliament, it seemed to them, was violating the very principle on which its own authority rested.

Isolating constitutional arguments from reality makes it plausible for Draper to portray the Americans as scarcely knowing or admitting to themselves what they really wanted when they disavowed a desire for outright independence and contended that they wanted nothing more than a return to the relationship that existed before 1763. That relationship had been marked by little constitutional conflict, except as implied in the clashes between governors and assemblies. A ramshackle system, it had nevertheless worked until Parliament tried to fix it and in doing so led the colonists to define the constitutional principles that had made it satisfactory to both parties. Draper's emphasis on the British expectation of a colonial bid for independence leads him, I think, to exaggerate the colonists' flouting of imperial policy under those principles before 1763. Later royal governors were not quite as helpless as those whose letters Draper quotes at length from the early part of the century. In the two or three decades before 1763 many governors enjoyed an accretion of power that made the implementation of British colonial policy less precarious than it once seemed. If the colonists were growing in strength, so in many ways was the imperial control exercised by royal governors through traditional channels.

In Massachusetts, for example, later to be a center of revolutionary activity, the royal governor had gained not a dominating but at least a respectable power in the colonial assembly itself. As the historian John Murrin has shown, he had been able to use his prerogative of appointing justices of the peace to influence a sizable bloc of representatives and to shift a good deal of governmental power to the county courts where the justices presided. Disputes over the governor's salary came to an end after 1735, when the assembly, while declining to grant a permanent salary, agreed to make an annual grant the first business of every session. "In effect," Murrin tells us, "the governor obtained a guaranteed salary, which he had never had before, while the House agreed never again to use its most effective weapon. This settlement took constitutional questions out of politics for the next generation, guaranteed the governor's political independence, and thus inaugurated the royal era of Massachusetts history."[2] Not every colony experienced such a "royal era," but in many of the colonies that later participated in the Revolution the British were able to establish salaries for governors independent of assembly control.³ Thus, when the colonists offered a constitutional definition of the relationship that existed before 1763, they were demanding restoration of a system that had worked for England as well as for themselves and that generated neither discontent nor aspirations of independence.

Draper sees the colonists, even before 1763, as straining at the leash, impatient with the restrictions imposed by parliamentary regulation of their trade and manufactures, violating those restrictions at every opportunity. But the economic growth that made the colonies strong and ever stronger took place within the limits established by Parliament in the so-called Navigation Acts of 1660 and 1663, which required the colonies to purchase all European products *from* England and to sell their major exports *in* England. It is misleading to claim that "one of the most cherished colonial freedoms had been the freedom to smuggle," that is, to evade customs duties or to import European goods directly from foreign countries and export to them the commodities, such as sugar and tobacco, that were supposed to be sent to England. Smuggling undoubtedly existed, and smugglers do not leave the archives needed to measure their activities, but enough records of legitimate trade survive for historians to assign the prosperity of the colonies to it.

In the vain attempt to define a limit to Parliament's authority over them, colonial spokesmen left intact its authority to regulate their trade. Even when they came to the point of denying Parliament any authority at all, as they generally did by 1774, they continued, in the Continental Congress of that year, to express a willingness to submit voluntarily to such regulation. And in the Declaration of Independence, when compiling their long (and inflated) list of grievances, they were careful to exclude the Navigation Acts. Before the fighting began, it was not unrealistic for the colonists to hope that the struggle for power could be settled within the Empire. They had a greater knowledge of the way the empire had worked and a greater knowledge of themselves than Draper gives them credit for.

The Revolution was indeed a struggle for power. And Draper's account is a forceful reminder that the arguments over the limitation of power took place only because power itself was in dispute. His book restores to a central place in the Revolution the simple clash of wills that can be neglected in searches for a larger meaning. Yet there was a larger meaning. It can be found in the constitutional limitation of power that the Americans thought they had enjoyed before 1763 and affirmed as their right thereafter. They knew what they wanted from the beginning, and it was precisely what they said they wanted: not power alone but just power derived from the consent of the governed. That was the objective to which they ultimately and successfully pledged their lives, their fortunes, and their sacred honor.

March 21, 1996

CHAPTER EIGHTEEN

The Fixers

The Republic of Letters: The Correspondence Between
Thomas Jefferson and James Madison, 1776–1826
James Morton Smith, editor

THOMAS JEFFERSON and James Madison were, in the words of one historian, "the two greatest philosopher statesmen of the American Enlightenment." Who can deny it? Jefferson wrote the Declaration of Independence; Madison wrote not only the United States Constitution, or at least most of it, but also the most searching commentary on it that has ever appeared. Each of them served as president of the United States for eight years. What they had to say to each other has to command attention. And they had a lot to say. They first met while serving in the Virginia state legislature in 1776, when Madison was twenty-six and Jefferson thirty-three, and within a few years began a correspondence and collaboration that ended only with Jefferson's death on the fiftieth anniversary of his great Declaration, July 4, 1826. During that time they exchanged 1,250 letters that have been preserved, and here they are, in chronological order, from small enigmatic one-liners to lengthy discursive ruminations.

The editor, James Morton Smith, has divided them into chapters, each with an introduction furnishing the background of events and issues that prompted the exchanges. It is no accident that the introductions, taken together, form a running political history of the United States in its first half century, for the letters themselves are devoted almost entirely to politics—they include a very little about natural history, a little about books (each procured them for the other), a little about the weather, scarcely anything about art, literature, science, history, or even political philosophy. Jefferson and Madison wrote to each other about politics, the day-to-day business of running the government, whether of Virginia or the United States.

Their letters have long served as a principal source for historians studying the period. Complete scholarly editions of each man's papers have been under way for fifty-odd years; and biographies and monographs are abundant, including Dumas Malone's six volumes on Jefferson and Irving Brant's five volumes on Madison. The relationship between the two men is itself the subject of a classic study by Adrienne Koch,[1] written when most of the letters published here were available only in manuscript. What these volumes offer is a chance to explore that relationship for ourselves, to observe the operation of what is commonly called "Jeffersonian democracy," though it could as well be called Madisonian. By whatever name we call it the written exchanges of the two men suggest that it was not the monolithic product of a mutual admiration society. While the two held views similar enough to enable them to work together for fifty years, they brought to their work, as one can see in these pages, different objectives and different strategies for reaching them.

The differences are most apparent in the early years, the 1780s, when they both knew that the government of the United States needed fixing but neither had yet fastened on a satisfactory way to fix it. During much of that time (1784–89), Jefferson was in France, representing the United States and pondering the superiority of the republican governments he had known at home to the monarchies he had to deal with in Europe. Madison, meanwhile, immersed in the Virginia government and the Continental Congress, was becoming obsessed with the irresponsible capriciousness of the state governments, the impotence of Congress, and the difficulty of giving republican government the stability needed to make it last. He did succeed in getting the Virginia legislature to pass Jefferson's statute of religious freedom (for which he actually deserves more credit than Jefferson).

But his early thoughts on giving stability to the national government were uncharacteristically naive: he proposed that the faltering United States Congress send a warship or a body of troops against any state that failed to comply with its requisitions—which would have been a quick way to dissolve the union altogether.

Jefferson's way of strengthening the national government was equally unrealistic. Although he seems not to have discussed his solution in letters to Madison, he expected, as representative of the United States, to make commercial treaties with European countries. Since the Articles of Confederation gave Congress no power to regulate trade, but did give it sole power to make treaties, he would use treaties to regulate trade on a national basis. But when Jefferson tried to negotiate treaties, he found himself in a Catch-22 situation: other countries would not deal with the United States because it lacked the power Jefferson was seeking for it. Madison, of course, was finally able to solve the problem with the Constitution of 1787.

Jefferson came to accept that solution, but his first doubting reaction to it contrasts markedly with Madison's own initial misgivings. Jefferson, like many others, was dismayed by the Constitutional Convention's disregard of its instructions in creating a whole new union with a new government, instead of merely revising the Articles of Confederation. To Madison he confessed, "I am not a friend to a very energetic government. It is always oppressive." The new one promised to turn oppressive quickly, he thought, because it lacked a bill of rights, lacked rotation in office, and created a president who would transform himself into a monarch. Madison, on the other hand, had engineered the bold stroke of the Convention but was disappointed that he had been unable to get his colleagues to make the government *more* energetic. As the sessions drew to a close in September he confided to Jefferson the conviction that his Constitution, "should it be adopted will neither effectually answer its national object nor prevent the local mischiefs which every where excite disgusts against the state governments."

For Madison, the irresponsibility of the states was enough "to alarm the most steadfast friends of Republicanism," and he had tried again and again at the Convention to arm the new national government with an absolute veto on state laws. The proposal was about as realistic as his former notion of sending troops or ships against them. The Convention never came close to accepting it, and Jefferson made no bones about indicating that he too would have been against it.

The different approaches of the two men were apparent in other exchanges during this early period, not least in Jefferson's formulation of the concept that the earth belongs to the living and in Madison's reaction to it. The germ of the idea came to Jefferson when walking in the country around Fontainebleau in 1785. He told Madison how his encounter with a peasant woman "led me into a train of reflections on that unequal division of property which occasions the numberless instances of wretchedness which I had observed in this country and is to be observed all over Europe." The outcome of his reflections at this point was that "the earth is given as a common stock for man to labour and live on. If, for the encouragement of industry we allow it to be appropriated, we must take care that other employment be furnished to those excluded from the appropriation. If we do not the fundamental right to labour the earth returns to the unemployed."

By the time he returned to America, Jefferson had carried his reflections a step further. Just before leaving Paris, he wrote a long letter arguing against the unequal distribution of property imposed on the living by the dead. If the earth was a common stock for man to labor and live on, it belonged not to the dead but to the living. And from this premise he reached the conclusion that no person had the right to acquire debts that could not be paid in his own lifetime. Similarly no government could acquire debts that could not be paid within the lifetime of a majority of its members. And going still a step further, no government could make laws or constitutions that would extend beyond that lifetime. He calculated by actuarial tables that a majority of any population would expire in nineteen years. "Every constitution then, and every law, naturally expires at the end of nineteen years. If it be inforced longer, it is an act of force, and not of right." Jefferson urged Madison to apply this principle to the government of the United States, "particularly as to the power of contracting debts." Madison's response, like Jefferson's letter, was the closest thing to a discussion of political philosophy that either man presented in their correspondence. To put Jefferson's theory into practice, Madison said, would mean that no government could undertake debts for purposes that would benefit posterity, that "all the rights depending on positive laws, that is, most of the rights of property would become absolutely defunct; and the most violent struggles be generated between those interested in revising and those interested in new-modelling the former state of property." In other words, forget it.

Madison was interested in maintaining the stability of republican government, Jefferson in making that government subservient to its citizens. It was a difference of attitude and emphasis, not of contradiction, for their relations were continuously cordial, if always a little careful. Jefferson was the more impulsive, Madison his quiet control. And while Madison, as the junior partner, always phrased his differences in a deferential manner, he did not conceal them. Jefferson, knowing perhaps his own tendency to fly off half-cocked, generally acceded to Madison's advice. When he was out of office and Madison in, he did not hesitate to offer advice himself, but Madison seldom asked for it and did not feel obliged to follow it when given.

The difference of attitude, as might be expected, showed itself when the two contemplated rebellion, even rebellion against a republican government. Madison regarded Shays's Rebellion in 1786 as "distressing beyond measure to the zealous friends of the Revolution";[2] but he refrained from even mentioning its existence to Jefferson. Jefferson, who heard about it from other correspondents, wrote to Madison in another famous letter that he thought "a little rebellion now and then is a good thing, and as necessary in the political world as storms in the physical. Unsuccessful rebellions indeed generally establish the encroachments on the rights of the people which have produced them. An observation of this truth should render honest republican governors so mild in their punishment of rebellions, as not to discourage them too much." Madison's only reply was to report the measures taken by Massachusetts, including an amnesty conditioned upon the disarming and temporary disfranchisement of the rebels. A great proportion of the rebels, Madison heard, had refused the amnesty, and it was said "that they not only appear openly on public occasions but distinguish themselves by badges of their character. . . ." Moreover "this insolence" was countenanced by popular favor and election to public office. In Madison's view, it would seem, their punishment had been far too mild. It is perhaps of interest that George Washington thought disfranchisement too severe, a view that aligned Jefferson more closely with Washington than with Madison.

On the occasion of another rebellion, the so-called Whiskey Rebellion of 1794, after Jefferson had served and retired as secretary of state under Washington, Madison, sitting in Congress, sided with a much more severe Washington who called out fifteen thousand troops to put down the rebels. Madison told Jefferson that "the insurrection was universally and deservedly odious" and was concerned only to counter any attempt to associate his and Jefferson's Republican Party with it. To another correspondent he made the same observation that Jefferson had made about Shays but drew a different conclusion: "The result of the insurrection ought to be a lesson to every part of the Union against disobedience to the laws. Examples of this kind are as favorable to the enemies of Republican Government, as the experiment proves them to be dangerous to the Authors."[3] Jefferson on the other hand, from his retreat in Monticello, was outraged by the heavy-handed suppression of the rebels. He told Madison that "you are all swept away in the torrent of governmental opinions." He could not see that the supposed rebels "according to the definitions of the law, have been any thing more than riotous."

As Jeffersonian or Madisonian democracy took shape in opposition to Alexander Hamilton and the Federalists and then in the presidencies first of Jefferson and then of Madison, it continued to exhibit their differing perspectives. By 1798, when the infamous Alien and Sedition Acts were passed, forbidding, in effect, public criticism of the government or its officers, Madison could rejoice that his proposal for a national veto on state laws had never been adopted. The states now offered the only counterweight to an overenergetic national government, and he and Jefferson had to consider something like a rebellion of the states against the national government. Jefferson took the lead in getting the Kentucky legislature to pass resolutions declaring the Sedition Act to be "altogether void and of no force." Madison followed by getting similar resolutions passed in Virginia, but Madison's resolutions stopped short of inviting defiance to the act by simply declaring it to be "unconstitutional."

The distinction was more than verbal. If it came to a showdown, Jefferson leaned to the view that a state could be the final judge and nullify an act that it considered unconstitutional. Madison, still looking for national stability, thought that the final arbiter of constitutionality must be the Supreme Court of the United States. No final arbiter was required in the case of the Sedition Act, because it expired in 1800, as Jefferson took over the presidency. But the question would emerge again shortly before Jefferson's death, when Congress passed laws for building roads and canals, assuming a power that both Jefferson and Madison considered an unconstitutional usurpation of powers belonging only to the states. This time Jefferson proposed from Monticello that the question be submitted to the amending process provided by the Constitution and that meanwhile Virginia, to show attachment to the union, and at the same time assert its own sovereignty, should repass the laws as its own. Madison dissuaded his friend from placing the proposal before the legislature; and when a greater showdown came after Jefferson's death, Madison supported Andrew Jackson in his firm suppression of South Carolina's attempt to nullify a federal law.

The fifty-year collaboration of the two men is a memorial to the success of Madison's Constitution in furnishing stability to a union that would ultimately come to arms over the very differences that the two were able to contain in friendship. (They did not differ over slavery, which is scarcely mentioned here.) The correspondence, published with all the scholarly apparatus needed to make it intelligible, offers solid evidence of that friendship and of the way it operated. But it has to be said that, taken by itself, most of it gives only the faintest clues to the character of the men who wrote it. During the years when they were separated by the Atlantic and to some extent during the years after retirement when they were separated by the distance between Montpelier and Monticello, they put much of themselves into their letters. But from the time Jefferson returned to the United States in 1789 until he retired from the presidency in 1808, if the two men exchanged significant ideas, they must have done so face-to-face in their almost daily contacts. The bulk of the letters from these years, occupying nearly nine hundred pages, are the routine communications between two government officers about daily business, appointments to minor offices, meetings with subordinates, problems of protocol and precedent.

Both men were writing serious letters and state papers at this time, but not to each other. We have Madison's brief suggested revisions in wording for Jefferson's messages to Congress, but without the text of the messages, the words don't tell us much in themselves. During the political contests with Hamilton and the Federalists, Jefferson continually urged Madison, "For god's sake take up your pen . . . set apart a certain portion of every post day to write what may be proper for the public." (He never explained why he did not do it himself.) Madison often obliged with pamphlets and newspaper columns, but since they were not a part of his correspondence with Jefferson, they are not included here; and since Jefferson could read them in print, Madison felt no need to tell him what they said.

The two men faced some problems that required a good deal of thought, such as the purchase of Louisiana, which in Jefferson's own view exceeded the powers that Madison's Constitution gave to the federal government. Jefferson recorded his scruples about the purchase in letters to other friends,[4] but he and Madison (his secretary of state) evidently talked the matter out. They drafted possible amendments to the Constitution which are printed here, but they did not present them to the public and did not need to write each other about them. The only surviving trace in their correspondence is Jefferson's comment that "the less we say about constitutional difficulties respecting Louisiana the better." The lengthiest discussion of any question in their letters for these years was a ten-page report by Madison in 1804 on the momentous issue of whether the United States consul at Santo Domingo should be compensated for expenses he claimed for a mission there in 1799.

The two great philosopher statesmen, like other statesmen, had to spend much of their time dealing with trivial problems and trivial people, of which their correspondence gives painful proof. No wonder they both welcomed retirement from public office, when in their remaining years they could help each other in starting the University of Virginia as they had helped each other in starting the United States and in rescuing it from the Federalists. They must have found time for some real conversation about their philosophical differences during their years in office, but for whatever reason they put precious little of it into the correspondence now presented to us.

This will come as a disappointment to anyone who has enjoyed Jefferson's scintillating correspondence with John Adams.[5] Since Jefferson and Madison were kindred spirits, and Jefferson and Adams were not, one looked for a more revealing exchange. But Adams's mocking wit and playful manner drew more thoughtful responses from Jefferson than Madison's carefully phrased and deferential disagreements. It may be that a correspondence between two friends as intimate as Madison and Jefferson can never tell us as much about either man as we expect to find. Madison's genius lay in politics and political thought, but though he wrote to Jefferson almost solely about politics, his published writings and even his letters to other correspondents often give his political views more explicitly than he allowed himself to do with his old friend. And Jefferson, whose mind ranged far more widely, if less sharply, than Madison's, also let himself

go more freely with others. For a more balanced firsthand understanding of either man, of the relation between them, and of the kind
of democracy which bears their names, we still have to await the
complete editions of their papers, under way at Princeton and
Charlottesville.

March 2, 1995

CHAPTER NINETEEN

The Great Political Fiction

Commons Debates 1628. Vol. I: Introduction and Reference Materials.
Vol. II: March 17–April 19, 1628. Vol. III: April 21–May 27, 1628
Robert C. Johnson, editor

Letters of Delegates to Congress, 1774–1789. Vol. I:
August 1774–August 1775. Vol. II: August–December 1775
Paul H. Smith, editor

The Documentary History of the Ratification of the Constitution.
Vol. I: Constitutional Documents and Records, 1776–1787.
Vol. II: Ratification of the Constitution by States, Pennsylvania
Merrill Jensen, editor

The Documentary History of the First Federal Elections, 1788–1790. Vol. I
Merrill Jensen, editor

IN THE LATTER PART of the twentieth century a large cadre of American historians directed their research to a new kind of social history that revealed things about the past that the people who lived in it are not likely to have known about themselves, things like the mean or median age at which they married, how much longer they could expect to live at any given age, how their wealth was distributed, in what ethnic or geographic or economic patterns they cast their votes, and so on. In the midst of all this counting and computing a number of historians and archivists have been quietly carrying forward a work that contributes very little to it but that tells us more completely and more reliably than ever before what some people in the past did know, and what they thought, about themselves and the world they lived in.

The first great enterprises of this kind in our time were the new editions of the papers of the founding fathers, Jefferson, Adams, Franklin, Hamilton, Madison, and Washington, editions that include the letters a man received as well as those he wrote, so that the reader can follow the course of his thinking and his exchange of thoughts with his contemporaries. These ongoing editions have already made it possible to get inside the mind of eighteenth-century America in a way that was never before available to any but the most assiduous student.

With the publication of these volumes, we begin to get the first fruits of another kind of editorial enterprise that offers extraordinary excitement to anyone who still cares what people in the past thought about themselves and in particular what they thought about the way they were governed. These are editions, not of the papers of a particular man, but of the surviving documents that concern crucial political episodes or developments, editions that offer the reader virtually all the surviving evidence of what was said and done. Here are four of the first examples, and a splendid achievement they are.

The first of them may seem out of place in this essay. Why consider debates in the English House of Commons in 1628 along with documents on American developments in the late eighteenth century? The juxtaposition is not capricious, because the Commons during this period generated many of the ideas that were later embodied in the government of the United States. This is not the place to pursue that lengthy line of descent. Instead, merely to suggest the richness of these collections, it may be enough to draw from them a few of the fictions by which Englishmen and Americans have governed themselves from the seventeenth century to the present.

All government, of course, rests on fictions, whether we call them that or self-evident truths; and political fictions, like other fictions, require a willing suspension of disbelief on the part of those who live under them. The suspension is seldom total, and when it is the results are disastrous. For the individual, total suspension of disbelief in any fiction spells insanity, an inability to distinguish the real world from make-believe; and in politics total suspension of disbelief can lead to a *1984* scenario, with autocratic governments ruling over autistic subjects. A fiction should not be mistaken for a fact, and the mistake is sometimes easy to make, since ideally the one should be seen to approach the other. For a political fiction to be acceptable to sane men and women it must, while remaining a fiction, bear some resemblance to fact. There has to be at least a kernel of truth in it, which government must nourish by trying to make facts resemble it; and both governors and governed must join in a benign conspiracy to suspend disbelief without mistaking fiction for fact.

Englishmen and Americans have generally managed to sustain such a conspiracy, but occasionally either governors or governed have taken a fiction too literally, have taken it for fact, and in so doing have destroyed it—and sometimes destroyed themselves. Our own favorite fiction, the sovereignty of the people, the fiction that the people are masters of their governors, has lasted now for three centuries and gives no signs of giving up the ghost. But in 1628 it had not yet made its appearance in the Anglo-American world. The *Commons Debates* of that year can give us some perspective on it and on ourselves, because the Commons would have found it a laughable concept (though most of them would cry themselves into it by 1642). The favorite fiction of 1628 was, at least seemingly, quite different: it was the divine right of kings.

On the face of it this seems today so absurd a fiction that we find it difficult to believe anyone in his right mind could have suspended disbelief in it. It was particularly absurd in the persons of its principal English exponents, James I, who reigned from 1603 to 1625, and Charles I, who reigned from 1625 to 1649 (when the Commons terminated the fiction by chopping off his divine head). James, who expounded the divine right of kings at greatest length, assuring his people that he was the maker of all laws and the giver of all good things, was a slob and a bit of a crook. He drank almost to the point of alcoholism and was frequently befuddled. He stank, because he did not like to bathe. In an age of Puritanism (and the Commons was loaded with Puritans) he shocked everyone by kissing and fondling his young men in public. He lectured the members of the House, many of whom were his intellectual superiors, as though they were schoolboys, and occasionally he lied to them. His son Charles was more attractive in his person but more of a crook. He was always demanding that Parliament rely on his royal word and he lied and lied and lied. How anyone could speak of either of these two louts as God's lieutenant and keep a straight face is hard to see. The *Commons Debates* of 1628 show how it was done.

The edition includes all the surviving records, many of which have remained in manuscript until now: private diaries kept by members, notes, transcripts, and other miscellaneous documents, besides the official journal kept by the clerk. The editors have arranged them day by day, to put before the reader, in one place, all the evidence of what was said and done on a particular day. For important speeches there are usually notes taken by several different listeners and sometimes the speaker's own notes, so that the reader can put together as complete a version of the speech as is now possible. This was the session of Parliament that produced the Petition of Right (the grandfather, along with Magna Carta, of all modern bills of rights). The speeches of the men who drafted and adopted that document are worth listening to.

They all seem to have believed in the divine right of kings, but not in quite the same way that James and Charles did. The Commons did not say, "The king is God's lieutenant, therefore we must do what he wants." Instead, they said, "The king is God's lieutenant, therefore he must want what we want, because we want only what is right." The king, being all wise, all good, the acme of perfection, could do no wrong—that was part of the fiction. Therefore if his government did something wrong, it must be without his authorization. It was the business of the Commons to bring these wrongs to the king's attention and to bring the offenders to punishment by the courts or by the House of Lords or by the king himself.

Charles did not make it easy for them. If they went after one of his underlings or favorites for what they took to be a violation of the rights of subjects, Charles would declare the man to be acting on his orders. It was thus necessary for the Commons to be hard of hearing. They could not have heard the king say quite what he seemed to have said, or if he did say it, cunning counselors must have fed him false information. He certainly could not have meant to authorize anything wrong. The Commons knew what he must really want better than he knew himself, confused as he may momentarily have been by the satanic lies of those who always stood ready to confound the best of kings. The Commons would rescue him, and in 1628 he clearly needed rescuing.

He needed rescuing because the previous year he had seemingly authorized a forced loan, requiring subjects to lend him the money that the Commons had been unwilling to give him. Those who would not lend, including several leaders of the Commons, had been imprisoned; and the king's courts had refused to release them, even though the king and his ministers had declined to name charges against them after a writ of habeas corpus was served on the jailers. The Commons, acting on their heady assumption of royal rightness, apprised the king of how gravely he disapproved of these wrongs committed by his unworthy servants, and they drafted a definition of the rights of subjects to security of property and liberty of person (the Petition of Right) so that the courts could never again ignore the king's true wishes.

Sir John Eliot, fresh from imprisonment for refusing the forced loan, which he was much too astute to think was not the king's own doing, insisted that the king could have known nothing about it: "The goodness of the King," he cried, "is like the glory of the sun, not capable in itself of any obscurity or eclipse, but only by intervenient and dark clouds it may seem to be eclipsed and diminished to us. So by interposition of officers the goodness of the King may be darkened to us." And Sir Edward Coke, the greatest jurist of his day, grew rapturous: "In him is all the confidence we have under God. He is God's lieutenant. Trust him we must." But this was prelude to an argument not to trust the royal word but to insist on the king's formal approval of a written statement of rights.

It looks a little ridiculous, the Commons posing as champions of the king's honor against the king himself. But it worked, at least temporarily. Give a king a good name and then make him live up to it. Because the king badly needed the money that only the Commons could get for him (the forced loan had not been enough), they were able to make him accept the words of the Petition of Right as what he wanted; and the words went on the statute book where the courts would have to accept them too.

The Commons throughout maintained the posture of subjects. They were, they insisted, the king's subjects par excellence, the representatives, and the only representatives, of all his other subjects, sent to keep him informed of their needs and rights. This, of course, was another fiction. We know that the Commons were not, by our standards, representative, nor were they mere subjects. They were gentlemen of fortune who had elbowed their way into the House, mostly from boroughs with a small voting population. Many of the famous "rotten boroughs" (constituencies with no voters or only a handful) were rotten at the time of their creation. Even in the larger constituencies the voters were seldom offered a choice of candidates, and most elections consisted of a mere ritual shout by those who were standing about the hustings.

But the fiction was not quite so distant from reality as has usually been supposed. Recent scholarship has shown that the qualifications for voting (though not the actual voters in any given election) in English counties and boroughs in the early seventeenth century embraced from a quarter to a third of the adult male population, a larger proportion than those enfranchised by the famous Reform Act of 1832.[1] What is more significant, the Commons took the fiction of representation (and all representation is fictitious) seriously enough to try to bring the facts closer to it. The number of genuine elections, where there was a choice between candidates, increased markedly during the 1620s.

The defeated candidates in these contests usually cried foul and appealed to the Commons to upset the election. In judging the disputes the Commons favored the widest possible interpretation of the voting requirements, which differed from borough to borough accord-ing to local custom. In 1628, in the volumes before us, they went on record for a principle which could have led to universal suffrage, namely "that the election of burgesses [i.e., members of Parliament] in all boroughs did of common right belong to the commoners [i.e., the free inhabitants] and that nothing could take it from them but a pre-scription and a constant usage beyond all memory." A constant usage would be very difficult to demonstrate. The purpose of this generosity may have been to favor candidates who would side with the majority of the Commons against the king's wicked ministers, but the result was nevertheless to make the Commons more truly representative.

The fictions of 1628, however absurd they may seem today, were not beyond belief in seventeenth-century England. Yet they were not in danger of being mistaken for fact. They were workable fictions. No one, except perhaps Charles I, could really suppose that Charles I could do no wrong. And no one could really suppose that the gentlemen who assembled in St. Stephen's Chapel at Westminster had really been authorized by everyone else in the realm to act for them. By accepting the fiction as fiction and working with it, the House of Commons was able to shape reality, to make the facts resemble the fiction.

It could be argued that they did not succeed. In the next year, 1629, when they tried again to make the king do the right that God's lieutenant must always do, he dismissed them and ruled for a decade without having to be told his own mind by a crowd of country gentle-men. But he did not get away with it. By the time he called them back in 1640 (again because he needed their money) he had made the fiction of divine right unworkable by treating it as fact. Political fictions treated as fact invite disbelief by the sane and can be sustained only by incessant propaganda and vast power. Charles I did not have that kind of power, and his propaganda machine was no match for that of the gentlemen who opposed him.

A CENTURY and a half later, when the Continental Congress met at Philadelphia to protest against what the House of Commons was then doing to Americans, the divine right of kings had been replaced in England as in America by our modern fiction, which was much more nebulous and in many ways less credible than divine right. The sovereignty of the people presupposed a "state of nature," in which men, hitherto living in unaccountable isolation, formed a "social compact" with one another and then proceeded to create a government. The government they had supposedly created in England still had a hereditary king and House of Lords and an elected House of Commons, but none of these had access to divinity. All three derived their authority from the people; and in place of the fiction that the king *could* do no wrong there had developed the fiction that the people, rightly informed, *would* do no wrong, a fiction especially dear to those (including the American colonists) who cherished the revolutionary legacy of the seventeenth century.

The new fiction worked somewhat like the old one. The will of the people was no easier to ascertain than the will of God; and each of the different branches of government claimed to know what the people wanted (they would only want what was right), just as the Commons had formerly known what the king wanted better than the king did. But in this new epistemology the claim of the Commons, allegedly elected by the people, was more plausible than that of the hereditary king or the hereditary House of Lords. The Commons, no longer considering themselves mere subjects, had become the dominant element in the government, and neither of the other branches was in as good a position to withstand them as the Commons had been to withstand the king in 1628. Only the people themselves, at a general election, could effectively correct the House of Commons when it erred.

The people were now supposed to be the masters of government, not its subjects, the fiction that still guides us. Since it has lasted so long, it is evidently an easy fiction to accept, even when its divergence from fact grows wide. But the divergence may be more evident when viewed from a distance than it is to those nearby, and the government of eighteenth-century England as viewed from the American colonies increasingly exhibited traits that put severe strains on the fictions that had sustained English authority over the colonists for so long.

As the power of the Commons had grown in the eighteenth century, power derived from its supposed representative character, the fiction of that representation had become more and more tenuous. No one (at least no one in government) was trying to make the facts resemble the fiction. Burgeoning new towns and cities went unrepresented. The electorate encompassed a smaller proportion of the people in 1774 than in 1628, and the House had become even more of a gentleman's club, with no interest in opening the doors wider. In 1774 the idea of a "common right" to vote would have been laughed to scorn at Westminster. In its place the members were becoming attached to a more refined fiction, that of virtual representation. Each member, it was argued, instead of representing the people who elected him, stood for the whole country and was therefore not responsible to his immediate constituents. On this basis Parliament translated the sovereignty of the people into an authority to legislate not merely for Englishmen in England but for Englishmen everywhere, including the American colonies. Although the colonists had had no hand in choosing members of Parliament, the House of Commons nevertheless claimed to represent them and therefore to legislate for them.

Even before the fiction of virtual representation became common, Parliament had occasionally legislated for the colonies; and despite uneasiness about some of the legislation the colonists had not made strenuous objections. They thought of themselves as Englishmen, as part of the English people, and they were content to let the government by Englishmen "at home" make a few laws for them. But they had not forgotten the Petition of Right of 1628 or the other occasions on which Englishmen had made their government accept its subjects' definition of right. By 1774, as they saw it, the House of Commons had violated right in taxing them without consent, in curtailing trial by jury, in placing a standing army among them, and in reducing the popular element in one of their provincial governments. Neither the king nor the House of Lords had tried to stop the Commons (nor could have), and what was worse, neither had the English people. When the First Continental Congress assembled at Philadelphia in 1774, its members faced the problem of making the government of a sovereign people do right. And that problem in turn required them to ask whether they were a part of that people—that distant people, three thousand miles across the ocean.

The journals of the Continental Congress have long been available in print, but like the journals of most assemblies they tell us little about what the members said or how they thought about the measures they adopted. Early in this century Edmund C. Burnett conceived the idea of attempting to reconstruct the proceedings and debates by publishing the surviving letters and diaries of the members, arranged day by day, from the first meeting in 1774 until the Congress dissolved in 1789 to make way for the present United States Congress. Burnett published the results of his work in eight volumes, which ever since have guided historians in trying to understand the American Revolution.

By the time he reached the last volume Burnett had already discovered many new papers from the earlier years, and since then a great many more have turned up. As part of its contribution to the Bicentennial the Library of Congress undertook a new edition, of which the first two volumes appeared in 1976 and 1977 (the final, 26th volume in 2000). Some idea of the extent of new material may be gained from the fact that the two volumes cover in 1,254 pages the period (August 1774–December 1775) which in Burnett's edition required only 291 pages. Part of the increase is the result of printing in full letters from which Burnett extracted excerpts, but much of the material is wholly new, including the texts of some important speeches.

The most exciting reading in these new volumes, at least for one interested in political fictions, comes in the opening session, from August through October 1774. At this point the members did not yet have a war to run and could afford to spend time contemplating the large question of who they were and what they were up to. In doing so, they had to reassess some of the fictions that had grown up around popular sovereignty since 1628. Because they had already rejected Parliament's claim to represent them "virtually," they were particularly sensitive about stretching the concept of representation in any way. They did not, in fact, consider themselves as a representative assembly, because none of them had been elected by popular vote. And they rejected a plan of conciliation with England that would have given legislative authority to an intercolonial assembly chosen by the various colonial representative assemblies. Such an assembly would have been composed, they said, of "representatives of representatives," and they did not think the fiction of representation would bear that great an extension (neither, for that matter, did John Locke, who denied that a representative could delegate the powers entrusted to him).

But many of them were eager to promote a new fiction that went by the name of America. Although they displayed strong regional loyalties, they had come together in a common cause, and they began talking at once about "American liberty," "the rights of America," the "common good of America," and even "an American bill of rights." Patrick Henry in a burst of enthusiasm exclaimed, "I am not a Virginian, but an American." There was a good deal of talk about being thrown back to a state of nature, with government dissolved and the opportunity to create a new people as well as a new government. In these pages we can watch an American people in the process of creation before our eyes; we see national identity developing in the usual negative manner of dissociation from others, in this case the English.

Americans had been proud of being part of the English people, and they moved only reluctantly to repudiate the designation. Even after the fighting began, John Adams noted the "strange Oscillation between Love and Hatred" for the mother country. But with increasing frequency after Lexington and Concord we find the members of the Continental Congress denouncing the wickedness and corruption not merely of the English government but of the English people, who had failed to stop their representatives from invading American rights. Thus Samuel Ward, after tracing the origin of the English people and

the English Parliament out of a state of nature, went on to demonstrate that the American colonists, when they emigrated, had separated
themselves both from Parliament's authority and from their English
brethren. And fortunately so, for, he said, "The People of England,
formerly a sober frugal industrious and brave people, are now
immersed in Luxury Riot and Dissipation." There was an element of
self-righteousness in American nationality from the beginning.

Perhaps there had to be. Until they had convinced themselves that
they were not Englishmen, resistance to England's government would
seem to challenge the fiction on which they thought all rightful government now rested. The sovereignty of the people had often been
justified on the grounds that the people, rightly informed, would do no
wrong. For centuries Parliament had been the accepted voice of the
people. Now it had done wrong, and it was becoming ever more clear
that the people of England were not going to correct it. To be sure,
Parliament had been led astray by a corrupt ministry (as the ever right
king had been in 1628), but it began to appear that the corruption had
sunk into the English people themselves. And if a people could do
wrong, who was left to correct them?

Only, it seemed, another, better people. The only way to save the
rights that Parliament had enshrined in 1628 was for Americans to cut
loose both from Parliament and from the people who chose it.
Continued association with England might infect the Americans with
the same vices as the English, and the rights so hardly won in the seventeenth century would expire on both sides of the Atlantic. It was
thus essential for Americans to persuade themselves that they were
indeed another people, and continual denunciations of the dissolute
English were the most effective form of persuasion.

The long delay at Philadelphia before Congress could take the
final step of independence came partly from a reluctance to admit that
the English had truly become so corrupt and partly from a fear that
Americans would not accept so novel a fiction as that of their own
nationality. John Dickinson, who led the opposition to independence,
feared that there could be no American people, that independence

would result in civil war, that only the strong hand of England kept the colonists from flying at each other's throats. Even among those eager to take the risk, there was fear for the fragility of American virtue and of the union it supported, so that the members had continually to reassure themselves of their countrymen's separate righteousness. Thus, ironically, in the moment of independence the revolutionaries harbored doubts about the fiction of popular sovereignty: even if Americans could be persuaded that they were indeed a people, would they be able to assert their mastery over government any more successfully than the English had? Was their virtue any safer from ultimate corruption? What was to prevent an American government from escaping popular control as the English government had?

Beneath these questions, never quite surfacing, lay an uneasiness about popular sovereignty itself, an uneasiness about the fiction that a people, bound together in a social compact, can act apart from their elected government, that the people as masters of their governors can direct and control them. The swift tide of events after April 19, 1775, kept the doubts from rising and nourished the fiction by demonstrations of popular control over government. As the Revolution progressed, every state saw popular conventions gather to replace the colonial governments with new ones that reaffirmed and exhibited the origin of all government in the people. At the same time doubts and uneasiness about the fiction were drowned in the emerging mystical sense of identity that we call nationalism.

The war for independence proved a hothouse for the growth of national feeling, especially among those who directed it. But when the war ended, national feeling momentarily subsided, and the idea of popular sovereignty on a national scale began to appear more and more implausible. The only central government was still based on the Continental Congress, which was still composed of the representatives of representatives. It was at the local, state level that popular control of government seemed most easy to believe. And perhaps even the states were too large. A small people, it seemed to many, had a better chance of controlling their government than a large one, a view supported by

Montesquieu, the most fashionable political philosopher of the time. And indeed the idea of a people created by social compact, able to act independently of government, able to create a government or restrain it or correct it, was on the face of it far more plausible when applied to a small group, say a town or neighborhood, than when applied to a continent. In a group small enough to meet together in one place, the facts could be made to approach closely to the fiction. It was much more difficult to pretend that the people of a continent could give directions to a continental government.

Popular sovereignty thus seemed to be at odds with government on a national scale, and Americans let their Continental Congress slump into impotence. During most of the 1780s they were torn between their wish, on the one hand, to make popular sovereignty plausible, to make the facts of their political life resemble the fiction (which seemed possible only at the local, state level), and, on the other hand, their wish to retain the sense of national identity which had grown with their rejection of Englishness, and which was threatened by the decline of the national government. It was the task of the Constitutional Convention of 1787 to reconcile the two, to create a government that could embody national pride and yet sustain the fiction of popular sovereignty, a national government over which people could believe that they had control. Since we still live with the result, its terms are familiar, and for the most part we still find it possible to suspend disbelief in the notion that "we the people of the United States" control our governors. It may be, however, that our nationalism has submerged our doubts more deeply than we recognize. It is instructive to turn to three new volumes of documents covering the years from 1787 to 1789 and discover the pangs that accompanied the rituals whereby our forebears persuaded themselves to suspend *their* disbelief.

THE CONSTITUTIONAL CONVENTION had been called by the members of the Continental Congress, and the members of the Convention, chosen by the state legislatures, were similarly representatives of representatives. If a constitution framed by representatives of representatives were presented to Americans by a Congress of representatives of representatives, hostility and conflict were predictable. To sustain the fiction of popular sovereignty, the Constitution would have to be seen as an act of the people, independent of government. Hence the Convention provided for ratification of the Constitution by special, popularly elected state conventions. The proceedings and debates of these conventions, so far as they could then be collected, were first published in 1861. By the late 1970s. the first two volumes of a much more ambitious collection of documents relating to ratification, including not only the debates in the conventions but private letters and newspaper articles were published. Accompanying these was the first volume of similar documents, never before assembled, relating to the first election of representatives, senators, and the presidential electoral college. The two series go together, for the debates over ratification of the Constitution were continued in the first election contests.

Although these volumes are only the first installment in each series, they contain the full documentation for Pennsylvania, the second state to ratify and the first to hold federal elections. As it happens, Pennsylvania also had a state constitution that exceeded any other in provisions designed to give the people continuing control of their state government. As a result, the debates and discussions in Pennsylvania, both public and private, brought out most of the issues that the federal Constitution presented to Americans in its attempt to reconcile national government with popular sovereignty.

Those who thought the Convention had succeeded included those who set the highest value on a strong national government, but they seized the name of "Federalists" (suggesting decentralizing) and fastened the negative epithet "Antifederalist" on those who thought that the new national government would escape popular control. Strong supporters of the Pennsylvania state constitution were Antifederalists from the start, partly because the Federalists included the principal leaders of a Pennsylvania party that regarded the Pennsylvania state constitution as ineffective. Both in the debates over ratification and in

the first election campaigns we witness some of the paradoxical positions that the fiction of popular sovereignty has imposed on American
politics ever since. We see the most ardent former advocates of popular
sovereignty in Pennsylvania arguing for the sacred powers of the state
government, while their opponents, whom they accuse of "aristocratic
principles, aspiring ambition, and contempt of the common people,"
argue against state power and in favor of the supreme power of the people: "How comes it," demand the Federalists, "that these state governments dictate to their superiors, to the majesty of the people?"

The Antifederalists were forced by such queries to argue that
Pennsylvanians had left the state of nature and having delegated their
powers to the state government and the Continental Congress could
not simply retrieve them at will. The Federalists, though they included
men who could argue privately that popular government was "both
foolish and feeble," were able to stand forth as champions of a popular
sovereignty that remained in the people regardless of whatever powers
they might for the moment entrust to their governments. The power
of the people, they said, was "paramount to every constitution, inalien-
able in its nature, and indefinite in its extent." The people could return
to a state of nature and act apart from their government whenever they
felt like it. If they found errors in their government, they had "the
right not only to correct and amend them, but likewise totally to
change and reject its form."

Confronted with this radical populism coming from men whom
they identified as "the well-born or their servile minions," the
Antifederalists argued frenetically that the new government, even if
adopted by the people, would fall into the hands of "a lordly and prof-
ligate few" and that the people would be unable to do anything about
it. The scale was too large for the people to act apart from their government and bring it to heel. What the Antifederalists were saying, in
effect, was that they could not suspend disbelief in popular sovereignty
when it was applied on a continental scale. But they could scarcely
admit to doubts about popular authority as such. Instead, they turned
their efforts toward reaffirming the rights (with a number of additions)

that the House of Commons had extracted from God's lieutenant in 1628. They demanded a bill of rights.

Since the Antifederalists could not admit that government had any powers other than what the people gave it, the Federalists could demolish the Antifederalist arguments for a bill of rights with apostrophes to the sovereign people. Yes, said James Wilson, a true Philadelphia lawyer, a bill of rights was necessary to protect subjects against a monarch who held his throne by divine right, and so the Petition of Right had been a step toward popular liberty. But the Petition of Right was something that the king granted to his subjects. The case was quite otherwise when the people created their own government. Why, it was asked, "should the people by a bill of rights convey to *themselves* what was their own inherent and natural right?" Benjamin Rush, the learned Philadelphia physician, was beside himself at the very thought: "Would it not be absurd to frame a formal declaration that our natural rights are acquired from ourselves, and would it not be a solecism to say that they are the gift of those rulers whom we have created, and who are invested by us with every power they possess? Sir, I consider it as an honor to the late Convention that this system has not been disgraced with a bill of rights. . . ."

The Federalists could argue that the new Constitution was itself "nothing more than a bill of rights—a declaration of the people in what manner they choose to be governed." And James Wilson belabored the Antifederalists with the fact that the Pennsylvania constitution which they loved so dearly had never been submitted to popular ratification, and that the Continental Congress, for which the Antifederalists expressed a continuing allegiance, was not elected by the people, while the new national House of Representatives would be.

For anyone who accepted the fiction of popular sovereignty these were compelling arguments, and they served to get the Constitution adopted without amendment. But the Antifederalists had a point, and they knew it. The point was that popular government must in the end be a fiction, and to take the fiction literally is dangerous. Although the new government was to be ostensibly the creature of the people, it would be safest for the people to provide their creature with a muzzle in the form of a bill of rights. Because of continuing pressure from Antifederalists the first Congress under the Constitution took the necessary steps to add a bill of rights in the first ten amendments. James Madison, who drafted them, initially considered them to be inconsistent with popular sovereignty. And so, in a sense, they were and are. Indeed they have generally operated at the insistence of that branch of government whose members are appointed for life.

But consistency in the application of fictions can lead to political schizophrenia. The sovereignty of the people, taken literally, can generate a more autocratic government than the divine right of kings did. The power of a James I or Charles I never approached that of modern despots who rule in the name of the people. Our own government purports to be of the people, by the people, and for the people, but all governments are of the people, all governments purport to be for the people, and no government is in fact by the people. In early Massachusetts the Reverend John Cotton, fresh from the England of Charles I, rejected democracy as a poor excuse for government, for, he asked, "if the people be governors, who shall be governed?" Today we dismiss the question as sophistry, coming from a man who had never witnessed the benefits of popular sovereignty. But even as we strive to bring the fiction of government by the people closer to reality, even as we strive to shape fact by fiction, we should perhaps admit with John Cotton, in some private recess of the mind, that governors and governed can never be the same. It is safe to suspend our disbelief up to a point, but when we suspend it altogether we are ripe for tyranny. The Antifederalists did have a point. The sovereignty of the people is a fiction.

March 9, 1978

CHAPTER TWENTY

Power to the People?

—◆◇◆—

The Debate on the Constitution: Federalist and Antifederalist Speeches,
Articles, and Letters During the Struggle Over Ratification
Bernard Bailyn

IN 1787 many Americans were convinced that the "perpetual union" they had created in winning independence was collapsing. Six years earlier in the Articles of Confederation the thirteen state governments had surrendered extensive powers to a congress of delegates from each state legislature. Six years had proved the powers surrendered to be not enough. With no power to tax or to enforce its decrees, the Congress had been helpless to restore the credit of a nation heavily indebted to foreign powers, helpless to halt runaway inflation, helpless to prevent trade wars among the states. The famous Convention of 1787 met in Philadelphia to define the additional powers needed to enable Congress to do its job effectively. Instead, the convention proposed a brand-new national government. In the year that followed publication of its proposals in September, Americans had to decide, state by state, whether to abandon the old Articles of Confederation for this new Constitution, which was to go into operation when and if nine of the thirteen states approved it. Within a year ten states had done so.

That year was marked by fierce debate, in public assemblies, in the press, in private letters, and most importantly in the popularly elected state conventions through which, by the terms of the Constitution, official approval or disapproval was to be reached. Having lived through a revolution, the men and women who engaged in this contest brought to it more experience in making and breaking governments than any previous or subsequent generation of Americans. Their arguments, dissecting the terms of the document that still defines our government, are still worth listening to. In these volumes Bernard Bailyn has given us a sample of what they had to say, 1,862 pages of it (limited to the period from September 1787 to August 1788), along with 525 more pages of related documents, helpful notes explaining obscure references and allusions, an extensive chronology of related political events from 1774 to 1804, and brief but detailed biographies of the participants.

To serious students of the period, few of the texts will be new. Three hundred eighty-eight pages are devoted to selections from the well-known *Federalist Papers* by Madison and Hamilton (the few by John Jay are omitted). Most of the pieces opposing the Constitution have been reprinted relatively recently in the seven volumes of Herbert Storing's *The Complete Antifederalist*.[1] And the whole collection is heavily indebted (as the editor generously acknowledges) to the volumes that have appeared in the ongoing *Documentary History of the Ratification of the Constitution*, published by the State Historical Society of Wisconsin.

That the Library of America thought it worthwhile to bring out this collection, evidently intended for the general public, shows the continuing vitality of the subject. Although it seems unlikely that many readers will persevere through the whole 2,387 pages, anyone who goes very far in them will indeed encounter a discussion in which assessment of the Constitution reaches to fundamental questions of how any government obtains or deserves the consent of the governed.

The immediate purpose of each article or essay when first published was not so cosmic; it was simply to persuade its readers to accept or reject the Constitution. In general those who were for it (Federalists) maintained that the nation's very existence was so threatened by the impotence of the existing Congress that any delay in setting up a true national government would spell anarchy, disunion, and disaster. Those who were against adoption (Antifederalists), while acknowledging the need to give Congress more power, argued that the national government proposed in the Constitution would substitute tyranny for mere disorder and inconvenience. The terms of the debate were dictated largely by the Antifederalists, who included such prominent revolutionaries as Samuel Adams of Massachusetts and Patrick Henry of Virginia. They could fix on particular provisions of the Constitution and project dire consequences from each of them: the federal judiciary would preempt the functions of the state judiciaries and abolish trial by jury, the new government's taxes would swallow up the country's whole resources and eventually eliminate the state governments, the presidency would turn into a lifetime office and the senate into a hereditary aristocracy. Federalists, in response, had to justify provisions that some of them would privately have preferred to alter. They could not acknowledge any defects for fear of opening the whole document to revisions that would cripple the national government they hoped to establish.

What nevertheless elevated the debate was the agreement of both sides on principles of government that they had all become familiar with in the preceding years of revolution and constitution making. They all agreed that the only kind of government for Americans, the only kind Americans would accept, was republican. And in republican government, they agreed, all power derived from the people. Ideally and originally the people exercised power themselves in assemblies attended by the whole population. But such direct democracies were a thing of the past, not feasible in any republic embracing more than a small territory and unthinkable in a country as large as the United States or even in its smallest states. In a republic of any size the people must delegate their power or a part of it to a few of their number to exercise for them. The great problem of republican government was to devise ways to keep those few honest, to prevent them from betraying the trust reposed in them. No constitutional device could offer complete protection against the ingenuity of human corruption; what a constitution had to do was make betrayal as difficult as possible.

This much Federalists and Antifederalists agreed on, and their debate over the Constitution was in large measure a debate over whether specific provisions made betrayal likely or unlikely. As they argue the case in these pages, it becomes apparent that while they agreed on basic principles, they differed not merely on whether the Constitution adequately embodied those principles or offered adequate protection for them: they differed in their understanding of the principles themselves, their understanding of what precisely they thought happened or ought to happen in the creation and operation of republican governments.

They had all seen such governments created in the several states after the Declaration of Independence in 1776. In a sense they could all feel that they had shared in the creation. Indeed republican theory required that they and all other Americans feel it. But in fact the state governments had been created, not by assemblies of the people but by assemblies of their representatives, and those assemblies had been chosen by no more than the 20 percent of the population who were adult white males. It required a certain stretch of the imagination for most people to feel that they had participated in transferring the power of the people to the few who governed.

The Antifederalists were less willing to make the stretch than the Federalists and consequently more reluctant to see any government as their own creature. For Antifederalists government remained always something other. They accepted the unfeasibility of direct democracy, but they regretted its unfeasibility and wanted government to resemble it as closely as possible by making the few who governed resemble in every way the many they governed. Hence frequent elections (more frequent than the proposed Constitution provided) and rotation in office (not provided at all in the Constitution) were favorite Antifederalist devices for improving the document. Not the expertise gained from experience in office, but the common humanity gained from experience out of office was what qualified a person to govern. The most trustworthy part of the government was a large, annually elected legislative assembly, designed to sit briefly and then return its members to their farms and workshops. Most of the existing state governments, in which the legislatures dominated, fitted the picture, and the new national government provided by the Constitution did not. In a sense the Antifederalists could be said to put a premium on mediocrity. They did not want to be governed by people who were smarter or richer, better spoken or better bred than their neighbors.

The Federalists, on the other hand, had no trouble in seeing the government they proposed as the creature of the people, however remote it might be from any direct action of actual people. They were quite happy with the fact, only grudgingly allowed by Antifederalists, that the only way the people could create or participate in government was through representatives. For the people to act directly in government was as undesirable as it was unfeasible, for as one Federalist put it, "the people themselves are totally unfit for the exercise of *any* of the powers of Government." Alexander Hamilton thought that, contrary to the standard view, "the ancient democracies, in which the people themselves deliberated, never possessed one feature of good government." Another Federalist, Fisher Ames of Massachusetts, contended that the only thing the people by themselves could do about government was to destroy it.

The great advantage of representative government over direct democracy, in the Federalist view, was that it enabled the people to delegate power to persons as unlike most of themselves as possible, to persons distinguished by their abilities and talents, by the very talents that would lead voters to favor them. Hereditary aristocracy, agreed, was a bad thing, but among every people there were "natural aristocrats," people with greater virtue, greater talent, and, perhaps incidentally, greater wealth than their neighbors. It was they to whom the people should trust their government, for they would know what the people wanted better than the people themselves could. They would be too astute, James Madison argued, to be "misled by the artful misrepresentations of interested men," they would not be overcome by "irregular passion," and they would resist misguided popular pressure "until reason, justice and truth, can regain their authority over the public mind."

When the Constitutional Convention sought popular endorse-
ment of the Constitution, in order to rest it more directly on the people than mere approval of the state legislatures would have provided,
they did not submit it to a popular referendum. They specified that it
be judged by popularly elected conventions, where a small number of
delegates of the people could decide for them. The wisdom of this
move became apparent when Rhode Island, which was dominated by
Antifederalists, refused to choose such a convention and submitted the
question to a direct popular vote. The result, though skewed by a
Federalist boycott of the election, was an overwhelming defeat of the
Constitution, 2,711 to 239. At Providence the Federalists in a town
meeting denied that this or any such referendum could be a valid
expression of popular will, precisely because it was not the act of a representative convention. Without the opportunity to meet together and
exchange views, no one could decide what was good for the whole
state. Since it was physically impossible for the people of the whole
state to assemble, they could express their true will only by electing
delegates from each town to a statewide convention, just as the
Constitution itself prescribed.

In no other state did the Antifederalists go to the extreme of trying
to place decisions on public policy directly in the hands of the people.
But in attacking the Constitution, Antifederalists everywhere focused
discussion on the remoteness from the people of the representation it
would create. According to the Constitution, there was to be no more
than one representative in Congress for every thirty thousand people in
a state. In the first Congress, the total number of representatives would
be only sixty-five, fewer for the entire United States than the number of
most state legislatures. (In 1787, only Delaware and New Jersey had
legislatures with fewer than sixty-five members.) Federalists thought
this number quite adequate. The larger the constituency (and thus the
fewer representatives), the more likely it was to contain a good number
of natural aristocrats for the voters to choose from. In large constituencies it would be, as James Madison put it "more difficult for unworthy
candidates to practise with success the vicious arts, by which elections

are too often carried; and the suffrages of the people being more free, will be more likely to centre on men who possess the most attractive merit, and the most diffusive and established characters."

Antifederalists could agree that large constituencies would very likely produce a Congress full of such men of established character. But that kind of Congress, in their view, would not be truly representative. In the New York ratifying convention Melancton Smith, though himself a merchant and lawyer of established character, explained the Antifederalist case most persuasively. Smith readily agreed that every society produces natural aristocrats, but he thought that "We ought to guard against the government being placed in the hands of this class—They cannot have that sympathy with their constituents which is necessary to connect them closely to their interest." A representative assembly, Smith said, should resemble the people represented. It should accordingly contain a few natural aristocrats, but a much larger number of ordinary "yeomen." As constituted, the number of representatives in Congress was to be so few that the office "will be highly elevated and distinguished" and one to which "sensible, substantial men, who have been used to walk in the plain and frugal paths of life" would not aspire. As a result, "none but the great will be chosen."

A representative, the Antifederalists argued, was supposed to bring the needs and wishes of his neighborhood to the government, the needs and wishes of people he knew and who knew him, and thirty thousand people could not be a neighborhood. It followed that republican government was as unfeasible in large territories as direct democracy. To represent properly the people of a country as large as the United States would require an assembly too large to work together as a deliberative body. The only way to extend republican government over so large a territory was by a series of republics (as the great Montesquieu had contended), which might be joined in the kind of alliance already provided by the Articles of Confederation.

The alliance could be made stronger than it was (as the Convention had been charged to do), but any government operating over the whole territory, such as the Constitution called for, though it might be republican in name, would be or become an oligarchy or dictatorship in fact. Its members, whether congressmen, senators, or president, would be unknown except by reputation to most of the people. They would be unable to win the trust that people gave willingly to friends and neighbors. Hence they would have to resort to force, and the fact that the Constitution allowed for a standing army seemed to be an acknowledgment of such an expectation on the part of the Constitution's authors. A columnist who signed himself "Brutus" put the Antifederalist argument soberly and effectively in a series of articles in the *New York Journal*:

> *The confidence which the people have in their rulers, in a free republic, arises from their knowing them . . . but in a republic of the extent of this continent [Americans already considered the continent theirs], the people in general would be acquainted with very few of their rulers. . . . The consequence will be, they will have no confidence in their legislature, suspect them of ambitious views, be jealous of every measure they adopt, and will not support the laws they pass. Hence the government will be nerveless and inefficient, and no way will be left to render it otherwise, but by establishing an armed force to execute the laws at the point of the bayonet.*

The Federalists, of course, could point out that by Antifederalist standards most of the existing states were also too large for republican government. But beneath the division between Federalists and Antifederalists lay a conflict within representative government, within the very concept of representation itself that can never be resolved, and continues to trouble the days and nights of anyone who serves as a representative, whether in a large republic or a small. The cry of "no taxation without representation" was still ringing in the ears of Americans in 1787. And the kind of representation intended by that slogan was the kind the Antifederalists intended. When the colonists had complained against taxation by Parliament, they had not asked for representation in that body, because they did not think such a representation was feasible: an effective representation of Americans would have added too many members to a Parliament that was already about as large as a deliberative body could be. Moreover, any representative sent overseas would lose touch with his constituents, cease to be truly one of them, and thus be unable to convey their wishes. A representative was supposed to be the agent of the people he represented. Only in the local colonial assemblies could such representation be found.

What no one wanted to say in contending against British taxation was that the representatives in colonial assemblies, like those in the British House of Commons, had always been much more than the agents of the people who elected them. Representative assemblies, despite the authority of royal governors, were the most powerful part of colonial governments, and after 1776 they were the dominant part of the new state governments. As such they had to make laws that served the interests and compelled the obedience of the whole population of a state. In doing so they might have to support measures that their particular constituents opposed. Indeed, as Robert Livingston reminded the New York convention, "There are a thousand things which an honest man might be obliged to do, from a conviction that it would be for the general good, which would give great dissatisfaction to his constituents." The validity of a representative's vote in a legislative assembly has never depended on the approval of his constituents. While serving as their agent, he also has to act independently of them as one of the sovereign rulers of a sovereign state. The two functions may often happily coincide, but conflict between them is inherent in representative government. If the representative loses his ties to his constituents, the government ceases to be representative; if he and his colleagues lose their responsibility to the whole state, the government itself ceases. Somehow the conflict has to be contained.

In the debate over the Constitution, the Antifederalists argued, in effect, that the scale of representation in a national government would obliterate local attachments and thus make the government unrepresentative and unrepublican. The Federalists in response argued that the state governments provided enough of that kind of representation and that the national government would benefit by the appropriately larger vision of representatives from larger districts. In the Federalist view the state governments had in fact been so dominated by the local attachments of the members that they had ceased to offer responsible government. Rhode Island was the favorite example, where legal-tender laws had sent debtors in pursuit of creditors to pay off debts in worthless scrip. The national government was needed, not only to preserve the union but to check the irresponsibility of the state governments.

In any immediate sense the Federalists won the debate: they persuaded the state ratifying conventions, though sometimes by narrow margins, to establish a national government in which representation was different in kind from anything Americans had ever known in their colonial or state governments. The new national government happily disappointed the Antifederalist predictions. However remote from their constituents the members might be, they did not have to rely on a standing army to enforce the laws they made. The confidence and trust of the people themselves that the Antifederalists had thought it impossible to extend beyond the familiarity of a neighborhood easily overleapt such bounds.

But while Federalists got the national government they wanted, its character exhibited less of the large, national vision, less of the freedom from local attachments that they had hoped for, and by the same token less of the remoteness from actual people that the Antifederalists had feared. The talents required for election to the national government proved to be not so very different from those required for success in a neighborhood. Even the "talents for low intrigue and the little arts of popularity" which Hamilton thought would prevail only in state contests have proved pretty effective on a national scale, whether in presidential or congressional elections. And the Antifederalist yearning for direct democracy has continued to surface in proposals for national referendums, rotation in office, and interactive televised "town meetings." It generates demands for limiting the discretion of officeholders by constitutional amendments to require balanced budgets or mandatory sentencing. It even threatens the stability of the national government in public opinion polls, lending power to that momentary "irregular passion" of the public mind that Madison hoped to overcome by the sober thoughtfulness of natural aristocrats.

The debate over the Constitution retains its vitality because the Antifederalists spoke for a populist element that makes representative government representative, while the Federalists spoke for a national interest that can require defiance of popular pressures. Republican government cannot survive the loss of either element. The representative who loses touch with his constituents loses office, but the representative who sacrifices the national interest to local prejudice or to the changing winds of popular opinion betrays all of the people for some of the people. Anyone walking this tightrope will find an uncomfortable familiarity in the arguments on both sides of the debate over the Constitution. The Federalists won, but the issues persist.

December 2, 1993

CHAPTER TWENTY-ONE

The Second American Revolution

———— ✳ ————

The Radicalism of the American Revolution
Gordon S. Wood

T HE AMERICAN REVOLUTION has always posed a challenge
to historians. Revolutions are supposed to be risings of the
masses against the tyranny of their masters. Even if the end result is
the new tyranny of a Cromwell, a Bonaparte, or a Stalin, a revolution
scarcely seems to deserve the name without the overthrow of an
oppressive ruling class by some kind of underclass. The first
American historians easily rose to the challenge by identifying the
British and especially George III as tyrants and the Americans as
oppressed. But the academic professionals who took up the subject at
the beginning of the twentieth century, priding themselves on a scientific objectivity, had difficulty finding enough evidence of British
oppression to explain the extent of American resistance. Instead,
under the influence, direct or indirect, of Marxist analysis, they went
looking for a local ruling class against whom a local working class
could have risen. Carl Becker, in an enduring epigram, described the
Revolution, in New York at least, as a contest not merely about home
rule but about who should rule at home, with an emphasis on the latter. Following Becker, a succession of historians throughout the 1920s
and 1930s translated every division among Americans (of which there
were many) into neo-Marxist terms of class struggle. The outcries of
colonial leaders against British oppression became mere window

dressing to cover the self-interest of a local ruling class, determined to resist interference by their betters in Britain or their inferiors at home. The resistance was successful in both cases, and the Revolution ended in Thermidorean reaction with the adoption of the federal Constitution of 1787.

After World War II a new generation of historians took a closer look at the supposed struggle over who should rule at home. Working in what an older critic called "the flush times of mid-twentieth-century capitalism," they were perhaps less sensitive than their predecessors to internal conflicts among the revolutionary Americans and so earned, unwittingly, the title of "consensus" historians.[1] The Revolution they described was one in which the Americans' resistance to Britain submerged and overwhelmed any lesser contests among themselves, but the quarrel with Britain was less about who should govern than it was about the limits of government itself. The distinguishing feature of the new historians was not really their assumption of consensus among Americans but their insistence on taking seriously what the colonial leaders said they were fighting about. If one supposed that people might have meant what they said, the many manifestoes and declarations of the revolutionists ceased to be window dressing and opened the way to a new understanding of what the Revolution was about and what it achieved.

What it achieved, in this view, apart from the independence of the colonies, was an enunciation of the principles that were supposed to guide and limit government, principles that rested the right to govern on the consent of the governed, principles that they thought the British had betrayed, thereby forfeiting the right to govern. Admittedly the British government had not engaged in any serious actual oppression of the colonies before 1774, but it had claimed powers not granted by the governed, powers that made oppression possible, powers that it began to exercise in 1774 in response to colonial denial of them. The Revolution came about not to overthrow tyranny, but to prevent it. In this reorientation of historical thinking, it was Gordon Wood's distinction in *The Creation of the American Republic*,

1776–1787 to show how the political ideas of the Americans developed in the decade after they declared independence, how they felt their way through the implications of their commitment to a popular origin and popular limitation of government.

Wood's *Creation*, published in 1969, has guided most subsequent study of that decade. But academic Marxism dies hard. Historians from the New Left, such as Staughton Lynd, Jesse Lemisch, Alfred Young, and Edward Countryman, with a good deal more sophistication than those of the Old Left, have uncovered abundant evidence of grassroots activities by mechanics and farmers that went beyond their leaders' denial of British authority and translated the popular origin and limitation of government into popular exercise of governmental powers. The implication of the New Left argument has been to discount again the Whig assertion of principle and to attribute popular activism to spontaneous resentment of upper-class rule. But such resentment, it must still be admitted, never reached revolutionary proportions and was easily brought under control, as the folks who had always ruled at home directed popular energies into the fight for independence.

Historical understanding of the American Revolution has thus been for some time a bit short of explaining why it deserves to be called a revolution. If it was simply a shrugging off of a novel British attempt to govern without consent of the governed, it looks more like a preservation of the status quo than a revolution. If it was in any way a struggle by the dispossessed over who should rule at home, the struggle was unsuccessful. And yet somehow we know that it *was* a revolution, that it changed things so radically that we *have* to call it a revolution. Enter, once more, Gordon Wood. In a book that has long needed to be written, free from anachronistic neo-Marxian or pseudo-Marxian formulas for understanding historical change, he gives us a revolution we can easily recognize as ours and shows us why it deserves the name.

The revolution Wood describes is a revolution in human relations, a revolution from social order to social anarchy, from hierarchy to equality, from a world where people knew their place to a world where they made their place. It was not a revolution that the revolutionists of 1776 had sought or envisaged or could approve: like other revolutions, it left its originators behind. In his earlier book Wood had already emphasized the dynamics of revolutionary thinking, how in the excitement of their new independence Americans expanded their understanding of what it meant to put the governed in control of their government, how they made every branch of government responsible to the people who chose it. In *The Radicalism of the American Revolution*, Wood reaches beyond politics and political thinking to examine the sweeping social changes that made the Revolution, in his view, "the most radical and most far-reaching event in American history." In a tour de force of historical revision, he trumps the New Left's unsuccessful effort to revolutionize the Revolution by making it far more revolutionary than they had ever claimed.

This takes some doing. To make his argument, Wood is carried into generalizations that invite dispute. His revolution begins well before 1776 and lasts into the first decades of the nineteenth century. He is constrained to allow that the changes he describes might have taken place without the American separation from Britain, but he rightly contends that that was not what happened, that they took place in the Revolution and as part of it.

The story begins with a picture of American colonial society as it was in the eighteenth century before the quarrel with England began, a society Wood characterizes as "monarchical." The characterization is more apt than it would have seemed a few years ago, for recent historians have discovered a multitude of ways in which colonial society, in the half century or more before the Revolution, was growing not more distinctively American and not more democratic, but more like English society. The power of royal governors was increasing; big merchants and planters were aping the English aristocracy, great families were intermarrying; lawyers were paying more attention to English law; social distinctions were hardening. To be sure, by English standards it was a truncated society: the most aristocratic colonists would have ranked as no better than middling gentry in England. But

social relations nevertheless fell into the vertical patterns of a monarchical society. Every community had its big men, to whom others
deferred, and on whom others depended for favors, for credit, for
work, sometimes even for the land on which they lived.

Dependency of this kind generated little class consciousness, but
rather a kind of loyalty on the part of small folk to those who had the
resources to help them. For example, when it was necessary to recruit
volunteers to serve in armed forces against the French and Indians,
officers' commissions had to be assigned to men, regardless of military
experience, who could command the loyalties of people in their neighborhood. Men would enlist only at the behest of those they knew and
respected as their social superiors. The same kind of allegiance prevailed in politics. Although colonial governments were dominated by
their popularly elected representative legislatures, and though the
majority of free white males could vote, they generally voted for their
betters. And with reason: a big man could do more for you in government than some small fry like yourself. Indeed, Wood argues, the
small-scale, face-to-face character of colonial communities could make
local dependencies even more significant than they were in the more
impersonally stratified society of England.

After ringing the changes on these vertical human relationships in
colonial society, Wood turns to the rise, both before and during the
Revolution, of republicanism. Here the eighteenth-century assimilation of the colonists to English culture remains pertinent, for an influential group of English thinkers and writers had long identified English
government as republican in all but name. The elevation of Parliament
to the supreme position in government distinguished England from
continental monarchies and likened it in the eyes of many to republican
Rome. In this idealized view of English society, the highest aspiration
of government and of those engaged in government must be the disinterested pursuit of the public good. And the greatest danger must
spring from the corruption of that aspiration by any kind of dependency in the governing class. Only persons of large means, the kind of
persons on whom others might depend, could afford the independence

and exhibit the public spirit needed to fulfill the aspiration.

Americans were not the first to suggest that the English government had succumbed to corruption, that its Parliament was filled not with great men of public spirit but with the minions of great men, not least of whom were the ministers of the king. A host of the so-called "eighteenth-century commonwealthmen" had been crying corruption for half a century before the Parliament they accused began its quarrel with the colonies. With the commencement of that quarrel, Americans discovered themselves to be better republicans than the English and their society better designed to sustain republican virtue. The web of dependencies that had governed social relations in America, Wood now shows, was far more fragile than its English model and becoming increasingly vulnerable as the Revolution approached. The exponential expansion of population, both from immigration and from a natural increase unprecedented in the Western world, threatened the stability of the hierarchy in local communities everywhere. Paternalism and loyalty lost their meaning in a society where everyone seemed to be on the move. Credit and debt were ceasing to be transactions between patrons and clients and becoming impersonal contracts between supposed equals. And the supposition of equality was less fictional in America's truncated society than it could be in England. Americans were on the move socially as well as geographically. It was much easier in America to move up the social and economic scale but also easier to fall down it. As a result Americans met one another on much more nearly equal terms socially and economically than the English.

In this volatile environment the republican ideas learned from England took on new meaning. Republicanism enshrined the personal independence on which public virtue rested; and despite the continuing though diminishing respect for rank, the vast majority, at least of white male Americans, enjoyed a greater degree of personal independence than the vast majority of Englishmen. In England landed property was the hallmark of that independence and the landed gentry the only visible repository of republican virtue; but most free Americans owned the land they worked and thus offered a much broader base for republicanism than England or any other country of the time could afford. As the quarrel with England progressed and the parliamentary assault on American liberties gave the lie to any English claim to republican virtue, Americans saw themselves as the true embodiment of that virtue. The local dependencies that had tied the members of a community together suddenly became suspect, and, in Wood's words, "the Revolution became a full-scale assault on dependency," loosening all social bonds that had characterized the earlier monarchical society.

Republican virtue in the new vision of Americans was to be the ideal, not simply of a governing class, but of a whole people. It was to be the new cement of society, the glue that held together people untrammeled by paternal obligations on the one hand or groveling gratitude on the other. The gentility and civility formerly conferred by birth must be spread to all through education available to all. People liberally educated would treat one another liberally, the selfishness that drove monarchical society would vanish before the liberated natural affection of human beings for one another. Even slavery, recognized as a contradiction and an evil stain, would eventually give way. It might take time for republican education to erase monarchical habits, but, again in Wood's words, "The natural feelings of love and benevolence between people could become republican substitutes for the artificial monarchical connectives of family, patronage, and dependency and the arrogance, mortification and fear that they had bred."

Such was the republican vision, reflected and embodied in the men who led the Revolution, men like Washington, Jefferson, and Adams. It held for long enough to break the hold of monarchical dependencies, to create republican governments in all the states, to foster equality in laws and constitutions that forbade hereditary aristocracy. But the social virtues that were supposed to grow from this foundation proved elusive. What made the Revolution truly revolutionary was not simply the dissolution of monarchical dependencies but the emergence of a kind of equality that republican leaders had never envisaged, an equality that validated selfishness rather than selflessness, an equality that mocked gentility instead of nurturing it.

The republican leaders had never thought of their Revolution as democratic. All men were created equal, but some always developed more virtue than others, some always had more talent than others; and a virtuous populace would place such natural aristocrats in charge of whatever government a virtuous society might need. Republican leaders were thus dismayed when the legislatures of the new republics filled up with men who showed no signs of gentility or of the social benevolence that was supposed to go with it, but rather a short-sighted pursuit of local interests.

Through the federal Constitution of 1787 faithful republicans hoped to outflank this heedless democracy of the states. But, as Wood sees it, they were too late. The leaven of equality, divorced from its republican association with public virtue, overwhelmed the idealists. The new cement of American society was not to be benevolent affections but an accepted pursuit of private interests competing in an open market for whatever rewards society or its government might offer. The qualification for public office, whether in the new national government or in the separate states, was not a disinterested commitment to a general public welfare, but a demonstrated commitment to the special private interests of a particular group of voters. The freedom won in the Revolution was a freedom to pursue one's own happiness, and happiness for most people lay in making as much money as possible as fast as possible. Working to make it became almost an end in itself, class differences submerged in the general competition for the bounty of the continent.

Wealth, Wood acknowledges, became more unequally distributed in post-Revolutionary America than it had been before, but the substitution of the cash nexus for older social ties, whether of patronage or the wished-for benevolence, made for a society where social distinctions all but disappeared. Servants became "help" and sat at table with their masters, whom they refused to call by any such name. Where gentlemen once prided themselves on superior education, superior manners, and freedom from the cares of labor, now it seemed to visitors from abroad that every white male in America thought himself a gentleman. And by the same token anyone who did not work for a living was suspect. Leisure was just another word for idleness. If a leisured aristocracy existed, it counted at best as only one among the multitude of private interests that made up the new society and deserved no more respect than the interest, say, of carpenters or blacksmiths. The ultimate source of property was labor, and labor accordingly had the highest claim to respect in a society where everyone was out to acquire as much property as possible. That some acquired much more than others may today seem the crucial fact of the time, but this, Wood argues, is anachronistic. What he wants us to see is that to understand the Revolution we have to get beyond the preoccupation with distribution of wealth that guides so much modern social analysis. Instead, we have to concentrate on the way people understood themselves and their society at the time. The widespread ownership of property had enabled them to think of themselves as republican, but the Revolution carried them beyond republicanism and republican virtue to a belief in equality that transcended every economic and social boundary. "Indeed," he writes in one of his most arresting passages,

> if equality had meant only equality of opportunity or a rough equality of property-holding, it could never have become, as it has, the single most powerful and radical ideological force in all of American history. Equality became so potent for Americans because it came to mean that everyone was really the same as everyone else, not just at birth, not in talent or property or wealth, and not just in some transcendental religious sense of the equality of souls. Ordinary Americans came to believe that no one in a basic down-to-earth and day-in-and-day-out manner was really better than anyone else. That was equality as no other nation has ever quite had it.

It is possible to fault a number of details on which this analysis rests. The book becomes almost a polemic as Wood's exuberant discovery of social change sweeps him into a celebration of it that sometimes leaves the reader behind. Again and again, in describing the characteristics of his three successive societies—monarchical, republican, and democratic—he insists that it would be difficult to exaggerate this or that component of each. Some readers may feel that he has overcome the difficulty.

The most conspicuous example is his depiction of a transformation in attitudes toward work. In the pre-Revolutionary, monarchical society, he tells us, people labored only "out of necessity, out of poverty." Labor was therefore associated with slavery and servitude. Indeed slavery often seemed to be only "another degree of labor," not all that different from free labor. Labor as such, he believes, did not achieve dignity or come to be valued as a productive source of wealth until the Revolution. There may well have been a change in this direction, but to see it as so dramatic is to ignore at least two centuries of what Max Weber called "the Protestant Ethic." The dignity of working at one's calling may have been magnified by the Revolution but was certainly not invented by it or even by John Locke's labor theory of value, which was already a century old by the time of the Revolution.

In his zeal to magnify the Revolution's assault on "monarchical" social relations, Wood also exaggerates the extent to which royal patronage had penetrated colonial society. The very use of the word "monarchical" to describe that society can be justified only figuratively. To claim that "the great social antagonists of the American Revolution . . . were patriots vs. courtiers" is to attribute an inordinate significance and power in colonial life to courtiers, that is, to "persons whose position or rank . . . ultimately flowed from the crown or court." Certainly royal office holders were the first local targets of the Revolution, but their numbers were few and their expulsion or suppression instantaneous. The number of their dependents was also small. One of the perennial complaints of royal governors was that the small number of government offices under their patronage prevented them from building a local following of the kind that the king's ministers in England enjoyed.

The elimination of royally derived patronage thus effected relatively little social change. The departure of the loyalists, colonists who preferred not to live in an independent America, was more significant, but less so than Wood suggests. It was once thought that the loyalists were drawn from the highest ranks of colonial society, and it may well be that the upper crust was represented among them in a larger proportion than in the population at large. But the most careful studies have found the loyalists to constitute a pretty fair cross section of the population. It may be, as Wood argues, that the removal of loyalist leaders "disrupted colonial society to a degree far in excess of their numbers," but the numbers were small enough to make the disruption less than revolutionary.

In short, Wood sometimes seems to be carried away by the excitement of his theme. But the theme is truly exciting and his treatment of it eloquent. His discovery of a social revolution where modern aficionados of revolution have looked for it in vain will doubtless raise eyebrows among the lingering left of academia. But this is a book that could redirect historical thinking about the Revolution and its place in the national consciousness. When every exception has been taken to Wood's overstatement of his case, that case is still convincing and particularly so to anyone familiar with the events he deals with.

The Revolution did revolutionize social relations. It did displace the deference, the patronage, the social divisions that had determined the way people viewed one another for centuries and still view one another in much of the world. It did give to ordinary people a pride and power, not to say an arrogance, that have continued to shock visitors from less favored lands. It may have left standing a host of inequalities that have troubled us ever since. But it generated the egalitarian view of human society that makes them troubling and makes our world so different from the one in which the revolutionists had grown up. It was not a Marxist revolution, not the overthrow of a ruling class, not the rising of an oppressed class. But if we can escape from the stereotypes that have governed our thinking about it, we will recognize that it is time to stop apologizing for its conservatism (or praising it) and see it as indeed "the most radical and most far-reaching event in American history."

June 25, 1992

CHAPTER TWENTY-TWO

The Genuine Article

Founding Father: Rediscovering George Washington
Richard Brookhiser

IT IS HARD for anyone who discovers George Washington not to write about him, perhaps because he is so hard to discover and such a surprise when you do. That featureless face peering harmlessly from the dollar bill and a thousand other places becomes hardly noticeable, protected like the purloined letter by its meaningless visibility. To discover him, moreover, requires persevering beyond the bare record of his achievements, for what did he actually do, when you come right down to it?

He was the general who won American independence on the field of battle. Yes, but he lost most of the battles at which he commanded. He was not present (not yet even appointed) at Lexington, Concord, and Bunker Hill. For years after 1776 he avoided any serious engagement of the enemy whatever. He had virtually nothing to do with the northern campaign in which Horatio Gates forced the surrender of John Burgoyne at Saratoga in 1777, the real turning point of the war. He commanded at the siege of Yorktown in 1781, which effectively ended the war, but French forces outnumbered American at Yorktown, and it was only the presence of the French navy that made the siege possible at all.

Washington presided at the Constitutional Convention of 1787 and is often credited with its success. But he had no known part in drafting its provisions. He did not even speak about any of them, except to support, on the last day of the Convention, a motion to change the ratio of representation in Congress from one for forty thousand persons to one for thirty thousand. In the struggle over ratification, though he had signed the document and privately praised it, he conspicuously refrained from any public statement of support, not even attending Virginia's crucial ratifying convention.

As the first president (and the only one ever to win a unanimous electoral vote) he launched the new government. But his policies provoked the first opposition, led by Thomas Jefferson and James Madison, who had originally guided him. His own most prominent action as president was to take the field again at the head of an army, to suppress a rebellion in which no rebel force made an appearance to get itself suppressed. He is credited with some important state papers, but most of them, including the famous "Farewell Address," were drafted by others (Madison wrote both his first message to Congress and the congressional answer to it).

The record does not look so great. Yet people at the time obviously thought it did. Throughout his long career Washington earned the adulation not merely of ordinary people but of the other luminaries whom we now hail as "founding fathers." Benjamin Franklin, his only senior in age among them and the man most responsible for securing the indispensable French assistance, had no hesitation in honoring Washington's use of it. He wrote him from France in 1780, at a time when the American cause seemed to be faltering under Washington's direction, that "the old generals of this martial country . . . join in giving you the character of one of the greatest captains of the age." Franklin evidently shared their opinion and in his will bequeathed him "my fine crabtree walking stick, with a gold head curiously wrought in the form of the cap of liberty. . . . If it were a sceptre, he has merited it and would become it."[1]

Immediately after the war Jefferson and Madison collaborated to have the French sculptor Jean-Antoine Houdon prepare a marble statue of Washington, commissioned by the Virginia legislature and still gracing the capitol at Richmond. Madison's proposed caption for it proclaimed Washington as "an immortal example of true glory."

Before the statue was finished, Madison withdrew this in favor of a Latin inscription favored by Jefferson, which Jefferson translated as, "Behold, Reader, the form of George Washington. For his worth ask History: that will tell it, when this stone shall have yielded to the decays of time." Fifteen years after Washington's death, despite Jefferson's leadership of the opposition to his presidential policies, Jefferson could write to a friend that Washington was "in every sense of the words, a wise, a good, and a great man," who belonged "in the same constellation with whatever worthies have merited from man an everlasting remembrance."[2] John Marshall, the great Chief Justice of the Supreme Court, devoted five volumes to a biographical eulogy.

All these people knew Washington personally. Some knew him as well as he let anyone know him. And they were all, by most standards, his intellectual superiors. Indeed they have themselves had few equals in that respect among their successors in American public life. If they were so awed by Washington, they must have found something in him that is not immediately apparent in the public record. Two hundred years later it can still be found, and the search can be rewarding if arduous. Those who make their way through the thirty-seven volumes of his *Writings*, edited by John C. Fitzpatrick, are likely to be frustrated by the absence of the incoming letters, without which the answers to them are often incomprehensible (and a large proportion of the letters are answers: Washington did not initiate many exchanges). Fortunately the complete correspondence and other surviving papers are now in the process of publication in a definitive edition, fully annotated (forming with the similar editions of the papers of other "founding fathers" the major scholarly achievement of American historical scholarship in the twentieth century).[3]

It is possible to discover Washington without reading all of these volumes, but once glimpsed the man is addictive. The fact that he is not an original thinker in any usual sense makes it the more enticing to examine the way he thought and acted in the many situations where the outcome depended on him. What he brought to the American Revolution and the creation of the republic was not creative genius, not brilliant maneuvers, not some profound insight. It was something much more mundane but at the same time so elusive, so difficult to define, that when it emerges in one situation after another, we begin to see what his contemporaries saw and to be overwhelmed by it as they were. What looked in the historical record like shortcomings are transformed into triumphs.

As the realization dawns, so does the need to share the discovery, and hence the host of books that have become almost an American literary genre. Most are biographies, big ones beginning with Marshall's, then Washington Irving's five volumes, and in the twentieth century Douglas Southall Freeman's six and James Flexner's four. Interspersed are numberless smaller ones, including one by his aide-de-camp, David Humphreys. Written in different stages before 1789, it remained unpublished until 1991, when Rosemarie Zagarri reconstructed it from the scattered fragments.[4] What all the biographies seek to do, Humphreys's included, is to embody the secret of Washington's unique reputation in the narrative of a career that placed him at the center of so many critical passages in the creation of the United States. Attempts to humanize or debunk him as just another man, full of human weaknesses, miss the point, not so much because they are wrong as because they are irrelevant. There is plenty of material in his writings from which to reconstruct his day-to-day pursuits, to show that he was genuinely interested in farming and almost obsessively concerned, even during prolonged absences, with the management of his plantation at Mount Vernon. Washington the farmer is easily perceived, easily understood, and easily forgotten. That Washington is not the one who matters. But the one who matters is so closely identified with the creation of the United States that any biography, long or short, easily drifts into a history of the period.

Since the historical record, as suggested above, scarcely explains in itself why Washington mattered so much, the shorter biographies can seldom show as effectively as the longer ones that he did matter or how he mattered. And the longer ones are so long that we may need some preliminary incentive before tackling their bulk or the greater bulk of the new *Papers*.

The incentive can be found in some recent monographs that attempt to recover Washington's public persona without following him through all the events of his public life. Paul Longmore, in *The Invention of George Washington* (1988),[5] goes directly to Washington's own conscious creation of the reputation that so dazzled his contemporaries and continues to dazzle anyone who studies him long enough. Longmore confines his closely argued treatment to Washington's early years, before his national career and prominence began. Washington's sensitivity to what the public thought of him has been noticed by all his biographers. What Longmore shows is that Washington's preoccupation began when he first became a public man in Virginia in his early twenties.

Washington seems to have been born with a thirst for public respect of a special kind. He wanted nothing more than honor, and he had identified its ingredients so clearly that he knew he would miss getting it if he showed himself wanting it as badly as he did. He wished to be honored by deserving it. If his neighbors placed a high value on graceful ballroom dancing or fine horsemanship, he wanted not simply to have the reputation but to *be* the most graceful dancer and the finest horseman. If they honored physical courage, he would give them courage, leading Virginia's militia against the French when he was only twenty-two. In the contest with England he found the larger cause he needed to gain larger honor and deliberately placed himself in a position to win it by command of the Continental Army. In the end his own successful quest won him the prestige to honor the cause that had honored him. Longmore is not a debunker. He, too, honors the man, because he sees that Washington continually sought to make nature imitate art, to make his life conform to the perfection of character and conduct that was his ideal.

Longmore's is probably the best account of Washington's character in the making. If it leaves us still a little puzzled, unable to explain why Washington was so successful in getting the honor he craved without performing the exceptional feats generally expected of magnificent heroes—the triumphs over odds, the ascents of Everests, the messages carried to Garcia—Barry Schwartz offers an answer in *George Washington: The Making of an American Symbol* (1987).[6] As Schwartz sees it (drawing on the sociology of Emile Durkheim), Washington did not invent himself by himself; he was a construct fashioned by society to meet its own changing social and political needs.

Washington's simplicity of mind and poker-faced reserve made it possible to project on him the image first of a great military commander and then of a great political leader. His impassive devotion to duty made him the perfect vessel into which all the other admired public virtues could be poured. Washington was quite ready to cooperate in the process. If, as Longmore shows, his consuming passion was to be honored, he was also alert to recognizing what would be most honorable and most honored in whatever situation confronted him. Schwartz examines not only the situations but the political culture in which they occurred and the way in which the elevation of Washington satisfied the successive demands of that culture.

Thus when the colonial resistance to British policies turned to war in 1775, society needed a collective symbol to embody the radical change of direction in the public mind. Washington's appointment to military command filled the need and made him "the best-known and most admired man in the colonies" before he had to do anything but look the part. Nor did he have to do much more to sustain and magnify the role thrust upon him. "The idea of George Washington," more than the man himself, "was essential to America's militant arousal and to her incipient national consciousness." And so it went. After the war, when the Union was in danger of collapse, "loyalty to Washington the individual held the government together until the people could learn to be loyal to the government itself." When the new Constitution was proposed, it must be identified with Washington in order to succeed; and he must preside over the new government, for "the public's image of Washington had blended so deeply into its image of the presidency as to make the two virtually inseparable." His reputation became so elevated as to be something of a handicap: anything he did as president that seemed less than godlike could generate a disappointment that easily turned into an exaggerated hostility, which he felt, Jefferson noted, "more than any person I ever yet met with."[7] But for most Americans disappointment was unthinkable and hostility a sacrilege. In Washington they could see only the public virtues they wished to see in themselves.

Schwartz's analysis is perceptive, but it tells us more about the sociology of hero worship than about Washington himself, whose image was more malleable than the man could have been. Garry Wills, in *Cincinnatus: George Washington and the Enlightenment* (1984), offered a more searching explanation of what it was in Washington that made his pursuit of honor so successful. Wills opens his meditation—for that is really what his book is—with an observation that he pursues through the familiar passages of Washington's career (assisted by the painters and sculptors who tried to open the secret on canvas and in marble): "He was a virtuoso of resignations. He perfected the art of getting power by giving it away."[8] The obvious example is the resignation of his commission after the war: his refusal to seize the power that a Caesar or a Cromwell would have grasped. That refusal earned him an international prestige and domestic power that no other American before or since has ever approached. Wills cites Benjamin West, the American painter exiled in England during the war, who was asked by King George III (Farmer George to many of his subjects) what Washington would do if he should win. When West said that he would probably return to his farm, the king allegedly replied, "if he does that, he will be the greatest man in the world."[9] He did and he was. He was Cincinnatus in an age when people knew who Cincinnatus was and what he did.

Wills does not contend that Washington was hungry for power and used devious means of gaining it by pretending to spurn it. On the other hand, it is clear, as Longmore shows, that Washington always valued his prestige and by no means disdained the power that it carried. He cultivated the aloofness that still surrounds him, with full awareness that it supported the personal authority which seemingly required him to direct the nation while renouncing its direction. His first significant resignation came not at the end of the war but at the beginning, when he chose to serve as commander in chief without compensation, a gesture that contributed to his hold over the soldiers who served under him. He never lost an opportunity to strengthen that hold, whether by using his rank or by refraining from using it. The furthest thing from his mind, however, was to appear in the character of a popular commander. His great achievement in the war was to keep his army in existence, despite a feckless Congress, despite superior British forces continually threatening him, and he did it by the force of example and the loyalty it engendered.

As Wills puts it, "Others might *use* armies better; but Washington best grasped that the problem was to *create* an army, to keep it in existence, by embodying its cause."[10] He knew that success in war depended on destroying the enemy's army. But he also knew that the republican principles animating the Revolution (the demands of the political culture) depended on the army's subordination to civil power, however inept and irresponsible that power might be. He kept his own army from destruction by dodging the British, becoming a master of retreat—another kind of resignation—until he was in a position to destroy *them*, and then he swept his troops back to their farms as he went back to his. His resignation of command would have meant little if he had not been able to carry his men, unpaid and underpaid, with him. The old French generals recognized him for a great captain because he did not let a superior force destroy his army. The world recognized him for a great man, because he did not let his victorious army turn loyalty to him into a military dictatorship of the United States under his direction.

The interval after the war that ended with the adoption of the Constitution offers Wills the most impressive example of Washington's exercising power by not exercising it. Washington knew that the United States desperately needed an effective government, but he refrained from any public activity to bring it about and even hesitated until the last moment before agreeing to attend the Convention that created it. It was the people around him, especially James Madison, who did the job but did so in full knowledge that their success depended on his silent support. He must be seen to preside at the Convention and sign the document, but neither participate in debating its provisions nor publicly advocate its adoption. To do so would lessen the force of his approbation by making him a partisan rather than a gift-giver. The Constitution was hailed everywhere as his work, and he would have suggested the possibility of its being something less if he had stooped to praising it. By leaving the people to decide its fate without engaging himself in the debate over it, he became, Wills points out, the embodiment of Rousseau's ideal legislator, who "shall not use either force or argument," but "resort to another kind of authority entirely, an ability to lead without compelling and persuade without proving."[11]

Washington probably never read Rousseau, but he needed no model and no instructor. Although he was probably not above thinking of himself as Cincinnatus or Cato, he acted or refrained from action out of an instinctive, deliberate dignity that never deserted him. He was a virtuoso not merely of resignation but of understatement, indeed of silence. No one, not even Freeman or Flexner, has caught this cryptic quality better than Wills.

The discovery of Washington continues, and discoverers continue to write about it. The latest entry is Richard Brookhiser, who previously squandered his talents on a jeremiad for the demise of WASP hegemony. In Washington, Brookhiser has found a subject more worthy of those talents, which are considerable. Brookhiser can pin down character traits in a few phrases, sometimes glib but often brilliant, as in his dismissal of Washington's early advisers in the presidency: "Hamilton was a know-it-all, who (even worse) often did know it all. Madison, beneath a layer of intense shyness, was equally headstrong, while Jefferson had the deep deviousness that is given only to the pure of heart."

Pureness of heart is what contemporaries preferred to ascribe to Washington, but deviousness, deep or shallow, did not accompany it. Washington's was a less transparent nature than Jefferson's, not susceptible to simple characterization and not easily penetrated. Brookhiser knows that. He has glimpsed Washington, seen enough to recognize that "his patterns of expression and thought reveal themselves slowly," that his writings offer a clue, but "the effect they make is cumulative," that they require "time and effort—as much time and effort as it takes to decode his deeds." Brookhiser has given the requisite time and effort, assisted in no small way by the previous interpretations of Wills and Longmore, and has given us his own brief decoding of words and deeds. He rightly rejects the debunkers and humanizers who try to turn the man into someone like us. "We must look for the man," he says, "in the glare of public life," and begins with a graceful recitation of his career, occupying half the book but still too sketchy to reveal the elements that made it so puzzlingly triumphant.

In a second part of the book Brookhiser tries to identify those elements, which, he has assured us, give the life of Washington "the power to inspire anyone who studies it." Here he hits first upon some superficial and obvious things that, though often noticed, tend to be slighted in more sophisticated analyses of Washington's power. The first is simply physical. Washington was a big man, six feet two or three, in an age when that was a towering height, and he made the most of it in an erect and commanding posture that seemed to dwarf everyone around him, of whatever size. As Benjamin Rush put it, in words dear to every biographer: "There is not a king in Europe that would not look like a valet de chambre by his side." Washington wanted honor, and he carried himself as though he merited it. It was especially true of the way he rode a horse, which everyone seems to have remarked upon.

It would be easy to belittle the importance of so everyday a thing as personal appearance in the conduct of government, but we judge people by their looks and demeanor more than we usually realize. If we could see Washington in the company of the other founding fathers, especially if they were on horseback—which is where they often were—we would know who was number one without a word said. In case there should be any doubt, Washington would be wearing a smart military uniform of his own design that would make the others look shabby.

As he was careful of his appearance before other people, so he was also careful to mind his manners. Though he was short-tempered, he did not fly out at other people but rather followed the ancient precepts of politeness and self-command. And Brookhiser, after describing Washington's habits in social intercourse, shrewdly observes that "Politeness is the first form of politics."

But good manners and an imposing appearance are scarcely sufficient to inspire those of us not directly exposed to them. When Brookhiser gets beyond appearances to "the importance to Washington of right ideas," we hope and expect to get to the heart of the matter, especially since Brookhiser tells us that "it was in the name of right ideas about politics and government that he commanded his countrymen." Possibly so, but for a man who could express himself in speech and writing with extraordinary clarity, Washington's ideas about politics and government remained diffuse and inarticulate, to be found only in conventional phrases here and there in his writings. Washington accepted the prevailing view of other American colonists that the British government was corrupt and bent on tyranny. He clearly thought that republican government was superior to monarchy. But he did not say why and wrote virtually nothing on the subject. His contemporaries could not believe that he ever read much on that topic or any other, probably because his speech and writing so seldom reflected any reading. Longmore offers proof, in a long appendix, that Washington read more than acquaintances realized, and Brookhiser follows Longmore in reciting how many books and newspapers Washington kept. But exactly what ideas meant so much to him is not to be found in any distinct exposition of them by Washington himself or by Brookhiser.

Instead of trying to decipher what his ideas may have been, Brookhiser is reduced to telling us how important to Washington were the Anglican church, the Bible, Freemasonry, and the theater, an analysis which hardly distinguishes him from his Virginian compatriots. His religious conceptions, such as they were, have to be discerned in a few mentions of "providence," his familiarity with the Scriptures in a handful of quotations that were commonplace clichés of the day, like "every man under his vine and under his fig tree." Devotees of Freemasonry were supposed to be secretive about their cult anyhow, and Washington, as we have seen, never found discretion or silence to be a heavy yoke. And the theatrical performances he witnessed, apart from Addison's *Cato*, seem to have been designed simply for entertainment. Washington did not gain his power to command by reading the Bible, going to church or the playhouse, or engaging in Masonic ceremonies. If right ideas were what mattered to him, he was not much given to talking about them.

Brookhiser closes his book with a more fruitful disquisition on fatherhood and Washington's role as father of his country. Washington doubtless cherished the title, given him as early as 1778. But, more important, he identified the honor he sought so assiduously with the country and the people who gave it to him and whom he himself regarded as his offspring. His final resignation of power becomes the more meaningful, as Brookhiser stresses, because it meant giving up his most cherished possession. This time he was not giving up power in order to keep it. He was a father turning out his sons and daughters to make it on their own.

What emerges from all these books is a Washington in conscious pursuit of honor and power by means of deserving honor and power. He got them and deserved them by identifying himself wholly with the people who conferred them. What makes him so difficult to discover and the discovery so surprising must be the completeness of the identification. Patriotism is so often a disguise that the genuine article is always surprising. How it could propel a man of ordinary talents to the unique position Washington attained among Americans is more than a surprise. It remains a kind of mystery that yields itself to view only gradually. The great biographers and a few commentators like Wills can take us close to it, but in the end there is no substitute for the *Papers*. The route through them is long, but it is not dull. For Washington, whether or not he did much reading, knew how to write. He had a great many amanuenses, and the quality of his writing is often attributed to them, but the consistent force and clarity have to be the expression of a single mind. It was not the mind of an intellectual, but it was a mind whose simple power is reflected in his every move. Its workings can be found in every volume of his *Papers*. A recent one, for example, covers most of the year 1786, when Shays's Rebellion in Massachusetts had everyone worried. Washington's friends suggested that he come to the scene and use his influence to calm the rebels. His reply was typical:

> *Influence is no government. . . . My humble opinion is, that there is a call for decision. Know precisely what the Insurgents aim at. If they have real grievances, redress them, if possible, or acknowledge the justice of their complaints and your inability of doing it, in the present moment. If they have not [real grievances], employ the force of government against them at once.*[12]

The "right ideas" that gave Washington the power to command have to be deduced from passages like this throughout his *Papers*. They are not susceptible to profound analysis nor do they need it; but the cumulative effect, as noticed by Brookhiser, leaves the reader in no doubt about what made Washington *the* founding father. Funding for these splendid volumes has always been precarious, but fifty-two had appeared by 2003, with many more to come if the project is enabled to continue. Read the *Papers*.

February 29, 1996

Part Four

QUESTIONS OF
CULTURE

THESE LAST TWO essays reach beyond early America because I wanted to say something about the national culture that early Americans helped to create. As a student of the New England Puritans, I gained a high regard for the role they gave to sermons. Early American intellectual history came to life and generated its permutations in sermons. Sermons reflected and sometimes directed the later course of American public life. It troubled me that what could be seen as a definitive collection of them gave no hint of their historical and cultural significance.

The final essay, written with Marie Morgan, who knows a great deal about the American past that I do not, treats what we both see as a defining moment in American culture. Twenty-four volumes is a bit long for a manifesto. Their impact has not yet been appreciated. But their publication in 1999 announces a revolutionary change in the way we think about our past and about who and what matters in it.

CHAPTER TWENTY-THREE

Persuading the Persuaded

---∞∞∞---

American Sermons: The Pilgrims to Martin Luther King Jr.
Michael Warner, editor

WITH THE PUBLICATION in 1999 of a volume of sermons ranging over three and a half centuries, the Library of America entered new territory. None of the previous 107 volumes in the series, which "is dedicated to preserving America's best and most significant writing," had included anything religious or theological. Until the appearance of this volume, the authors had been selected for their literary distinction or, in a few cases, for their political significance (writings of Washington and Jefferson, the debates on the Constitution). The format of the series has required that there be no introduction explaining or justifying the selections and none has been needed. There would be no point in cluttering the texts of William Faulkner or Nathaniel Hawthorne with yet another analysis of what they really said or meant or why they are worthy of the imprimatur of the series. The same might have been true of a volume allotted to, say, Jonathan Edwards or Reinhold Niebuhr. The sermons in this work are similarly presented as though their intrinsic merit were obvious. It is not. The publication itself is a kind of statement that sermons played an important role in American life, but why or how is not self-evident and does not become so in reading this collection of them. Edwards and Niebuhr are both here, but in strange company.

The editor, Michael Warner (his name, as in other volumes, is excluded from the title page), had a more formidable task of selection than any previous editor in the series. Before the twentieth century sermons accounted for a large percentage of all published writing in America. They were certainly the largest single category in the 39,000 known titles printed by 1800, from which Warner has selected 26. He must have had to choose the others of his total of fifty-eight from an even larger mass. So the volume has to be his work; no other editor in this series has had to pick so few from so many. We are left to guess how he did it.

What did not dictate his selection is more apparent than what did. The table of contents includes many famous names, along with some unknown ones, but very few famous sermons. I count only three that may have been included simply because modern readers are likely to have heard of them: John Winthrop's "A Modell of Christian Charity" of 1630, preached while en route to New England; Jonathan Edwards's "Sinners in the Hands of an Angry God" a century later; and Martin Luther King Jr.'s sermon in Memphis on the day before he was killed. Not present are any sermons in which a religious leader signaled a new direction in theology or in church organization. Solomon Stoddard and Increase Mather led opposing religious movements at the end of the seventeenth century, but each is represented here by a sermon that either of them could have written and that has nothing to do with their arguments over church membership, which divided New Englanders for a century after them. Cotton Mather, Increase's son and the most influential minister of the late seventeenth and early eighteenth centuries, is represented not by anything characteristic of his special pietistic and chiliastic doctrines, but by two sermons, one affirming in platitudes that Christianity is reasonable, and the other an untimely warning against the presence of witchcraft, the worst thing he ever wrote, published just when the rest of New England was trying to forget the delusions that produced the Salem trials.

Other religious leaders suffer similar offbeat treatment. The selection from Charles Chauncy, who led a fierce opposition to the Great Awakening of the 1740s, is a funeral sermon reflecting on the shortness and fragility of human life. It could have been preached by any minister of any denomination at any time. William Ellery Channing, whose "Baltimore sermon" in 1819 became a manifesto of Unitarianism, is represented not by that sermon but by an ordination sermon in 1828. Ralph Waldo Emerson announced his desertion of Unitarianism in his famous Divinity School Address of 1838, which became one of the landmarks of Transcendentalism, but he is represented by an 1832 sermon in which he resigned his ministry at his Boston church before his views had matured. His contemporary Horace Bushnell, America's most original and most eloquent theological thinker after Edwards, is not represented at all. With so many great sermons to choose from, why would an obscure, anonymous tract against swearing, almost certainly never preached anywhere, be included? Why a sermon refuting Hosea Ballou, the founder of Universalism, but none by Ballou or any other Universalist? Historical or theological significance has obviously not been Warner's criterion.

The success of any minister's sermons in moving large numbers of people has also had no apparent influence on the selection. The sermon was the engine of the periodic revivals that have characterized American religion since the early eighteenth century. Warner has chosen examples from the popular evangelists of the late nineteenth and early twentieth centuries: Dwight Moody, Billy Sunday, and Aimee Semple McPherson, but nothing from the great Methodist preachers of the early nineteenth century, whose sermons brought more Americans to their churches than those of any other denomination. George Whitefield, the itinerant preacher who sparked the Great Awakening, may have been omitted because he was English, though a pallid depiction of him in the pulpit oddly graces the dust jacket. But if Whitefield is excluded because he was English, though his best-known sermons were preached in America, why does the volume open with a sermon by an Englishman, Robert Cushman, delivered in Plymouth Plantation in 1621 during a visit that lasted just over a month? And why is John Cotton represented by a sermon preached in England before he left? Most unaccountable is the absence of Charles Grandison Finney, unquestionably American and arguably the most popular and most powerful preacher in all of our history. His sermons in the 1820s and 1830s, in a new vernacular style, inspired the abolition movement, filled churches of all denominations, and served as a model for later American revivalists. Only Whitefield before him had so wide an influence.

What we have is a seemingly arbitrary selection. Political correctness may have had something to do with it: there are sermons by three rabbis, two women, and two former slaves. Famous names may have had something to do with it. The editor's literary taste doubtless had something to do with it. A few sermons reflect historical events: one by Samuel Cooke in 1770 can be seen as foreshadowing the American Revolution; Theodore Parker denounces the Mexican War and all wars in 1846; Henry Ward Beecher denounces slavery and defends the Union in 1861. But otherwise there are no sermons addressing the great public issues that agitated the churches and caused deep schisms within some of them, no abolitionist sermons, none on missions, imperialism, labor, evolution. There is simply no apparent rationale for assembling these sermons and no intrinsic theological, historical, or literary significance in most of them. It does not follow that the sermon has not occupied a major place in American culture. For much of American history, delivering sermons, listening to them, and discussing them were the principal intellectual activities for most people. Publication of the volume is a recognition of that fact; and the miscellaneous character of the selections, whether by accident or by design, raises the question of what gave the sermon such vitality through the changing circumstances of American society over so long a time.

We can speak of the sermon in the singular, because these sermons, along with the thousands of others from which they have been drawn, are all recognizable as exemplars of a single genre. They all have, in one way or another, the same subject: the goodness of God and His unfulfilled expectations of human beings. They all approach the subject in a hortatory mode, trying to persuade people what to believe and how to behave. They almost all derive their arguments, sometimes by rather circuitous routes, from a verse or set of verses in the Bible. What is most important is that they were all prepared for oral delivery to an assembly of people gathered for the purpose of listening to them. Many, including some in this volume, were written down only by an auditor during their delivery. Some ministers made a point of not knowing what they would say in a sermon before entering the pulpit, and many more spoke only from brief notes. Sermons were more persuasive when they were spontaneous, and persuasion was always their purpose.

Different ministers had different techniques of persuasion. We know that Jonathan Edwards delivered his sermons, whether of God's anger or of God's love, in a toneless manner, the more effective perhaps because of his matter-of-fact presentation. Other revivalists of his time and later needed a multitude of histrionic gestures to give a sense of urgency to their words. Perhaps because they lose so much in print, few of the sermons here are revival sermons. Most are formal discourses addressed to reasonable men and women seated quietly at the feet of a minister in church. But they were not presented simply as instruction. Even the most didactic are instruments of persuasion. They aim to persuade people who wish to be persuaded, people who, it is safe to assume, enjoyed persuasion, and found in it a fulfillment different from what they could get in church ceremonies alone.

The kind of fulfillment that came from sermons, though it may have had different meanings for different people at different times, has been what Americans have sought in religion from the beginning. While sermons are certainly not unique to American churches, no other people in the Western world has shown so long or so strong an attachment to them. It began with the Puritans, whose sermons occupy nearly a quarter of this work. Before leaving England they had made a nuisance of themselves by demanding more sermons than the church was willing to offer. They wanted the Church of England to give up most of the ceremonies prescribed in its Book of Common Prayer and to give up all church officers—bishops, archbishops, and a host of lesser functionaries—except for the parish ministers who preached sermons. When they organized churches of their own in New England, they held all rituals to a minimum in favor of lengthy, cerebral sermons, both morning and afternoon every Sunday.

Sermons, they believed, were the instrument of God in conferring the Holy Spirit, and anyone interested in eternal life had better seek maximum exposure to them. The conferring of the spirit was a decisive, once-in-a-lifetime experience, a new birth, a "conversion," which ceremonies might celebrate but only sermons could bring about and future sermons make intelligible. Later evangelicals attributed the same power to sermons that the Puritans did and made it visible in the way their preaching shook people into strange trances and tremblings at revival meetings. But even among those who believed that God operated on men more quietly, the sermon remained the mode of explaining who He was, what He did, and what people ought to do about it.

The variety of the explanations, as exhibited in this volume, as in the thousands of sermons on which it rests, suggests that the act of listening, of being persuaded, may somehow have mattered as much as the substance. A sermon expounding free will could have much the same effect on listeners as one expounding predestination. The sermons that produced the Great Awakening of the 1740s were Calvinist expositions of predestination. The sermons of the great revivals of the next century were "Arminian" expositions of human ability to win salvation by wanting it and working for it. In both cases, sermons coming from the lips of a charismatic minister could overwhelm a congregation with a sense of divine presence, sending the most susceptible into something resembling a coma, a phenomenon that often proved contagious. There is no record of anyone being so physically struck by reading. The distinctive and crucial experience came from hearing and from hearing in the presence of others. Listening to sermons in a Unitarian church or a Universalist one was doubtless something different from listening to an evangelical one, but it was still a collective experience. And that experience, of whatever kind in whatever church, carried an invitation to return for a repetition of it, for more sermons, more persuasion, not just in a pastoral visit but from the pulpit in the company of the whole congregation.

In America the invitation was not encumbered by the compulsions or the limitations that surrounded sermons in the European world from which most Americans or their ancestors arrived. In that world, membership in the church was a corollary of citizenship in the state, and membership in a variety of other institutions was also determined more by birth than by choice. The absence of such established institutions has often been noted as a distinctive feature of American life, especially in the first two or three centuries after English settlement. While Americans were engaged in occupying the continent and ousting the native inhabitants, institutions could not keep up with the exponential growth of the population. Not only was there no established church, but there was no hereditary aristocracy, no standing army, no business monopolies, fewer of any of the institutions that elsewhere posed limits on what an individual could do, fewer even of the social customs and taboos that so often dictate human behavior, and necessarily fewer of the rites and ceremonies through which institutions identify themselves and their members. In this environment the persuasive power of sermons took the place of institutional compulsions and reduced the significance of ceremony, of feasts and fastings, sacraments and prayers, and every other liturgical rite.

The very absence of ceremony as an emblem of identity emphasized the collective experience of attendance at sermons, an experience we cannot recapture in print. It is fair to see the sermon as a literary genre and to read it as such, but its importance in American history was not literary. Its significance lay both in the inexpressible collective religious experience it provided and also in its capacity to affect the stance people took on public issues, even on issues not specifically mentioned in it. Warner seems to have avoided the many sermons directed explicitly at public issues, perhaps because the format of the series made impossible the introductions needed to explain controversies less well known than the Civil War. But every sermon took its meaning from the people it addressed. It would require an extraordinary immersion in the times that produced a seemingly routine sermon to grasp the many meanings and implications it may have had for the people to whom it was addressed. A couple of examples from the book may suggest why.

When in 1709 Cotton Mather extols the reasonableness of Christianity and cites how reason requires a church to show "Respect unto the countenance of any *Neighbouring Churches*," it seems to us merely an illustration of an obvious proposition, but everyone in the meetinghouse would have known that he was trying to co-opt them into a plan propounded unsuccessfully by himself and his father to bring the New England churches into a semi-presbyterial organization. It was a lost cause, but Mather may have structured the whole sermon in order to get in that plug for it. When Jonathan Mitchell in 1667 urges New Englanders to be faithful to the principles of their forefathers ("Oh seek and keep it, and hold it fast"), we read it as a standard exhortation to stick to the good old ways, but the congregation could hear him coming down hard in favor of the novel and highly controversial "Halfway Covenant" of 1662, extending baptism to children whose parents had never experienced the new birth necessary for full membership in the church. When he says, "Prize and hold fast the Covenant of God to you and yours," the seemingly innocent "yours" is directed at those who did not accept this innovation. He makes his condemnation of them explicit when he goes on to say, "To leave the *Children* of non-scandalous Orthodox Christians *Unbaptized*, will (I doubt not) be one day found a thing displeasing unto Jesus Christ." This, coming from the man who was probably the most respected Congregational minister of his time, would have been a red flag to opponents of the "Halfway Covenant" and a cause for cheering to its advocates. The sermon was an instrument of persuasion in more ways than one, and its effectiveness cannot be gauged from its appearance in print.

One form of its effectiveness, however, is obvious: the expansion of population and the proliferation of sects opened church membership in America to a competition conducted through sermons.

Ultimately the existence of every church came to depend on the persuasiveness of the minister's performance in the pulpit. After American independence, even the Church of England, cut off from English support and English law, had to rely more on sermons and less on ceremony. As the Protestant Episcopal Church in the United States, it placed even its bishops in parish pulpits and expected them to preach, and many of its priests and deacons on their own initiative neglected the liturgical ceremonies prescribed in the Book of Common Prayer in favor of unprescribed sermons and exhortations. Without sermons the Episcopal Church might have expired altogether, and its die-hard High Church members might have merged with the Roman Catholic Church. The Catholic Church has always augmented its membership in America from the immigrants who remained faithful to it, but even they felt the need for more sermons than had been customary in Europe. In many of the large cities where they gathered in the decades before the Civil War, lay trustees of particular churches claimed the power to appoint priests in defiance of their bishops and insisted on more evangelical sermons.

The sermon has retained its preeminence in American churches during most of the present century. But in the last twenty or thirty years, while fundamentalist fanaticism has been on the rise among so many of the world's religions and while Americans have continued to frequent their churches more regularly than Europeans do, the sermon seems to have been losing its central place in religious experience and activity. Protestant churches in general have been giving more attention to liturgical formalities and to peripheral social activities. Religious energies have been diverted to education, to single-issue politics, to picket lines and protests and soup kitchens. Zeal for salvation has moved to Pentecostal movements, where the sermon has become a spontaneous interactive performance between preacher and congregants. It is perhaps appropriate, then, that the Library of America should issue a volume of sermons at this time. Although it is difficult to see how this particular selection of them can meet the description of "America's best and most significant writing," it does meet what is evidently another requirement. As with the other volumes in the series, the authors are all dead. The sermon as a genre may already have passed its best days, and the experiences that gave it meaning cannot be recovered in print. But it still deserves a better epitaph than this strange work provides.

September 23, 1999

CHAPTER TWENTY-FOUR

Who's Really Who

—∞∞—

American National Biography (24 vols.)
John A. Garraty and Mark C. Carnes, general editors

TWO PEOPLE NAMED John Adams, one born in Braintree, Massachusetts, in 1735, the other about twenty miles west of Braintree in Medway in 1812. The first was a leader of the American Revolution, helped write the Declaration of Independence, and succeeded George Washington as president of the United States. The second made a career of capturing and training grizzly bears in the Sierra Nevada Mountains for exhibition around the country in the 1850s. You can read about the first John Adams in the *American National Biography* (*ANB*) and also, at somewhat greater length, in the older twenty-volume *Dictionary of American Biography* (*DAB*). You can read about the second John Adams, better known as Grizzly Adams, only in the *ANB*. That, in short, is the difference between these two reference works. But it is a difference that reaches well beyond the fun of finding so improbable a character as Grizzly Adams while looking for his more famous namesake.

Not that the fun should be discounted. The contrasting of personalities joined by alphabetical juxtaposition is enough to jolt anyone into exclamations of "Only in America!" Look up Margaret Fuller, the New England Transcendentalist, and find her in a pack of Fullers not much like her. Alfred Carl Fuller, the original Fuller Brush Man, resembled her a little in doing a lot of traveling. Buckminster Fuller, the inventor of the geodesic dome and various other engineering marvels, shared with her an absorption in cosmic problems. But we get pretty far from Margaret with Blind Boy Fuller, "probably the Southeast's most important and influential blues artist." Blind Boy started out as a street singer and guitarist, teaming up with Bull City Red, a washboard player, and Sonny Terry, another blind street singer, who specialized in the harmonica. Before Blind Boy died at the age of thirty-three in 1941, he had cut 135 titles like "Rag, Mama, Rag" and "Truckin' My Blues Away" for Decca and other major record companies. And don't miss Jesse "Lone Cat" Fuller, a drifter who worked variously as a circus roustabout, yard hand for the Southern Pacific, and shipyard welder before making the big time on TV and film with his one-man-band performance on the harmonica, kazoo, washboard, cymbal, double bass, and twelve-string guitar ("he employed a northern Georgia/Piedmont picking style and could play in open-tuned slide style as well"). Only in America, indeed, and only in the *ANB* will you find them joined, not just for fun but in serious recognition of what they all did to make America whatever it is.

What gives the volumes their unique significance is the vision that guided the two principal editors and the associates who helped them in choosing persons for inclusion and establishing guidelines for writing about them. *American National Biography* is an editorial work of art, different in kind from any preceding study of American history. It could perhaps be compared to the many historical series of books in which twentieth-century publishers have periodically enlisted experts to rewrite the history of the United States, as perspectives have changed over time: the *American Nation* series, the *New American Nation* series, the *Chronicles of America* series (edited by the original editor of the *DAB*), the *History of American Life* series, *The Chicago History of American Civilization*, the *Oxford History of the United States*. Each has sought to offer the latest in historical interpretations by the latest experts. But none of them approaches the reconception of American life in the *ANB*.

The *ANB* was originally projected as an update of the *DAB*, and an update it certainly is. Quite apart from any larger significance, it presents, through its new depictions of individual lives, all the advances in historical understanding that have occurred since the *DAB* was published between 1928 and 1936 (some of which were already evident in the supplementary volumes issued periodically from 1944 to 1995). More than any of the historical series, in which each volume is the work of a single author, both the *DAB* and the *ANB* represent a collective effort of the historical profession by a wide spectrum of its members.

The profession had just come of age in the 1920s and early 1930s when some of its then leaders cooperated with the American Council of Learned Societies to put together the *DAB*. Few of the entrepreneurs had the time or the inclination to work extensively on the biographies themselves. Carl Becker did a classic one on Benjamin Franklin. But Charles Beard and Frederick Jackson Turner, whose interpretations dominated American history at the time, contributed none. Nor did Charles McLean Andrews, the dean of colonial studies. The editors, first Allen Johnson, then Dumas Malone and Harris Starr, had to call on a couple of thousand people, many of them just beginning their careers, to undertake more biographies than any of them could bring a degree of expertise to. Interpretation of large areas of history rested more on assumption than research, and the assumptions of most of the profession at the time were "progressive." American history was seen as a continuing struggle for betterment by the common man against the dominance of usurping superiors. That view is not in itself without merit, but a close look at any time, place, or person has generally revealed a situation that does not yield to explanation by previously accepted suppositions.

Since the 1930s several generations of historians (historiographical generations are pretty short) have been taking closer and closer looks at every part of the American past, and there are now several times as many professional historians doing it as were present or available in the 1920s or 1930s. They have singled out narrower and narrower segments of the past and disclosed new complexities that require continual revising or reversing of previous suppositions. The revisions and reversals are often exaggerated, resulting in a kind of pendulum swing, from emphasis on conflict to emphasis on consensus, back to a more complex conflict and forward to a different kind of consensus, and so on. The swings sometimes follow corresponding swings in public opinion, or at least academic opinion, about current issues that may have no immediate bearing on the subject. But the net result is a much more sophisticated understanding of the American past and of the people in it than would have been possible in the 1930s. The difference is evident in the *ANB*'s handling of people also covered in the *DAB*. In general, the new treatments take more space: the *ANB*, with twenty-four volumes instead of twenty, over three hundred more pages per volume, and more words to a page, is almost twice as long as the DAB, but it contains only 22 percent more entries (17,450 as against 13,633). In general, also, the new sketches show greater interest in and understanding of what people thought, give a little less attention to genealogical origins, public careers, offices held, honors received. And they show far greater familiarity with the sources from which the stories they tell have to be drawn.

A good example can be found in the treatment of figures from early New England. Seventeenth-century Massachusetts exhibited several conflicts in which liberty-loving democrats could be seen as arrayed against tyrannical aristocrats. Thomas Hooker, who led an exodus from Massachusetts to found Connecticut, becomes in the *DAB* "a born democrat," as evinced by writings in which he placed the origin of government in a social contract, while the leaders of Massachusetts "opposed democracy tooth and nail." The *ANB* notes Hooker's reputation as a pioneer of democracy and deflates it by showing that his views on the origin of government were shared by all Puritans. His statements about it were merely reminders to readers "of conventional truths of political theory they already knew." Similarly, Roger Williams in the *DAB* was banished to Rhode Island because his ministry at Salem "roused the fears of the governing class for their own supremacy," and his opposition to oaths of allegiance endangered their attempts "to bind the lower orders to strict submission." The *ANB* sets the record straight in showing that Williams's offensiveness to the Massachusetts authorities lay in his intransigent insistence that the colony's Puritan churches were not pure enough. He never found one that was, for "in his heart he was a congregation of one."

A similar study in contrasts arises in examining the cluster of individuals whose lives converged in southern Montana during the Indian wars. General George Crook's column of one thousand troopers, as well as his Crow and Shoshone allies, were defeated by a large force of Sioux and Cheyenne led by Crazy Horse at the Battle of the Rosebud. Only eight days later, five companies of the Seventh Cavalry, led by George A. Custer, were wiped out by Lakota Sioux and Cheyenne warriors. Here the *ANB* offers a markedly different version from the *DAB* of the people and forces which brought about the collision. The 1920s' take on Indian warfare was very much influenced by William James Ghent, an editor of the *DAB* with a specialist interest in western history. Ghent, who wrote many articles for the *DAB*, admired Custer as a gentleman of the old school: "In personal habits he was abstemious; except in the peace-pipe ceremony with Indians he did not use tobacco." The character of Sitting Bull he sums up as "wily, untrustworthy," comparing his spiritual gifts to those of a table-turning fake medium. Sixty years on, Robert M. Utley makes the observation that "had Custer been killed at Appomattox, he would be remembered as a great cavalry general, second only to Sheridan among Union horsemen." As an Indian fighter, however, "the fame came as much from newspaper attention and from his own writings" as from victories on the field of battle. Noting the endless controversies that still swirl around the Battle of the Little Bighorn, Utley laconically concludes: "The soldiers lost because the Indians won—although in victory lay the seeds of their ultimate defeat."

Joseph C. Porter, who profiles General George Crook, praises the sympathy with which he studied Indian ways of life, for Crook "appreciated that American Indians fought to preserve their cultures and lands." Whereas the *DAB*'s G. J. Fiebeger deemed it important to establish that Crook was "never profane, indulged in no intoxicating liquors, and was clean of speech," Porter analyzes his soldiering in some detail. Highly skilled in logistics and strategy, he was implacable in his pursuit of hostile Indians—whose villages he ruthlessly extirpated to weaken their ability to wage war—but magnanimous toward those he conquered. He campaigned tirelessly to persuade the federal government to grant them civil rights. "The southwestern press vilified Crook for his evenhanded treatment of the Apaches," who suffered terrible oppression at the hands of Crook's successor, General Nelson Miles.

A like evenhandedness informs the *ANB* portraits of the principal Indian actors in the Little Bighorn disaster, Crazy Horse, Gall, and Sitting Bull, whose personal attributes and leadership roles are analyzed with care and sensitivity. In evaluating the now common accusation that Gall, an Episcopalian convert and opponent of the native Ghost Dance religion, was "a pawn of white culture who sold out the reservation Sioux for personal gain," Neil C. Mangum declares that "this perception is not entirely accurate." Calling Gall "a visionary" who understood all too well the overwhelming force white America had at its disposal, Mangum explains that he "accepted reservation confinement because to resist meant defeat and death."

Nothing dates the *DAB* as markedly as its treatment of charismatic religious leaders who flourished outside mainstream Protestantism. In the late 1920s the fact that Mary Baker Eddy was a New Englander, had established a thriving "Mother Church" in Boston, and had a following of educated and mostly affluent men and women must have worked in her favor with the editors of the *DAB*. But it is hard to see why she was accorded an article nearly the length of Jonathan Edwards's, and especially one that harps on her "little airs," her "little court," and her propensity for bitter litigation. Even then it must have been apparent that Christian Science was a religion that appealed to few, as compared with Mormonism, whose founder, Joseph Smith, was given short shrift by Bernard DeVoto in a *DAB* article cast as a quizzical look at a phenomenon at once grotesque and hardy.

It is inconceivable that any serious historian of today would exhibit the degree of scorn that DeVoto visited on Smith. While acknowledging his great influence upon others, DeVoto sums him up by saying,

"He was at his best in situations that could be personalized and drama-tized, but he lacked intelligence and his judgment was almost uni-formly bad." DeVoto even attaches a show of legality to the murder of Smith and his brother Hyrum by a lynch mob, in the bald statement that they were "arrested and lodged in the jail at Carthage, Ill., whence they were taken on June 27 and shot." Religious ideas are taken much more seriously by the authors of the *ANB*, who strive to place them socially and intellectually in context, while paying particular attention to the institutional forms of religious life and the transformations of the social structures which give rise to them. A fine example of this is the article on Dorothy Day of the *Catholic Worker* movement. James Terence Fisher describes the tension between Day's personal piety, which found redemptive power in a life of spirituality and voluntary poverty, and the demands laid upon her as the chief organizer and public symbol of a lay movement dedicated to succoring the jobless and the homeless.

Another subject which modern historians treat with a candor uncommon in the 1920s and 1930s is sexuality. The highly respectful profile of the poet Amy Lowell in the *DAB*, while discussing her per-sonal life in some detail, states without further explanation that she ded-icated her poems to A.D.R., identified as Mrs. Harold Russell, who served as her literary executor. The *ANB* has no difficulty in saying, "The friendship between the two women has been described as platonic by some, as lesbian by others; it was, in fact, a 'Boston marriage.' They lived together and were committed to each other until Lowell's death."

The *ANB*'s updating offers many contrasts to the *DAB* of this kind but not always so directly. The only other area we have found where the clash of interpretations figures so obviously is in the treatment of people involved in the Reconstruction governments of the South after the Civil War. The historians at work on the *DAB* were beneficiaries of many studies of Reconstruction, in particular studies done under the direction of William A. Dunning at Columbia University. In all of them the Radical Republicans who wrote new state constitutions and ran the governments under them before 1878 came in for denunciation, while the resumption of white dominance after that date was viewed as a restoration of order and decency. Studies completed since 1934, based on a wider range of sources, have emphasized the achievements of the Reconstruction governments and the overt racism of their successors. Biographies in the *DAB* and the *ANB* exhibit the differences. For example, the *DAB*, quoting Ulrich B. Phillips, sums up the career of Rufus Bullock, governor of Georgia 1868–71, with the blanket judgment that "Bullock and his crew instituted a carnival of public spoliation." The *ANB* allows that there were numerous "allegations of fraud and malfeasance" but finds that "these charges obscured the unquestioned contributions of Bullock's regime," among them, albeit temporary, "the inclusion of blacks in Georgia politics."

THE CHANGED VIEW of Reconstruction represents a closer look at the evidence, but it is hard not to find something more than that behind it. The Dunning studies gave direct support to the efforts at North-South reunion carried out at the expense of blacks in the half century and more that followed the Civil War. The newer studies came in the wake of the civil rights movement and the resumption of black militancy in the 1960s and 1970s. The change in race relations in America since the 1920s is undoubtedly the most spectacular social development of the last half century, and along with the growth of the historical profession it has certainly affected the different ways the same people are treated in the two series. But it has affected more than that and is itself part of a larger development signaled in these volumes. The great achievement of the *ANB* does not lie merely in correcting old mistakes. The *ANB* delivers a message to Americans about themselves and what they have become, an announcement never stated as an argument, a prophecy, an analysis, or an interpretation, but incorporated inescapably in the record of lives lived.

A hint of what the editors have been up to lies in the different amount of space they allot to different kinds of people. The twenty-eight presidents of the United States who died before 1934 (the cut-off date for the *DAB*) occupy 213 pages of the *DAB* as against 116 in the

ANB. On the other hand, Oliver Wolcott Gibbs, a nineteenth-century chemist, recognized among scientists for his pioneering studies of chemical bonding, wins only a single page in the *DAB* but three in the *ANB*. Sanford Gibbs, a minor landscape painter of the Hudson River School, with a little over a page in the *DAB*, gets twice that in the *ANB*. And a good many chemists and painters, not to mention physicians, musicians, clergy, politicians, and lawyers, who earned a page or two in the *DAB*, have disappeared altogether in the *ANB*.

The editors have started from scratch, taking their pick of people who have affected American life from Christopher Columbus to the present, restricting their choice only to those who died before the year 1996. They chose about half of those who had made it to the *DAB*, but also took a good many from the years before 1934 whom the *DAB* had not included, Grizzly Adams and Scott Joplin for example. They cut down on the space for the twenty-eight presidents in the *DAB* but made room for twenty-four of their "First Ladies," only three of whom are in the *DAB*. And they made room for people who affected American life without becoming part of it, like Alexis de Tocqueville, whose analysis of us 150 years ago retains an uncanny relevance today, and the Jamaican Bob Marley, whose tours of the country with the Wailers established reggae as a significant musical form. A few of these outsiders with inside influence never set foot in the country, like Charles Fourier, the nineteenth-century Utopian theorist who inspired American communal experiments like Brook Farm, and the Marquis of Rockingham, the British minister who won fame in America by presiding over the repeal of the Stamp Act. (Incidentally neither George Grenville, the author of the offensive act, nor King George III makes it.) Rockingham's name nestling next to Knute Rockne's is another of those intriguing juxtapositions that make the volumes so engrossing. And it can serve to remind us that this assemblage of names in effortless, alphabetical order conceals the imaginative taste and judgment behind what amounts to an extended manifesto of American civilization as it has become in the twentieth and twenty-first centuries. This is what we are and what we have been, the editors are saying, and it is a long way from what we were sixty years ago or perhaps from what other people may think we are now. We are not what we were before the Great Depression of the 1930s, before the New Deal, World War II, the atomic bomb, rock 'n' roll, the Vietnam War, the civil rights movement, the modern feminist movement. But these highly visible events and developments, bearing heavily and immediately on the lives of everyone who lived through them, coincided with an explosion of artistic creativity, technical innovation, and scientific discovery whose full impact has yet to be felt.

Recognition has had a large part in the achievements of the people whose lives are celebrated in these volumes. It has been particularly powerful in art and music, where many major figures would never have created the works that command our admiration and respect without earlier recognition of their talent by people who mattered, by critics and patrons, by producers and impresarios and showmen, by galleries and collectors and connoisseurs. The artists recognized here—artists in the largest sense of the word—are dead, their work done and already noticed by someone who mattered, or at least mattered to the editors. But their inclusion in the *ANB* and its evaluation of their work means a much larger kind of recognition, not only of their particular talents but of the genres in which they worked, not all of which have hitherto enjoyed the status that the *ANB* will confer.

Recognition can come at many levels and usually has to begin with someone's furnishing the wherewithal for a person to do what his or her talents make possible and still eat. Many great artists, as the biographies in the *ANB* make clear, had to scrounge for a living before, and often after, someone recognized what they were capable of. Jackson Pollock's first job after finishing art school was as a janitor, a not uncommon choice for people of talent. Mark Rothko worked as a garment cutter. Big Bill Broonzy, king of the blues in Chicago in the 1940s, had to keep a day job to stay alive. Louis Armstrong delivered coal. Charlie Parker washed dishes. Muddy Waters picked cotton. Billie Holiday was a prostitute.

Pollock and the other Abstract Expressionists who moved the center of modern art from Paris to New York in the 1950s were already well established when they did so, but only the Federal Arts Project made it possible for many of them to develop their talents during the Depression years. The "Pop" artists who seized leadership of American and world art from them almost all owed their success to recognition by a single gallery owner, Leo Castelli, who died in August 1990. Many of his now famous protégés are still alive, but the stature of the Pop movement is suggested by the four and a half pages devoted to Andy Warhol in the *ANB* (about the same as for Thomas Eakins and Winslow Homer and a bit more than for Pollock).

As Castelli's influence attests, recognition in painting and sculpture, even when it is called "Pop," is not necessarily popular. But the evaluations applied in the *ANB* to popular culture as well as to high culture demonstrate a mingling of the two still under way. The whole Pop Art movement can be seen as a bid by high art for association with popular culture. From the other direction popular culture, at least in some kinds of music, has been winning a place in high culture. The person who, more than any other, effected that penetration of class, race, and artistic barriers was John Hammond, playing a role analogous in some ways to Castelli's. Hammond, working for Columbia Records, introduced the respectable white world to jazz and blues. He "discovered" Billie Holiday in a Harlem after-hours night club, as he also discovered Count Basie and untold others. Hammond, an ardent enemy of segregation, won respect for black musicians long before the civil rights movement won them recognition as human beings. (Billie Holiday, singing for Artie Shaw's band in the 1930s, had to enter a hotel's ballroom through the kitchen.)

Hammond's most spectacular success was in two concerts, titled "From Spirituals to Swing" at Carnegie Hall in 1938 and 1939, in which he introduced artists whose work had previously been known only on the "race" records sold by companies that targeted black buyers. Artists like Sister Rosetta Tharpe, Sonny Terry, and Big Bill Broonzy had already been discovered by scouts for a number of rival record companies that bargained in pennies for their services; the boogie-woogie trio of pianists Meade Lux Lewis, Albert Ammons, and Pete Johnson brought additional luster to the scene. Hammond won them recognition not only for their talents but for blues and jazz music, and prepared the way for the host of other musical genres that continue to multiply and mutate in popular culture. In a sense he helped to win the recognition of popular culture itself that the *ANB* now makes formal.

The line between art and entertainment can be a thin one, but the *ANB* has had to give far more attention to entertainment as such than the *DAB* had to, before television, computers, and other electronic media took over our daily lives and placed entertainment at the center of them. Entertainment has always had a place in American life, but before World War II it never occupied the position it has since taken. The *DAB* did not ignore entertainers, but the *ANB* has to weigh them in the context of a world that finds entertainment in anything that can be broadcast. Professional athletes are now as much entertainers as athletes. Because television has expanded exponentially the number of spectators for sports, the players who please the public earn a standing in popular culture that most former athletes could never enjoy in their lifetime and are not likely to achieve posthumously. Journalism and radio gave many boxers and a few other athletes, especially baseball players, a popular standing before 1934. But team sports and team fans have become the big thing they now are only in the past sixty years, and the timing makes for a difference in kind between choices for the *DAB* and for the *ANB*. Most of baseball's great players, including those in the Negro Leagues, lived beyond the 1934 terminus of the *DAB*. Josh Gibson died in 1947, and Satchel Paige lived until 1982. We have been able to find only eight baseball players in the *DAB*. The *ANB* has 171. The numbers for football and basketball, sixty-one football players and twelve basketball players in the *ANB*, none in the *DAB*, are smaller because more of their great players are still alive. There are no soccer players in either.

A similar difference in both timing and taste affects the choice of musicians. The *DAB* included opera singers, popular singers, and the composers who made up Tin Pan Alley. But while jazz and the collection of musical genres then called "race music" were going strong by the 1920s, many of their practitioners died too late for consideration in the *DAB*, though the great blues singers Bessie Smith and Ma Rainey were included in *Supplement Two*, published in 1958. The *ANB* had to search much more widely for those who deserved a place for their technical and creative talent and for popular recognition of it. The *DAB* lists 54 musicians, 108 composers, and 23 singers. The *ANB* has had to divide the profession into many more categories, among them 341 jazz musicians, 325 composers and arrangers, 125 songwriters, and 118 bandleaders, not to mention the numbers of swing, blues, rhythm and blues, country and western, gospel, ragtime, soul, reggae, rock, and not least opera (62) singers and musicians. In choosing its 194 actors and actresses, the *DAB* was confined mainly to the stage, again because most of the people in film were still alive, with the notable exception of Rudolph Valentino, who died in 1926 but was not deemed worthy of inclusion. The *ANB* lists 624 from stage and screen, in addition to 94 radio and TV personalities (there is some overlap here).

Obviously, with its recognition of popular culture, the *ANB* has had to give a person's mass appeal greater weight than was the case with the *DAB*. In both there is care to distinguish fact from fiction, but the ANB shows more interest in a person's popular image as itself worth recording. Jane McCrea, allegedly murdered by the Mohawks accompanying the British general John Burgoyne in the Revolutionary War, became a martyred heroine in popular legend. June Namias, in a lengthy account of the numerous depictions of her martyrdom by painters and poets, can assure us of only one fact: "There is no doubt that Jane McCrea lived and died." But she manages to draw a (somewhat strained) lesson in feminist history from McCrea's supposed intention to marry a loyalist at the time of her demise. The facts about Barbara Frietschie are equally scanty. She owes her place in the *ANB* to Mrs. E. D. E. N. Southworth and John Greenleaf Whittier for portraying her wholly imaginary confrontation with Stonewall Jackson. ("Shoot, if you must, this old gray head,/But spare your country's flag she said.") Nina Silber, after an extensive inquiry into the facts of Frietschie's life, insists that the two never met, much less bandied words about flying The Stars and Stripes, but Silber does not discount the effectiveness of the legend as a symbol for both North and South.

The *DAB* left out both these figures of popular culture, presumably because their actual achievements were nonexistent. Where popular icons were able to manufacture legendary images of themselves that left the facts behind, the *DAB* tends to stick to the facts, while the *ANB* gives equal credit to the showmanship. Parker Willis, writing about Buffalo Bill Cody in the *DAB*, gives a full report of Cody's achievements as a tracker and scout but only mentions his *Wild West Show* in a single sentence and warns the reader at length of the "gross indulgence in fiction" of his publicity agents. Rick Ewig in the *ANB* gives two appreciative paragraphs to the show and adds without disparagement that Cody's accounts of himself in dime novels "did not document his actual adventures." Davy Crockett's political career and death at the Alamo are covered in both profiles of him, but Michael Lofaro in the *ANB* relishes the mythmaking, delighting in the "outrageous stories" and "thrilling fictions" perpetuated in the movie portrayals by Fess Parker and John Wayne. Mike Fink, the keelboat hero and champion liar, is celebrated as such in the *ANB* but is left out altogether in the *DAB*.

In the cases where a person's popularity was not a kind of talent in itself but a reward for supposed musical or artistic achievement, the *ANB* undertakes to pass judgment on the match, as in the assessment of Ziggy Elman, a jazz musician, as "a talented technician" with "greater fame than his gift for invention warranted." Hawkshaw Hawkins, who lived and worked in the orbit of other, truly great, artists like Hank Williams, wins admission but with the reservation by his biographer that there was nothing distinctive or innovative about his music. Such judgments are valuable in all the accounts of musicians because they generally rest on actual recordings of their work. (The role of records and of the changing modes of recording in the development of modern music is a story in itself, parts of which can be read in the *ANB*'s biographies listed in its index under "Recording Industry Leaders.")

The same considerations of timing and the same weighing of popular reputation and talent in art and music reach into every field of endeavor, though in different degrees—to literature, science, engineering, politics, religion, law, and even crime. The *ANB* gives Wyatt Earp the space his notoriety warrants, but with a soberly factual recounting of his poor marksmanship and menial positions and the conclusion that his "only real genius was in self-promotion." In the article on Bat Masterson (the famous gunfighter) we learn that he did eventually become a deputy United States marshal. But it is a bit deflating to be told that his territory was the southern district of New York, where he died, seated at his desk, working up an article on boxing for a newspaper. On the other hand, Pat Garrett, the sheriff who shot Billy the Kid and earned a popular reputation as a "black-hearted villain" for doing so, gets credit as a "cool-headed, reflective lawman who kept his gun in his pants and tried to practice his trade in an efficient, businesslike manner." Billy the Kid himself gets fair treatment, but with the conclusion that in history he "rates hardly a footnote," his importance resting only in the legendary stature he had acquired even before his death.

What gives the *ANB* the authority that adheres to it is its treatment of the artifacts and artisans of popular culture as no less worthy of respect and analysis than those of high culture and high science. In the catholic appreciation of every kind of creative achievement, the editors have made their work a kind of *Who's Who* of American history and culture. Inclusion in the *ANB* will come to constitute formal recognition of a person's national significance. Many of the major figures of this century in every field are still alive, or were in 1996: George Kennan, Edward Teller, Murray Gell-Mann, Michael Jordan, Mohammed Ali, Ronald Reagan, Ella Fitzgerald, to name a few. That their absence seems conspicuous points to the position the *ANB* immediately assumes as an almost official arbiter of what place anyone should occupy in the national memory.

• • •

IT IS HARD to stand back from so monumental a work and see it as a product of the 1990s that may need redoing fifty years from now. Part of its monumental quality is physical. The production of the volumes by Oxford University Press, at a time when electronic publishing clouds the future of the printed word, is a model of good bookmaking. The design is excellent. The typeface is easy to read, with plenty of leading and adequate margins. Despite the size, the heavy volumes can be handled again and again, and inevitably dropped from time to time, without any signs of wear and tear. They won't have to be handled as much as other compilations of this kind, because readers will not have to shuttle back and forth from popular names to formal given names. If you want to look up Billy the Kid, find him under that name, not under "Bonney, William," which you are not likely to know was one of his real names. Each entry is followed by an extensive bibliography and by the full name of the author, instead of the *DAB*'s coy use of initials. The last volume contains an index of the people included by name, by occupation, and by place of birth, as well as a list of the authors and the persons each of them has written about. Finally, and not least important, when you open a volume anywhere it will open easily and stay open (a test that Alfred Knopf used to apply to his books as the ultimate criterion of good production). Will there be publishers sixty years from now who can do this kind of job?

Another feature that will be hard to duplicate is the style that the editors have somehow cultivated in their authors. The historical profession is not known for the readability of its members' prose, but the editors have extracted extraordinarily lively writing, in a genre, moreover, that generally encourages blandness and pomposity. One of the distinct pleasures of foraging in the *ANB* comes from seeing how much the authors have been able to do with the space allotted them. In many instances, the authors have published full-length lives of their subjects and in this, the short form, select those qualities or quirks that made the subjects attractive to them in the first place. Dwight Macdonald, we are told by Stephen J. Whitfield, "had a flair for seizing a bone of contention and classifying it in a paleontology of nonsense, for piecing together seemingly disparate parts into the looming presence of a dinosaur with a disproportionately small brain." James I. Robertson, Jr., describing the short-lived and gallant Stonewall Jackson, says of him: "He walked with long, ungraceful strides, enormous feet adding to the spectacle, and he sat a horse as if leaning into a strong wind."

Again and again the language has the ring of everyday speech. Since popular language evolves rapidly, it may be that the free use of vernacular expressions will date the writing, but it could hardly get more dated than the stilted avoidance of any kind of flair in the old *DAB*. The expressions that give life to the writing are not slang, which dates quickly, but colloquial and forceful. "Kept his gun in his pants" is a typical one. Sixty years ago—no, ten years ago—some editor would have transformed that into something like "was loath to resort to firearms." If anyone can produce a more readable encyclopedia sixty years hence, the written word will be in better shape than there is any reason to expect.

Still, we have to assume the mantle of objectivity to ask how much the editors' choice of names has been affected by passing fashions and how much by enduring values. About half of their selections, in a sampling of several volumes, lived and died between 1934 and 1996, suggesting that recent memories affected their choice, as was the case also with the editors of the *DAB*, where people who had died in the preceding sixty-two years constituted a bit more than half. (Most of those omitted from the *ANB* came from this group.) So there has been a certain presentism involved.

Since the contributors are almost all historians, most of them young, the current cult of social history, and particularly of racial, ethnic, and gender studies in the profession, along with the political correctness prevailing in academia, may have dictated the selection and treatment of some women, some blacks, some American Indians, who might not otherwise have made it, a kind of historical affirmative action. This is most evident in the choice of women, like many of the first ladies, whose principal claim to attention is their marriage. Lady Frances Berkeley, wife of the seventeenth-century governor of Virginia, scarcely deserves more space than her husband, when her reputed influence on him is the only apparent reason for including her. First ladies should, possibly, be given automatic entry to the *ANB*, but in most instances the historians and biographers assigned to write about them are hard-pressed to make them interesting in their own right. Not so, of course, with Eleanor Roosevelt or Jacqueline Kennedy, whose quite different lives may one day rank at least as high in interest as those of their quite different husbands. Both get the respect they deserve in these pages, as does Charlotte Masaryk, the American-born first lady of Czechoslovakia.

The inclusion of minority figures seems generally to rest on more substantial ground, even though the surviving records for slaves and for American Indians are thin. The *ANB* lists 113 slaves and former slaves, only a few of whom, like Amos Fortune and Jack Sisson, seem to have been selected simply because it is possible to document events in their lives. Fortune ran a successful tanning and bookbinding business in New Hampshire in the 1780s and 1790s. Sisson allegedly assisted in the capture of British general Richard Prescott in Newport in 1777 and otherwise left scarcely a trace of his existence. As with slaves, the principal surviving documentation for the lives of American Indians derives from their interaction with whites, but the *ANB* has made full use of what there is to sketch the lives of 166 "American Indian Leaders," as against 55 "Indian Chiefs" in the *DAB*.

Before dismissing any of these choices as aberrant or "unfair" to the deserving dead white males excluded from so authoritative a work, we have to ask of this history, as of any, what people may want to learn from it that they did not know before. The people to whom it is addressed have watched the status of women and minorities in American society change radically in recent decades, and the change can scarcely be regarded as complete or likely to be reversed. Both the *ANB*'s recognition of popular culture and its attention to women and minorities reflect ongoing developments that require a new usable past, a past encompassing areas of experience that left only faint traces in the records that sustain historical research. Extracting the history of the inarticulate from documents that make only incidental reference to them has occupied a generation of historians. Much has been learned about the lives, as a group, of slaves, of seamen, of artisans, of housewives, of American Indians, but to pluck individuals from anonymity and place them beside the likes of John Adams or Margaret Fuller may have benefits for national memory comparable to those that affirmative action has demonstrably had in American society at large. There may not be much to say about an Amos Fortune, but it fills a blank space in the national memory to place in it a person with a name and not simply a generalized group.

The American Council of Learned Societies (ACLS) kept the *DAB* alive for sixty years after its completion with a staff that produced ten supplementary volumes covering people who lived through 1980. The *ANB* will enjoy a more rapid continuation in electronic form through a Center for American Biography, sponsored jointly by Oxford Press and the ACLS. We are promised "ongoing revisions and additions" on line, which will doubtless incorporate more discoveries of complexity behind suppositions we are not even aware of. But the present volumes set a standard in style, scope, and judgment that the profession will be challenged to sustain. *American National Biography* is not just a reference work. It represents a defining artifact, at the end of the twentieth century, for a culture that could exist "only in America."

with Marie Morgan
May 9, 2000

NOTES

PREFACE

1. John Smith, *Travels and Works*, ed. Edward Arber (Edinburgh, 1910), I, 140.

Chapter Two: HEAVEN CAN'T WAIT

1. *The Mathers: Three Generations of Puritan Intellectuals, 1596–1728* (New York: Oxford University Press, 1976).

Chapter Three: THOSE SEXY PURITANS

1. Roger Thompson, *Sex in Middlesex: Popular Mores in a Massachusetts County, 1649–1699* (Amherst, MA: University of Massachusetts Press, 1986).
2. John Cotton, *A Brief Exposition . . . Upon the Whole Book of Canticles* (London, 1655), pp. 4, 66.
3. *Winthrop Papers* (Massachusetts Historical Society), Vol. 1 (1929), p. 202.

Chapter Five: SUBJECT WOMEN

1. Perry Miller, *The New England Mind: The Seventeenth Century* (New York: Macmillan, 1939); *The New England Mind: From Colony to Province* (Cambridge, MA: Harvard University Press, 1953).
2. David D. Hall, *Worlds of Wonder, Days of Judgment: Popular Religious Belief in Early New England* (New York: Knopf, 1989).

Chapter Eight: OUR TOWN

1. See John Brewer, *Party Ideology and Popular Politics at the Accession of George III* (Cambridge: Cambridge University Press, 1976), and Linda Colley, *In Defiance of Oligarchy: The Tory Party, 1714–1760* (Cambridge: Cambridge University Press, 1982).

Chapter Nine: THE FALL OF THE GENTRY

1. *The Wind That Swept Mexico: The History of the Mexican Revolution: 1910–1942* (Austin: University of Texas Press, 1971).
2. See John Demos, *A Little Commonwealth: Family Life in Plymouth Colony* (New York: Oxford University Press, 1970), pp. 46–51. Cf. also essay #6.
3. James Essig, *The Bonds of Wickedness: American Evangelicals Against Slavery, 1770–1808* (Philadelphia: Temple University Press, 1982).

Chapter Ten: THE BIG AMERICAN CRIME

1. Reissued with a new introduction by Sidney W. Mintz (Boston: Beacon Press, 1990).
2. *From Sundown to Sunup: The Making of the Black Community* (Westport: Greenwood, 1972), p. 102.
3. William B. Willcox, et al., eds., *The Papers of Benjamin Franklin* (New Haven: Yale University Press), Vol. 23 (1983), p. 283; Vol. 22 (1982), p. 519.
4. Thomas Jefferson, *Notes on the State of Virginia*, ed. William Peden (New York: W. W. Norton, 1954, 1982), p. 138.
5. George Rawick, *The American Slave: A Composite Autobiography*, 41 vols. (Westport: Greenwood, 1972–79).
6. "Before We Apologize, We Should Learn What Slavery Means," *The Washington Post*, June 29, 1997, pp. C1, C5.

Chapter Eleven: PLANTATION BLUES

1. *Slavery: A Problem in American Institutional and Intellectual Life* (Chicago: University of Chicago Press, 1959).
2. U.S. Department of Labor, Office of Policy Planning and Research, *The Negro Family: The Case for National Action* (Washington, DC, 1965), p. 16.
3. *Time on the Cross: The Economics of American Negro Slavery* (Boston: Little, Brown, 1974), p. 264.
4. Paul A. David, et al., *Reckoning with Slavery: A Critical Study in the Quantitative History of American Negro Slavery* (New York: Oxford University Press, 1976), p. 28.
5. Particularly John Blassingame, *The Slave Community: Plantation Life in the Ante-Bellum South* (New York: Oxford University Press, 1972), and Herbert G. Gutman, *The Black Family in Slavery and Freedom, 1750–1925* (New York: Pantheon, 1976).
6. *Many Thousands Gone: The First Two Centuries of Slavery in North America* (Cambridge, MA: Belknap Press, Harvard University Press, 1998). See my review in *The New York Review*, December 3, 1998.
7. *The Sociology of Slavery: An Analysis of the Origins, Development and Structure of Negro Slave Society in Jamaica* (London: MacGibbon & Kee, 1967), p. 167.
8. *Slavery and Social Death: A Comparative Study* (Cambridge, MA: Harvard University Press, 1982), pp. 5–6, 190.
9. *The Ordeal of Integration: Progress and Resentment in America's "Racial" Crisis* (Washington, DC: Civitas/Counterpoint, 1997). See the review by George M. Frederickson, *The New York Review*, October 23, 1997.

Chapter Twelve: THE PRICE OF HONOR

1. Translated by W. D. Halls, with a foreword by Mary Douglas (New York: Routledge, 1990).
2. J. A. Pitt-Rivers, *The People of the Sierra* (New York: Criterion, 1954); J. A. Pitt-Rivers, *Honour and Shame: The Values of Mediterranean Society*, (Chicago: University of Chicago Press, 1966).
3. *Honour and Shame*, pp. 21–22.
4. *Encyclopedia of the Social Sciences* (New York: Macmillan, 1932), Vol. 7, p. 456.

5. *Slavery: A Problem in American Institutional and Intellectual Life* (Chicago: University of Chicago Press, 1959).

6. *Slavery and Social Death: A Comparative Study* (Cambridge, MA: Harvard University Press, 1982), pp. 211–17.

7. New York: Pantheon, 1974.

8. Richard M. Titmuss, *The Gift Relationship: From Human Blood to Social Policy* (New York: Pantheon, 1971), p. 215. The noted medical writer Dr. Richard Selzer pointed out to me in conversation that persons from whom organs are simply harvested after fatal road accidents are generally referred to as "donors."

Chapter Thirteen: HOW THE FRENCH LOST AMERICA

1. *Montcalm and Wolfe: France and England in North America*, Part Seventh, centenary edition (Boston: Little, Brown, 1925), Vol. 1, pp. 3, 5.

2. *The British Empire Before the American Revolution.* Vol. 6: *The Great War for the Empire: The Years of Defeat, 1754–1757* (New York: Knopf, 1946), p. 10.

3. *Montcalm and Wolfe*, Vol. 1, pp. 446–47.

4. Ibid., pp. 94–132, 243–95; quotations at pp. 254, 267.

5. *The British Empire*, Vol. 6, p. 343.

6. Anderson has discussed this topic more extensively in his earlier book, *A People's Army: Massachusetts Soldiers and Society in the Seven Years' War* (Chapel Hill, NC: University of North Carolina Press, 1984).

Chapter Fifteen: THE OEDIPAL REVOLUTION

1. Victor Turner, *The Ritual Process* (Chicago: University of Chicago Press, 1969).

Chapter Sixteen: SECRETS OF BENJAMIN FRANKLIN

1. Madame d'Houdetot to Thomas Jefferson, September 3, 1790, *The Papers of Thomas Jefferson*, ed. J. P. Boyd, et al., Vol. 17, p. 486 (Princeton: Princeton University Press, 1963).

2. Ibid., Vol. 19, pp. 140–72.

3. *The Diary and Autobiography of John Adams*, ed. L. H. Butterfield, et al., 4 vols. (Cambridge, MA: Belknap Press, Harvard University Press, 1961) Vol. 4, p. 118.

4. Cambridge, MA: Belknap Press, Harvard University Press, 1986.

Chapter Seventeen: DON'T TREAD ON US

1. E. G. R. Taylor, ed., *The Original Writings and Correspondence of the Two Richard Hakluyts* (London: Works issued by the Hakluyt Society, LXXVI, LXXVII, 1935), pp. 142–43.

2. John Murrin, "Review Essay," *History and Theory*, vol. XI, no. 2, (1972), pp. 226n–75. This essay has had almost as much influence on historical interpretation as the books it reviewed.

3. Leonard W. Labaree, *Royal Government in America* (New Haven: Yale University Press, 1930; New York: Frederick Ungar, 1958), p. 312–72.

Chapter Eighteen: THE FIXERS

1. *Jefferson and Madison: The Great Collaboration* (New York: Knopf, 1950).
2. Madison to George Muter, January 7, 1787, Robert A. Rutland, et al., eds., *The Papers of James Madison*. Vol. IX (April 9, 1786–May 24, 1787) (Chicago: University of Chicago Press, 1975), p. 231.
3. Madison to Hubbard Taylor, November 15, 1794, *The Papers of James Madison*. Vol. XV (March 24, 1793–April 20, 1795) (Charlottesville: University Press of Virginia, 1985), p. 378.
4. Dumas Malone, *Jefferson and His Time*, Vol. IV: *Jefferson the President: First Term, 1801–1805* (Boston: Little, Brown, 1970), pp. 310–15.
5. Lester J. Cappon, ed., *The Adams-Jefferson Letters: The Complete Correspondence Between Thomas Jefferson and Abigail and John Adams* (Chapel Hill, NC: University of North Carolina Press, 1959).

Chapter Nineteen: THE GREAT POLITICAL FICTION

1. See Derek Hirst, *The Representative of the People: Voters and Voting in England under the Early Stuarts* (Cambridge: Cambridge University Press, 1975).

Chapter Twenty: POWER TO THE PEOPLE?

1. (Chicago: University of Chicago Press, 1981).

Chapter Twenty-one: THE SECOND AMERICAN REVOLUTION

1. The term was applied to a wide variety of historians of different periods, including Daniel J. Boorstin, Bernard Bailyn, Richard Hofstadter, and Arthur M. Schlesinger, Jr.

Chapter Twenty-two: THE GENUINE ARTICLE

1. Carl Van Doren, *Benjamin Franklin* (New York: Viking, 1938), pp. 611, 762.
2. Irving Brant, *James Madison: The Nationalist, 1780–1787* (Indianapolis: Bobbs-Merrill, 1948), p. 321; Julian Boyd, et al., eds., *The Papers of Thomas Jefferson*, Vol. IX, p. 266; A. A. Lipscomb and A. E. Burgh, eds., *The Writings of Thomas Jefferson* (Thomas Jefferson Memorial Association, 1903–04), Vol. XIII, pp. 46–52.
3. W. W. Abbot, Dorothy Twohig, et al., eds., *The Papers of George Washington* (Charlottesville, VA: University Press of Virginia, 1976–). The edition is in five series: *Diaries, Colonial, Revolutionary War, Confederation*, and *Presidential*. The *Diaries* and the *Colonial* series have been completed in sixteen volumes. The other three are in progress, with fourteen volumes completed, as well as the completed single volume, *Journal of the Proceedings of the President, 1793–1797*.
4. Rosemarie Zagarri, ed., *David Humphreys' "Life of General Washington," with George Washington's "Remarks"* (Athens, GA: University of Georgia Press, 1991).
5. (Berkeley: University of California Press, 1988).
6. (New York: Free Press, 1987).
7. To James Madison, June 9, 1793, in W. T. Hutchinson, Robert Rutland, et al., eds., *The Papers of James Madison* (Chicago: University of Chicago Press and

Charlottesville, VA: University Press of Virginia, 1962–), Vol. XV, p. 27. The other quotations in this paragraph are all from Schwartz, *George Washington*.

8. *Cincinnatus: George Washington and the Enlightenment* (Garden City, NY: Doubleday, 1984), p. 3.

9. Ibid., p. 13.

10. Ibid., p. 130 (italics in the original).

11. Ibid., p. 162.

12. *The Papers of George Washington, Confederation* series, Vol. IV, p. 319.

INDEX

ABOUT THE AUTHOR

EDMUND S. MORGAN, who received his Ph.D. at Harvard University studying with Perry Miller, was born in 1916 in Minneapolis. He has written for the *New York Review of Books* for over forty years and has published over fifteen books, including *Benjamin Franklin; Inventing the People: The Rise of Popular Sovereignty in England and America*, which won Columbia University's Bancroft Prize in American History in 1989; and *American Slavery, American Freedom*, which won the Society of American Historians' Francis Parkman Prize, the Southern Historical Association's Charles S. Sydnor Prize, and the American Historical Association's Albert J. Beveridge Award.

Joining the faculty at Yale University in 1955, he trained a generation of students in early American history and was named Sterling Professor in 1965, retiring over two decades later in 1986. In 1971 he was awarded the Yale Chapter of Phi Beta Kappa's William Clyde DeVane Medal for outstanding teaching and scholarship, considered one of the most prestigious teaching prizes for Yale faculty. One year later, he became the first recipient of the Douglas Adair Memorial Award for scholarship in early American history, and in 1986 he received the Distinguished Scholar Award of the American Historical Association. Among other honors, he has received the National Humanities medal in 2000, and he currently chairs the board of The Benjamin Franklin Papers at Yale. A woodturner and furniture craftsman of distinction, he lives in New Haven with his wife, Marie Morgan.